WORKING
WITH ADULTS
IN GROUPS

Sheldon D. Rose

WORKING WITH ADULTS IN GROUPS

Integrating Cognitive-Behavioral and Small Group Strategies

 Jossey-Bass Publishers

San Francisco • London • 1989

WORKING WITH ADULTS IN GROUPS:
Integrating Cognitive-Behavioral and Small Group Strategies
  by Sheldon D. Rose

Copyright © 1989 by: Jossey-Bass Inc., Publishers
                      350 Sansome Street
                      San Francisco, California 94104
                                  &
                      Jossey-Bass Limited
                      28 Banner Street
                      London EC1Y 8QE

Library of Congress Cataloging-in-Publication Data

Rose, Sheldon D.
  Working with adults in groups.

  (The Jossey-Bass social and behavioral science series)
  Bibliography: p.
  Includes index.
  1. Cognitive therapy.   2. Group psychotherapy.
I. Title.   II. Series.
RC489.C63R67   1989   616.89′152   8945589
ISBN 1-55542-166-0 (alk. paper)

Manufactured in the United States of America

The paper in this book meets the guidelines for
permanence and durability of the Committee on
Production Guidelines for Book Longevity of the
Council on Library Resources.

JACKET DESIGN BY WILLI BAUM

FIRST EDITION

Code 8940

The Jossey-Bass
Social and Behavioral Science Series

Contents

Preface   xi

The Author   xix

Part One: Overview of Working with Groups

1. A Multimethod Approach to Working with Adults in Groups   1

2. Understanding Group Structure and Process   23

Part Two: Guidelines for Starting and Conducting Groups

3. Preparing for Group Therapy: Planning Treatment and Orienting Members   45

4. Assessment in Groups: Identifying Clients' Problems and Resources   72

5. Measuring and Evaluating Individual Achievements and Group Process   109
   with Richard M. Tolman

6. Setting Individual and Group Goals   137

7. Planning for Group Interventions   150

Part Three: Using Intervention Strategies in Groups

8. Changing Behavior Through Modeling, Rehearsing,
    Coaching, and Feedback   164

9. Using Cognitive Strategies to Cope with Stress
    and Promote Change   193

10. Involving Group Members in Relaxation, Breathing,
    Meditation, and Sociorecreational Activities   227

11. Resolving Problems in Group Structure and Process   243

Part Four: Beyond the Group Session

12. Extending Treatment into the Real World Through
    Extragroup Tasks   271

13. Principles and Strategies for Maintaining
    New Behavior   287

Part Five: Illustrating the Principles of Group Work

14. The Multimethod Approach in Action   309
       with Randy Magen

    References   329

    Name Index   347

    Subject Index   353

Preface

In the last ten or twelve years, an abundance of new techniques have been described for working with adults in groups—problem solving, reframing, cognitive restructuring, and group exposure, to mention just a few. Since the publication of my earlier book *Group Therapy: A Behavioral Approach* (1977), a great deal of research has been done on group process and on the group as the context of treatment. Indeed, the changes have been so dramatic that I felt that an entirely new book was called for. Among other things, I had come to realize the importance of the group as a treatment intervention in its own right. Furthermore, I felt that it would be most useful to integrate the new developments in a unified approach that would link specific therapeutic procedures to a general problem-solving paradigm for adults in groups. I have limited this book to adults because *Working with Children and Adolescents in Groups* (1987), which I coauthored with Jeffrey L. Edleson, was specifically devoted to techniques for working with children in therapy. Many of the strategies discussed in this book are also described elsewhere for dyadic and occasionally for family treatment. In *Working with Adults in Groups* I emphasize not only recognized group interventions but also ways to enlist group members' help in carrying out other methods of treatment.

The multimethod approach described in this book is an attempt to integrate different therapeutic approaches—behavioral and cognitive-behavioral methods, relational methods from the work of Yalom (1985), and small group methods from the work of Lewin (1951) and his followers—into one consistent, testable approach to therapy. I have attempted to explain this approach as fully as possible and to provide examples of all strategies suggested. Where possible, I have drawn on supporting research.

The possible applications of the approach are still under scrutiny. Research is increasing; the strategies for evaluating both outcome and group process are inherent in the approach and should contribute to its continued development. Unfortunately, few books on cognitive-behavioral group therapy consider the group as a treatment intervention. This book is intended to help fill that gap.

I have drawn on clinical experience and on recent research on small group and individual treatment procedures to develop concrete descriptions and generalizations about a multimethod group approach. This book is not a research summary, however. It is a clinical book, primarily for practitioners or students of practice. *Working with Adults in Groups* demonstrates the myriad principles that impinge on practice and proposes solutions to the problems that arise when one attempts to lead a group. Examples are drawn from a variety of groups with which I have had direct and indirect experience, primarily from those in which my colleagues and I have collaborated. These include stress, anxiety, and pain management groups; groups for men who batter, caregivers, parents (especially of adolescents), and the recently divorced; and general therapy groups. I have used excerpts from group sessions to illustrate how to implement the various principles of the multimethod approach. The approach is also applicable to many other types of groups besides those mentioned above.

Audience

I have directed this book primarily toward the group leader, the group worker, the group counselor, and other group practitioners who work in private practice, health and mental health clinics, family service agencies, halfway houses, recreation and community centers, occupational therapy workshops, correctional centers, and other residential settings. I have used the term *group leader* to refer to anyone who is formally employed to lead such a group. I could just as easily have used the terms *group worker, group therapist,* or *group counselor* (people with all these titles have led the types of groups described in this book), but I prefer the more generic term for its breadth of application.

Although not especially aimed at the researcher, *Working with Adults in Groups* emphasizes incorporating data collection into practice to increase the effectiveness of clinical decision making and evaluation of treatment progress and outcome. In formulating the principles that underlie the multimethod approach and in culling examples to illustrate their application, I have benefited from the experiences of hundreds of professionals and students, in courses and workshops throughout the United States and Europe, who have used the group as the context for treatment.

The book can be used by the experienced and the inexperienced practitioner alike. It will help therapists, social workers, and counselors who are experienced in dyadic treatment translate their experiences and knowledge base for use in the group setting. I have tried to provide enough examples so that the principles will also be understandable to neophytes and readily applicable to their group experience as it evolves. Advanced practitioners can use the book to compare their experiences with those of the author and other group leaders. Early drafts have served successfully as textbooks for both beginning and advanced classes in group work and group therapy. Although for such classes some familiarity with behavioral and cognitive-behavioral methods is helpful, it is not necessary, because most terms and principles are explained and exemplified in the text.

The multimethod approach can be described as a set of practice principles to be applied differentially in each phase of treatment. Although many of the components of the multimethod approach have been tested with both individuals and groups, only a few studies have incorporated most of the components into one package whose application for groups could then be compared in a control group with other approaches or with no treatment. Recently, studies by Tallant, Rose, and Tolman (1989), Subramanian and Rose (1988), and Tolman and Rose (1989) have provided modest support for the approach. Other studies now in progress may further broaden the base of support; however, extensive additional research is necessary.

Overview of the Contents

In Part One, the multimethod approach is explained in its entirety and the role of the group in that approach is described. This part is elaborated on in far greater detail in the subsequent parts.

Chapter One is an overview of the multimethod approach to group treatment of adults. It is called the multimethod approach because it combines the problem-solving, small group, coping-skills training, and empirical approaches to group treatment. This chapter presents the rationale for each of the orientations unified in the overall approach.

Some common targets for change with this approach are stress and anxiety, depression, social skill deficits, anger, pain, parenting problems, communication problems, eating disorders, and sexual disorders. In the multimethod approach, various methods are differentially applied during each of five overlapping treatment phases: planning, orientation, assessment, intervention, and generalization.

In Chapter Two, a distinction is made between group structure and group process. I consider several possible group structures with regard to their relevance for treatment outcomes: cohesion, norm structure, role structure, subgroup structure, and leadership structure. The changes in these structures over time constitute group development. I also define a number of emotional group processes and speculate about their relationship to group outcomes. Finally, the concept of group problems is introduced.

Part Two outlines the tasks of the group leader in the first phase of treatment.

In Chapter Three, I analyze the issues involved in organizing group treatment and orienting the clients to it. It is essential, in organizing a group, to decide on the type of group, group themes, the manner in which potential members will be recruited and eventually selected for the group, group composition, setting, frequency and length of sessions, and the number of leaders. This chapter presents and illustrates the principles for making decisions about these issues.

In Chapter Four, the general purposes of assessment and its place in the treatment process are set forth. Particular attention is

paid to the unique role of the group in that process. More specifically, I describe how the group leader helps the clients by carrying out
a situational analysis and defining specific concepts essential to a
situational analysis, such as situation-overt behavior, cognitions,
affective responses, critical moment, consequences, and situational
context. The chapter also deals with specific techniques for
identifying problematic situations, details training strategies for
familiarizing children with the concepts mentioned earlier, illustrates how to identify resources for and impediments to treatment,
and discusses the role of diagnosis in this type of assessment.

In Chapter Five, Richard M. Tolman and I analyze the role
that measurement and evaluation play in the treatment process. The
first part of this chapter focuses on techniques for measuring
change in individuals that can be used in groups. In particular,
we evaluated self-report tests and inventories, roleplay tests, self-
monitoring, extragroup observations, and problem cards in the
groups we worked with. In the second part of this chapter we
explore how certain data-gathering methods make it easier to gauge
what is happening in the group, and we look at case study designs
that practitioners can use to evaluate the significance of changes in
their clients.

In Chapter Six, I examine the function of goal setting in the
treatment process. Once clients have formulated goals, the group
leader can initiate treatment planning. I describe four different
kinds of treatment plans—individual, group, session, and generalization—and provide examples from actual treatment groups.

In Chapter Seven, concepts of group and individual intervention planning are presented. I illustrate how the four kinds of
intervention plans described in Chapter Six are related to specific
treatment goals and group goals.

Part Three covers intervention strategies designed to help
achieve group treatment goals.

In Chapter Eight, I discuss the modeling sequence as it is
applied in group treatment and review the prerequisites for effective
modeling, such as keen observation skills, incentives for observing,
and appropriate characteristics in the model. I outline the principles and variations on effective behavior rehearsal and group feed-

back—and discuss their advantages and disadvantages for different groups.

Chapter Nine presents cognitive procedures uniquely suited to group application. After discussing the steps in self-instructional training, I examine how cognitive restructuring applies to clients in groups. The focus is on identifying self-defeating statements and replacing them with self-enhancing ones, through disputation, cognitive modeling, and rehearsal, or variations on this approach.

In Chapter Ten, I show how relaxation and relaxation training can be introduced in groups to help clients achieve treatment goals. I examine three general relaxation procedures: neuromuscular relaxation, respiratory control, and meditation, emphasizing how sociorecreational and exercise activities can help clients become more productive and functional in their daily lives. I pay special attention to the role of the group in the teaching process.

In Chapter Eleven, I discuss methods for identifying group problems and dealing with their impact on the treatment process, including strategies for modifying group attributes such as cohesion, communication patterns, subgroup structure, group norms, role structure, leadership structure, group contagion, and productivity.

Part Four illustrates strategies and principles for generalization and maintenance of changes achieved in the group.

Chapter Twelve deals with the function and purpose of extragroup tasks in the treatment process. I present examples of different types of assignments—behavioral, cognitive, simulated, noninteractive, and self-observational tasks. Because getting clients to complete such assignments is a major challenge in treatment, this chapter also explains how to obtain the clients' compliance.

In Chapter Thirteen, I consider other procedures for maintaining and generalizing changes occurring in the group and explain the importance of giving multiple and varied examples. I illustrate how group members can gradually be given responsibility for their own treatment, and I emphasize the importance of moving the treatment program into the natural environment and involving significant others. I discuss ways in which clients can both be prepared for a hostile environment and potential setbacks and, at the same time, be trained to cooperate with others. And finally, I address the ways in which these principles can be integrated—with the assistance of the group—into a plan for generalization.

In Part Five (containing just Chapter Fourteen), most of the strategies discussed in this book are demonstrated by means of a case study: Randy Magen and I examine excerpts from the transcription of one group session in detail in order to illustrate the techniques discussed in the preceding chapters.

A Word of Thanks

Although as author I accept the responsibility for all that is written in this book, it is the product of the efforts of many people. Two of them actually coauthored chapters: Richard Tolman (Chapter Five) and Randy Magen (Chapter Fourteen). Others—for example, Karen Subramanian, Steven Tallant, and Dale Whitney—have contributed research or other scholarship to the book. I should like to thank them and also Ann Scobie, who was particularly helpful in adding the finishing touches to the manuscript in the last rush of its production. The many students and workshop participants who provided trials and criticism of the approach should not be overlooked when thanks are being handed out. And finally, most of all, I want to thank my wife, Cindy, and three daughters, Leah, Wendy, and Alisa, who bore with my absences as I labored to complete the manuscript and who supported me when I was discouraged and weary.

Madison, Wisconsin Sheldon D. Rose
July 1989

*This book is dedicated to
the memory of Lydia Rose,
who gave me life
and showed me how
to live it.*

The Author

Sheldon D. Rose is professor of social work at the University of Wisconsin, Madison, where he is also director of the Interpersonal Skill Training and Research Project. He received his A.B. degree (1950) from the University of Missouri in sociology, his M.S.W. degree (1952) from Washington University of St. Louis, and his Ph.D. degree (1960) from the University of Amsterdam, the Netherlands, with a major in social psychology. He has carried out extensive research on the effectiveness of various group approaches in the treatment of children and adults. In addition to numerous articles, he has written or edited five books on this topic: *Treating Children in Groups: A Behavioral Approach* (1972), *Group Therapy: A Behavioral Approach* (1977), *A Casebook in Group Therapy* (1980), *Working with Children and Adolescents in Groups* (1987), and *Research in Group Work* (1987, with R. Feldman). He is a coauthor of several manuals for group leaders on stress management, pain management, assertiveness training, and other topics. In addition, he serves as editor of the newsletter *Empirical Group Work* and as a member of the editorial boards for many psychology and social work journals.

WORKING WITH ADULTS IN GROUPS

ONE

A Multimethod Approach to Working with Adults in Groups

A group of clients who found it difficult to deal with the small day-to-day demands of job and family sought ways of reevaluating these situations. They practiced specific relaxation techniques and methods for improving relationships. Each week, each client brought in a description of a specific encounter he or she had had that triggered an increase in depression. These situations were discussed one at a time within the group.

A group of parents met weekly to find more effective methods of dealing with their teenage children. They shared with each other the different methods they had used in real-life situations. The group members supported each other and suggested alternate methods. Some demonstrated their suggestions by roleplaying. They provided encouragement for each other and were provided information by the group leader.

Men convicted of physically abusing their wives were referred by the courts to a group that met twice a week. They sought to improve communication with their partners. In addition, they studied and practiced new methods of handling anger in a wide variety of stressful situations by reevaluating their perceptions of these situations. Some first had to learn to take responsibility for their actions. At the beginning of each session each man reported to the group his progress in improving communication skills since the last meeting. The men also discussed the difficulties they had encountered and were offered suggestions on how similar situations could be handled differently in the future. At the end of each session, they planned what they would try out prior to the next session.

Five couples met weekly to explore new paths of interaction or to improve the quality of existing patterns. The meeting was both informational and experiential. The couples examined their present patterns of communication and offered both reinforcement and constructive criticism. These were skills that some members had to learn through group exercises and discussion of case studies.

After some preparation in a group setting, five women who suffered from agoraphobia together visited a department store. Afterward, they rode the elevators together. On their return to the clinic, they discussed the experience. The women praised each other enthusiastically for their accomplishments and planned to attempt similar excursions between sessions on their own.

The preceding excerpts are examples of only a few of the varied problems that have been addressed by the multimethod approach to group treatment and of the many intervention strategies used to help clients. In these examples, we note that clients work together to learn to deal more effectively with stress-inducing situations, to improve interpersonal relationships, to refine their parenting skills, to handle depression more effectively, to control the anger that is destroying their lives and the lives of their families, and to communicate more effectively with their adolescent children. This approach has also been used by those working to achieve more satisfying sexual functioning, resolution of phobic disorders, more effective pain management, and self-control in the areas of smoking, drinking, drugs, and weight loss. The major components of the approach described in this book have been used to provide skills to caregivers for the elderly, to help them resolve the many problems that accompany that role. At present, the method is being used to help recently divorced clients adjust to their new situation. A similar approach has been used with cancer patients and their families for this same purpose. (A comparable program has been described by Rose and Edleson, 1987, for use with children and adolescents.) One can discern in these examples a number of diverse orientations. The clients make use of the conditions of the group to enhance their learning. They acquire the skills needed to cope with their unique problem situations. They apply systematic problem-solving strategies to derive useful solutions. And they are trained to use the coping skills by means of many varied procedures. Let us look at these overlapping orientations to the multimethod approach to group therapy.

Orientation

Many basic overlapping orientations are inherent in the therapeutic paradigm presented in this book. First, a small group orientation is used because of the unique characteristics of and curative factors assumed to be inherent in group processes. Consistent with this orientation, the paradigm draws heavily on research on small groups and small group therapy as a basis for decisions about treatment planning and interventions. Second, multimethod group therapy is governed by a problem-solving orientation in which many diverse interventions are integrated into a basic problem-solving format. New behaviors and cognitions are learned in the service of resolving problematic situations. Third, as part of the problem-solving orientation, multimethod group therapy can also be considered goal oriented. Both individual treatment and common treatment goals are developed for and by each client and group goals are formulated concerning group conditions requiring change. The attainment of group goals should mediate the achievement of the treatment goals. Fourth, multimethod group therapy has an empirical orientation. As most intervention procedures and many theories are available to the group, the multimethod practitioner shows a preference for techniques and strategies for which empirical support exists. Fifth, this approach draws heavily from a coping-skill-training orientation. Clients are taught (and are involved in teaching each other) new strategies or they improve ineffective strategies for coping with problematic situations. These five orientations lead to a multitheoretical, multimethod approach. Many procedures derived from diverse theoretical frameworks are combined into a common plan to aid clients in helping one another to achieve their goals. Multimethod group therapy goes beyond cognitive and cognitive-behavioral strategies by incorporating procedures from various theories (such as operant conditioning, modeling, cognitive, relationship, networking, empowerment) into a unified though eclectic approach.

Small Group Orientation

Many skilled practitioners avoid the use of the group because of its apparent complexity and the perception that the interaction of members somehow interferes with the individuality of the client and the achievement of individual goals. This section describes the potential advantages as well as the difficulties involved in working with the group using a multimethod approach. How some of these difficulties can be dealt with is also suggested.

For many persons, the group dispels the sense of isolation felt from "being the only one with the problem." Listening to others who describe and solve their problems instills hope in the client that his or her problems are also resolvable. The group provides the client with a source of feedback about those behaviors that are irritating or acceptable to others and about those cognitions that can be viewed as self-defeating or self-enhancing. As a result, the group contributes to improved assessment.

Another reason for using groups is the frequent and varied opportunities for mutual reinforcement, which for clients is often far more powerful than reinforcement by the leader alone. Reinforcement is a highly valued commodity in our society; there is good reason to believe that as a client learns to reinforce others, she or he is reciprocally reinforced by others (see Lott and Lott, 1965). Each client is given the chance to learn or to improve his or her ability to mediate rewards for others in social interactive situations (with acquaintances, friends, family members, acquaintances in other groups, other group members, or employer). The group leader can create situations in which each client has frequent opportunity, instructions, and rewards for reinforcing others in the group. Also, special exercises have been designed to train groups specifically in mutual reinforcement, and often assignments are used to encourage practice of reinforcement skills in the real world.

In the group, a client must learn to deal with the idiosyncrasies of other individuals. Clients must wait while other people explain their problems. They must learn to tolerate what they perceive to be inadequate or even stupid advice. The client may be required to tolerate major differences with other group members and in some cases to deal with them and must learn to offer other clients critical feedback and advice in a tactful manner. In helping others, clients are practicing strategies they can use to help themselves and to help others outside the group. They are thus likely to improve their relationship skills.

Because of its similarity to natural friendship groups, therapy groups simulate the real world of most clients more closely than individual therapy, which is an interaction between a high-status adult and a low-status client. As such, the group eases transfer of the newly learned behavior from the therapeutic setting to the community.

Groups also provide an environment in which the group leader is able to use the many therapeutic procedures that are either unsuitable or less efficient in individual treatment. Among these procedures are the "buddy system," numerous group exercises (see, for example, Rose, Tolman, and Tallant, 1985b), multiple modeling, group feedback, group brainstorming, and mutual reinforcement.

Groups also provide each client with a large number of models, roleplayers for behavioral rehearsal, manpower for monitoring, and partners for the "buddy system." The group also provides a natural laboratory for the learning discussion and leadership skills that are esssential to good social relationships.

In the process of interaction in therapy groups, norms (informal agreements among members as to preferred modes of action and interaction in the group) are often established that serve to control the behavior of individual members. When these norms are introduced and effectively maintained by the group leader, they serve as powerful therapeutic tools. The group pressures deviant members to conform to such norms as regular attendance, peer reinforcement, self-disclosure, systematic and specific problem analysis, and assistance to peers with problems. Of course, if the group leader is not careful, antitherapeutic norms such as regular tardiness or refusal to participate in roleplaying may also be generated.

To avoid such problems or to deal with the problems should they arise, a group leader can draw on experimentally derived knowledge about norms and other group phenomena showing how individual behavior both influences and is influenced by the attributes of the group. (See Stockton and Morran, 1982; Shaw, 1976; Nixon, 1979, for a review of these relationships.) In addition to modifying the norms of the group, the group leader can facilitate the attainment of both individual and group goals by modifying the cohesiveness, the status pattern, or the communication structure of the group. Much of the power of group therapy to facilitate achievement of goals is lost if negative group attributes are permitted to fester.

For the most part, group therapy appears to be at least as effective and more efficient in terms of leader cost than individual therapy. Research comparing the various forms of group therapy with individual therapy with respect to the use of cognitive-behavioral procedures to treat lack of assertiveness, stress, phobias, and depression indicates far lower costs for similar results. (See, for example, Linehan and others, 1979; Teri and Lewinsohn, 1985; Toseland and Siporin, 1986, for reviews.) In the treatment of depression using Beck's (1976) paradigm, group therapy was found to be less effective than individual treatment (see, for example, Rush and Watkins, 1981).

Of course, groups are not without major disadvantages. In addition to the establishment and maintenance of antitherapeutic norms, mentioned earlier, such phenomena as group contagion and mutual aggression sometimes get out of hand in groups. Strategies for dealing with such group phenomena are available (see Chapter Eleven).

An important limitation is the greater difficulty involved in individualizing clients in groups than in individual therapy. For efficiency, the group leader continually seeks common goals and may therefore overlook the needs of an individual. Identifying, within the complex interaction of the group, the distinct needs of individuals requires a great deal of attention.

Confidentiality is more difficult to maintain in groups than in the dyad, although in my experience breaches of confidentiality are rare among group members, especially when the consequences of such breaches are discussed in early sessions.

Working with groups requires the unique and extensive skills of a trained practitioner. Unfortunately, such training is not ubiquitous in psychology, social work, counseling, or other professional training programs.

If the group leader is aware of these limitations, all of the previously mentioned potential problems can be avoided or resolved. Even the positive attributes of a group are advantages only if they are opportunistically seized upon by the group leader. Throughout this book, we point out how group leaders have dealt with the difficulties encountered in group interaction and how they have taken advantage of the unique and manifold assets of groups.

For the opportunities it affords, the group is a vital element in the approach proposed in this book. Yet it is not just the group that brings about change. As group problems are presented, a common concern is discussed and that concern is dealt with systematically.

Systematic Problem-Solving Orientation

Clients bring the problems that concern them to the group, which, under the guidance of the leader, attempts to help its members resolve their problems. It is systematic because the members follow (or deviate by plan from) specified steps. These steps are characteristic of the problem-solving process: orienting the members to the basic assumptions of problem solving, identifying and defining the problem and client resources for dealing with the problem, generating alternative solutions, evaluating and selecting the best set of solutions, preparing for implementation, implementing the solution, and evaluating outcome. Although not commonly found in the paradigms of others (for example, Spivack and Shure, 1974; Heppner, 1978; Goldfried and D'Zurilla, 1969), the intermediate step, preparation for implementation, is discussed here because merely identifying the problem and suggesting a solution often insufficiently prepare a client to carry out the solution.

Systematic problem solving is not only a general paradigm. It is a set of cognitive coping skills in its own right and should replace impetuous problem solving. By employing the problem-solving method, clients acquire the general skills necessary to deal with specific problems as they arise.

Goal Orientation

The categories of problems mentioned earlier suggest the general areas within which the group leader formulates the specific targets of change in the group. These specific targets, or goals, are concrete behaviors or identifiable cognitions in response to a given specified problem situation peculiar to a given client. As the achievement of goals will occur sometime in the future, a time frame should be included in the definition of a goal. The goals are either individual or, what is more likely in groups, common. Common goals are individual goals that are shared by some or all of the group members. Some specific goals toward which clients in various groups have worked are listed in Table 1.

Group goals refer to a future change in the interactive phenomena that occur in the group. Note these examples. "At the end of this session, all the members of the group will have actively participated in roleplays." "Members will establish the norm that extragroup tasks that the group agrees to will be completed by the end of the next session." "The attraction of the members to each other (as measured on a questionnaire) will have increased from the preceding session."

It is assumed that through achievement of their goals, the group members will begin to cope with problem situations more effectively. Thus, goal orientation is closely related to the coping-skill-training orientation.

Empirical Orientation

Available research on group therapy or any of the target behaviors, target populations, or interventions is incorporated into

Table 1. Examples of Treatment Goals Commonly Found in Groups.

Situation	Goal behavior	Time frame
1. The client perceives that she or he is being criticized by spouse.	1. Ask spouse to clarify the situation.	1. By next week
2. The client is with friends.	2. Increase verbal and affective participation.	2. Within three weeks
3. The client does not know how to solve a problem at work.	3. Ask others for help.	3. By end of month
4. The client is in a large department store.	4. Use elevator and escalator in store while talking positively to self.	4. By end of treatment
5. The client is with his mother.	5. Eliminate his vicious teasing.	5. Within two weeks
6. The client is alone and begins to think how depressed she is.	6. Reframe concern: "how calming it is to be alone for a change."	6. At least once tomorrow

goal setting and treatment planning. Moreover, data are collected throughout therapy to determine whether and in what kind of group a person should be included to determine the specific foci of therapy, to make clinical decisions, and to evaluate the effectiveness of therapy.

Coping-Skill-Training Orientation

The coping skills commonly sought in multimethod groups can be classified into at least two general categories: (1) cognitive and (2) active or behavioral. These are aimed both directly and indirectly at coping with specific problematic situations. Acquisition of these skills facilitates the attainment of specific therapeutic goals. Let us examine these general categories in terms of their relevance to the multimethod group therapy approach. Although in real life these skills generally overlap, they are discussed separately in this chapter for purposes of analysis.

Cognitive Coping Skills. Cognitions are thoughts, images, thinking patterns, expectations, self-statements (what one says to oneself), or private or covert patterns (such as excessive exaggeration or overgeneralization that may be inferred from verbal or other overt behavior). Cognitive coping skills are those cognitions that facilitate coping with internal and social phenomena, for example, the ability to analyze one's own cognitions, to label appropriately one's self-defeating self-statements, to observe and rehearse new, more appropriate self-statements, and to reinforce oneself covertly, and to make use of a systematic problem-solving paradigm. Though important skills in their own right, cognitive coping skills also mediate the attainment of the more observable social skills. Thus, the goal of increasing cognitive coping skills is important as a means of correcting anxiety-inducing and behavior-inhibiting cognitions and in improving social behavior (Meichenbaum, 1977). Self-statements such as "everyone thinks I'm strange" not only produce anxiety, they promote inaction. A different statement, for example, "Sure, I'm different from others in many ways, some things I like and some I'll change," may be a more accurate appraisal; it suggests avenues of change, implies greater self-respect, and, with much practice under a variety of conditions, may reduce anxiety and improve social behavior.

Self-management refers to those cognitive coping skills by which a client controls the environment to control his or her own behavior. Procedures involving the use of environmental cues, self-monitoring, self-instruction, self-evaluation, and self-reinforcement fall under this rubric. Although the data supporting the use of any one of these procedures are at best limited in scope, there is clinical evidence that these procedures may be effective after the use of more direct environmental strategies. In any case, the client will continue to struggle with various problems long after the group has terminated. These skills, when learned, constitute a set of strategies that the client can utilize even when only limited external support is available.

Cognitive coping skills are not, however, the only coping techniques available for dealing with stressful situations. Next, we discuss targets that are not exclusively cognitive but may also require overt behavior on the part of the client to cope with problems.

Active Coping Skills. Among the most common active coping skills are social skills, a set of learned performance behaviors that effectively relate an individual to others. "How should I deal with people in stressful situations?" is one of the most common requests of our clients. For this reason, it is one of the major targets of change. To be able to relax in stressful situations is another active coping skill. If clients can respond to stressful stimuli by relaxing, they are able to access other coping skills more effectively. Furthermore, mastery of relaxation may enhance a client's general quality of life. Another coping skill is the ability to escape or to avoid a highly stressful situation if appropriate.

Recreational skills may be regarded as active coping skills as well. Although some are social in nature, recreational skills may be regarded as a separate category. Groups can be taught both individual and group leisure time activities that may enhance the quality of their day-to-day life. Teaching of these skills affords opportunities to teach such social skills handling competition, getting involved and involving others, and giving and accepting criticism.

In the previous sections, we pointed out some major target behaviors and problems with which the multimethod group approach is designed to deal. In summary, these target behaviors include more effective management of pain, stress, anger, depression, or anxiety; reduction and/or elimination of excessive use of drugs, alcohol, or cigarettes; increased involvement in prosocial activities; job seeking; reduction of negative or self-defeating self-statements; reduction of avoidance behavior; skill in mediating rewards for others; skill in dealing with criticism of others; development of positive self-statements; increase in frequency of dating; use of condoms; development of assertiveness. Achievement of these goals may involve the learning of coping behaviors and/or coping cognitions. Some of these behaviors (for example, increasing positive self-statements) mediate the achievement of other behaviors (reduction of anxiety); others are targets in their own right (for example, getting a job). Because of the wide scope, intensity, and degree of observability of these behaviors, many different treatment

methods are required, hence the name "multimethod" approach.
Let us now examine some of the methods in the multimethod
approach.

The Multimethods

Extensive research has been carried out on methods of
teaching clients the various coping skills covered in this book. In
most of these studies, the intervention was limited to one or two of
the following methods: problem solving, cognitive-affective,
modeling, rehearsal, coaching, operant, stimulus control, sociorecreational, relational, small group, and extragroup. Even when
carried out in a group setting, most studies ignored both the group's
potential and the problems it could create (see Rose, Tolman, and
Tallant, 1986, for a review of those group studies dealing with
stress, anxiety, and depression). In the multimethod approach, we
attempt to integrate all or most of the methods. A method is
included preferably if it has some independent empirical foundation and if, at least in case studies, some relationship to the
previously mentioned targets can be demonstrated. A final criterion
for inclusion is whether a given procedure can be adapted to the
group; that is, the intervention is used to facilitate participation of
every member and to maintain or improve group cohesion. We
review each of these methods in terms of its contribution to the total
approach. In subsequent chapters, these methods are explained in
greater detail.

The Modeling Sequence. The modeling sequence, which is
one of the most commonly used intervention strategies in preparation for both overt social and cognitive skill implementation, is
designed to teach specific positive interactive behaviors. It includes
such techniques as overt modeling, behavior rehearsal, coaching,
and group feedback. Modeling is learning through observation of a
model, who might be the group leader, another member of the
group, someone in the client's environment, or an admired person
on stage, on screen, in novels, or in public life. Modeling may be
roleplayed in the group or may be observed directly in real life.
Modeling is often used to demonstrate how a situation problematic

to one or more clients in the group may be handled effectively. Behavioral rehearsal is a roleplay technique in which a client with a given problem practices more effective ways of handling that situation. Coaching refers to the instructions or verbal cues given to clients as they model or rehearse a set of behaviors in a given situation. Group feedback is verbal evaluation from others as to the effectiveness of a client's roleplaying or modeling. After the modeling sequence, the client prepares for and carries out extragroup tasks to practice the social skill in the real world. It is an excellent group procedure because each modeled situation offers multiple modeling and feedback opportunities.

Modification of Antecedents and Consequences. Modification of antecedents and consequences is derived from operant theory and involves procedures in which the immediate consequences of a given behavior are followed in some systematic manner by a reinforcing event. It may also involve procedures in which the immediate conditions that lead to or are parallel with a given behavior are changed to create circumstances more amenable to the performance of a desired behavior. The latter is often referred to as stimulus control.

Clients in groups receive many kinds of reinforcement for the performance of prosocial group behavior and the completion of extragroup assignments or home tasks. With adults, this reinforcement takes the form of praise (smiles, applause, approving nods, and delighted laughter) by the group leader or other group members. Reinforcement is withheld in response to undesirable behaviors. This is referred to as extinction and is an occasional group response to members who are frequently off-task or complain a great deal.

Modification of the antecedent conditions, or stimulus control, is exemplified by the use in small subgroups of group exercises that encourage intense interaction. A client who was working on nail biting wore thin gloves to prevent him from chewing on his nails. A client in the weight-loss group ate only at a set table and only food that had been cooked. A college student in the study-skill-enhancement program worked out a plan to study only at a clean desk and to do nothing but study at that desk. The client removed the telephone and food from the study room.

Operant procedures, especially reinforcement, lend themselves to the group setting provided that the leader trains and encourages members to reinforce each other and significant others outside the group.

Cognitive Change Methods. Cognitive change methods are used to train clients to evaluate problems more effectively. Many cognitive procedures are used in groups, often in combination with each other and with other procedures such as the modeling sequence. The most commonly used cognitive methods are restructuring, self-instructional training, and self-reinforcement.

Cognitive restructuring (Meichenbaum, 1977), the first step in increasing cognitive coping skills, is characterized as procedures that convert self-defeating or illogical patterns of thinking into self-enhancing or logical ones. It is assumed that in a given set of circumstances, cognitions in part mediate overt behavioral responses. These cognitions include self-image and covert patterns of response to a given situation. Clients are trained to identify self-enhancing and self-defeating thoughts in case examples or exercises. Later, they learn to identify their own self-defeating thoughts and those of their peers and to change these to self-enhancing thoughts. Clients are taught through covert modeling (modeling what the client should be thinking) initiated by the leader and covert rehearsal (practicing what they would think in a given situation).

Self-instructional training (Meichenbaum, 1977) combines cognitive restructuring and problem solving. Members are encouraged to verbalize step-by-step the problem ("What's wrong with the way I'm thinking about this?"), the problem focus ("What can I do about it?"), attention ("I should think about how that will get me in trouble"), coping ("If I keep relaxing I won't blow it!"), and self-reinforcement ("Wow! I did it! See, I can do it!"). To prepare for implementation of these strategies the group leader or another client demonstrates (covert modeling) what might be said to oneself. The client then practices by reading the coping statements aloud, then whispering, and eventually thinking them.

Group Exposure Methods. Group exposure methods have been used primarily in the treatment of agoraphobia (Hafner and Marks, 1976). They involve exposure, first together with other group members and then eventually alone, to frightening situations. For example, after preparation by cognitive restructuring and the modeling sequence, the group of agoraphobics together visited a department store several times. On their first visit, they went in the morning, when the store was almost empty; later, they went when there was a sale; and still later, they rode the elevators and escalators together. Finally, they practiced these same exercises with buddies and eventually by themselves. The procedures we use are derived from the descriptions of Hand, Lamontagne, and Marks (1974). Emmelkamp and Kuipers (1985) review the commonly used procedures and the current research that supports these methods.

Relaxation Methods. Relaxation methods are used to teach clients to cope with stress, pain, anger, or external environmental events for which no external coping behavior is available or for which cognitive coping behavior is insufficient. A modified version of the system developed by Jacobson (1929, 1978) is used in which various muscles groups are alternately tensed and relaxed. This is referred to as neuromuscular relaxation. In later phases the tensing is eliminated. Even later, clients teach, monitor, and reinforce each other to improve performance. Alternatives uniquely suited to various populations are also taught. Modest research supporting the use of neuromuscular relaxation procedures in reducing anxiety and stress is found in the studies of Stoyva (1977) and Lyles, Burish, Korzely, and Oldham (1982). Heide and Borkovec (1983) have shown that relaxation may increase anxiety in some people. Meditation and breathing exercises can be taught as alternatives to neuromuscular relaxation depending on individual preferences.

Relationship Enhancement Methods. Certain skills are crucial to any helping relationship (Goldstein and Myers, 1986) whether it be a dyad or a group. We have noted in our supervision of group leaders that despite possession of high level of technological skill in other methods, failure to possess these relationship skills results in high dropout rates, disinterest, and many group problems. In a sense, these skills are the solvent into which all the other methods are dissolved.

Many of these skills are used with the methods described earlier. For example, group leaders who comfortably and frequently provide their members with high levels of reinforcement tend to establish sound relationships with these members. Similarly, group leaders who model the skills that members are expected to acquire discover that group problems (high levels of conflict, low cohesion, low satisfaction, pairing off) seldom arise. Those group leaders who create stimulating sociorecreational activities together with their clients also enhance client–leader and client–client relationships. Because they are specific, these skills can be taught.

Some skills are unique to relationship building. For example, the use of humor with clients is not addressed with respect to other methods. Yet, to work with clients, one must be able to play with clients, to joke with them, and to permit oneself as leader to be teased.

Involving clients and the group in their own therapy is a skill that is essential to achieve generalization of change. This means helping clients to take the chance and answer the questions posed by other members, to suggest plans of action to each other, and to help each other clarify the basis of their problems and formulate appropriate goals. In each of the intervention chapters, we demonstrate how members can gradually assume responsibility for their own therapy. The more clients perceive themselves as deciding their own fate, the more likely they will make use of the intervention.

Listening to clients is a skill not covered earlier, yet its absence often results in the pursuit of the wrong targets. To be an effective listener, a group leader need not read the underlying meaning of a client's words; grasping the obvious meaning is sometimes a far more difficult task. In hastening to carry out a given agenda, leaders often interrupt or ponder the next step while a client is still speaking.

Attending skills refer to observation of nonverbal responses such as eye contact, body posture, and voice tone, which may indicate acceptance, warmth, and trust. Although these characteristics are difficult to define, observation of group leaders in action tends to indicate whether such skills are operating.

Often, the group leader is faced with a client's extreme affective response on entry into the group. Usually, this emotional outburst is a response to a perceived crisis that occurred prior to the meeting but falls outside the specific purpose of the meeting. Ignoring such crises inevitably results in passive or chaotic meetings. On the other hand, focusing all attention on the individual often results in failure to achieve preplanned objectives and broad participation. The way in which such situations are handled contributes to the nature of the relationship with the given client and the other group members.

Setting limits on disruptive or off-task behavior is another relationship skill that must be acquired if the goals of change are to be met in a safe environment. It is a difficult skill to acquire, yet is frequently required. Skill in reinforcement and the development of program activities that are attractive to members often eliminates the necessity for setting limits.

The methods for acquiring these (often-called) nonspecific therapeutic skills are not well worked out, although the work of Goldstein and Myers (1986) on dyadic interviewing and of Toseland and Rivas (1984) on group therapy point the way to training procedures. We suggest that modeling may be the best way to teach these skills to beginning group leaders. Although no one chapter is devoted to the application of relationship skills, their presence permeates most of the intervention chapters in this book.

Small Group Procedures. Because the multimethod approach is also a small group approach, advantage can be taken of the many procedures that are enhanced by employment in groups or are unique to the group setting. As mentioned earlier, modeling, cognitive restructuring, relaxation, and so forth are administered in such a way as to encourage broad participation. Some concrete group procedures also appear to be instrumental in helping clients move toward change or mediate the effectiveness of the other procedures. These include group discussion, roleplaying, subgrouping and the buddy system, group exercises, and sociorecreational procedures, all of which will be described. In the small group method, one or more of these procedures are used to facilitate the attainment of group goals or the resolution of group interactive problems.

Group discussion refers to client-client and client-leader verbal interaction. It is essentially how problems are laid out and considered, solutions are shared and evaluated, decisions are formulated and affirmed, values are deliberated, and friendships are made. Group discussion assumes that the maximum involvement of all group members is essential to cohesion and effective therapy.

Roleplaying, in its most elementary form, is defined as the practice of roles in simulated conditions. The group leader, acting as a guide and structuring the roleplaying, contributes to the process and, to a lesser degree, to the outcome. If the group leader is clear about the purposes of roleplaying, even through focused use, this technique can prove highly beneficial in promoting change, broadening participation, and increasing cohesion. In the modeling sequence, roleplaying is used both to demonstrate and to practice specific skills. Roleplaying is also used for assessment, to teach specific therapy skills, in role reversal, and in generalization training. Although, initially, some clients are reluctant to roleplay, eventually almost all members cooperate enthusiastically.

Subgrouping is working in pairs, triads, or larger subgroups to increase interaction among the members, to provide an opportunity to work without the oversight of the leader, and to practice leadership skills. In the *buddy system* (see O'Donnell, Lydgate, and Fo, 1979), a special subgrouping procedure, clients work together outside of the group. They transfer the knowledge gained within the group to the real world.

In *group exercises,* structured interactive activities are used to teach clients the skills that facilitate the achievement of therapeutic goals. For example, in the introduction exercise, clients interview at least two clients in the group and introduce them to the others. In another exercise, the clients study one case and discuss how they are different from the subject of that case. In still other exercises, clients are taught to give and accept both praise and criticism; usually at least one such exercise is carried out in every session. In the "round robin" exercise, modeling and rehearsal are employed at a rapid pace to provide multiple trials. For example, to teach help-asking behavior, Pete asks Don for help, then Don asks Robin for help, then Robin asks Jerry for help, and finally, Jerry asks Pete for help.

Sociorecreational procedures involve the use of physical games, board games, arts and crafts, storytelling, and drama to facilitate the achievement of therapeutic goals and increase group cohesion. Ross and Bernstein (1976, p. 127) state that "games and activities offer clients a workshop for discovering and developing new ways to manage obstacles." Although commonly used with children, these procedures, especially board games, are becoming popular with adults as well. More frequent, however, is the use of group exercises that are gamelike and provide clients with a highly satisfying set of stimulus conditions in which concrete skills can be informally practiced and reinforced. Sociorecreational activities in many groups form the initial basis for broad participation and increased group interest. Furthermore, such activities provide a context for practicing social skills that is more realistic than roleplaying.

Of greater importance with some clients is development of sociorecreational leisure time skills. Many clients have few opportunities to make friends or otherwise practice newly learned social skills. Their social networks are either limited or abusive. Therefore, clients are encouraged to identify and become involved in new sociorecreational interests. Group members support each other in this endeavor, which prepares them for outside activity.

Extragroup Intervention Methods. Vinter (1974) points to extragroup intervention strategies as important as those that occur within the group. Similarly, Pincus and Minahan (1973), in their classic social text, stress the importance of going beyond the individual and small group "systems" to maximize the effectiveness of therapy. These strategies involve the group leader with the family and other social units whose activities and policies impinge on the outcome of specific therapy. The strategies may involve reevaluation of policies, communication with representatives of these social units, and training of significant others in reinforcement or other techniques used in the group.

Most interventions that occur outside the group are performed not by the leader but by the client. The clients discuss with their families or friends what they might be able to do to help the clients to achieve their goals. The clients organize their own recreational programs. They may involve themselves in a social action project, for example, organizing a float in a local parade for handicapped children. The extragroup interventions are planned in the group. Some reinforcement and monitoring may also occur in the group. But the real action is in the community, where the client furthers his or her own interests.

Failure to go beyond the treatment group boundaries often results in the failure to maintain therapeutic goals once they are achieved. Because these issues are covered extensively elsewhere (see, for example, Sundel, Glasser, Sarri, and Vinter, 1985), we do not devote a chapter to these skills; however, the application of these skills is discussed in Chapter Thirteen. Extragroup interventions contribute heavily to achievement of generalization of change.

Some Remaining Issues

Many issues remain to be discussed; however, because of their centrality in guiding the leader, two issues should be introduced early in this book: Is the multimethod approach a form of training or of therapy? How structured is an approach in which maximum involvement of the client is essential and comprehensive prestructuring is carried out by the leader?

Training or Therapy? Review of the literature on groups reveals a distinction between therapeutic and training models. More often than not, these words are used interchangeably. Is there a distinction to be made? In general, we find it useful to place therapy at one end of a group intervention continuum and training at the other end. Basically, a training model provides the participant with information and opportunities to discuss and practice that information. The skills to be learned are generally narrow in scope, for example, relaxation or refusal responses. At the therapeutic end of the continuum, the focus is on broad-based learning. Moreover, more complex problems are dealt with in therapeutic programs than in training programs. Greater emphasis is placed on individualization; clients work not only toward common group goals but also toward individual goals. More effort is invested in simulated and real-world experiences so that new patterns of responses to difficult situations are well learned. Thus, therapy is more intensive, but not more important, than training. Most groups fall in the middle of the continuum. A factor crucial in determining where a group lies in the continuum is available time. It is difficult to provide therapy in an insufficient number of sessions. Groups that meet upward of eighteen sessions tend to move farther toward the therapeutic end of the continuum, whereas one-day workshops tend to be primarily educational or training. Those multimethod groups that meet for eight to twelve two-hour weekly sessions can be placed in the middle of the continuum. As more group leaders lean toward longer groups for the therapy of persistent problems, the program tends toward the therapeutic end. Regardless of the place on the continuum, the principles of teaching and learning in groups are the same.

It should be noted that this book has drawn from research (theoretical and clinical) and from the literature of social workers, psychiatrists, psychologists, social psychologists, and others in the helping professions and social sciences. The sources and the leaders of the groups exemplified in this book come from diverse professional backgrounds. The label most commonly attributed to work with groups to achieve sociotherapeutic purposes is *group therapy*. In many cases the labels *group work, group training, group treatment,* or *group counseling* could be used just as appropriately. We refer to the individual who leads the process as *group leader,* a label that cuts across the different professions. The group leader in many instances may just as readily be identified as group therapist, group worker, or group counselor, because the activities overlap considerably. We use *clients* and *members* interchangeably to refer to the persons in the groups, although in medical and some psychiatric settings, the word *patient* is used.

High Versus Low Group Structure. Because of the large number of interventions available to the group and because of the systematic problem-solving orientation of the approach, it would appear that the multimethod approach is highly structured and that its structure comes solely from the leader. (Compared with psychotherapeutic group approaches or Rogerian nondirective approaches, the multimethod approach appears to have a great deal more structure. If the level of leader-imposed structure is rated on a scale of 1 (the leader sits back and does nothing) to 10 (the leader performs all leadership functions and all interaction is directed at the leader), then the multimethod approach is initially 7, drops rapidly to 3, in subsequent phases, and increases slightly as the group approaches termination. The group leader must focus on providing increasing opportunity for members to intervene in changing their own behavior, assessing their own problems, and developing their own generalization plans. The leader demonstrates these activities, provides concepts, and recommends principles that members can use as a guide, but throughout treatment, the leader focuses on maximum member involvement. This principle is of sufficient importance to be illustrated throughout the book.

Summary

The multimethod approach is so named because it comprises a problem-solving approach, a small group approach, a coping-skill-training approach, a goal-orienting approach, and/or an empirical approach to group therapy. The rationales for these orientations are also discussed. This chapter introduces the reader to the basic concepts and procedures used throughout the text. It is important that the basic assumptions and definitions be presented before the specifics. The final chapter contains detailed excerpts from one group's sessions that illustrate many of the principles discussed throughout the book. The reader may find it useful to peruse that excerpt before continuing.

TWO

Understanding Group Structure and Process

The clients trickled into the room one at a time, five to ten minutes late. When the leader finally began the session most members participated in the discussion, but four men tended to talk only to each other for the first few meetings of the group and the women talked primarily to the group leader. Postsession questionnaires collected after the first two sessions revealed that satisfaction was moderately low but had increased from the first to the second week. Members tended to avoid talking about issues of great concern. Mr. Felonni and Mr. Rogers complained about how little the group was helping them. Ms. Hanssen made everything about the group sound useful and exciting. She was noticeably upset by Mr. Felonni's complaining. Ms. Carter wanted to tell about her son's accomplishments in math and science. And Mr. Hardcastel told her and others that they were off-task and should get back to the agenda.

From this example, we can postulate a number of group structural elements. We see broad distribution of participation but much of it is off-task. Subgroups have been established along gender lines. There appears to be a low level of self-disclosure. Also, mutual reinforcement is not apparent. Lateness appears to have become a norm in the group. Several member roles are beginning to evolve. One could surmise from the questionnaires that the cohesion within the group is low to moderate.

Structure Versus Process

As Lieberman, Yalom, and Miles (1973) note, group structure and processes play a significant role in group therapy whether or not salient attention is paid to them by the group leader. The significance of group process is further attested to by Whitaker and Lieberman (1964): "Process characteristics of the group as a whole are an intrinsic and inevitable aspect of all groups no matter what their size or function. In a treatment group, group processes not only 'exist' but are a major factor influencing the nature of each patient's therapeutic experience. The manner in which each patient contributes to, participates in, and is affected by the group process determines to a considerable degree whether he/she will profit from the group experience, be untouched by it, or be harmed by it."

There are data that support the preceding view. For example, increased group cohesion (Costell and Koran, 1972; Flowers, Booraem, and Hartman, 1981), group self-disclosure and feedback (Dies, 1973; Dies and Cohen, 1976; Kirshner, Dies, and Brown, 1978; Ribner, 1974), and group participation (Fielding, 1983) have all been associated with positive treatment outcome. For this reason, in the multimethod approach, the group is conceptualized as an active therapy component in itself and operates as both a means and a context for the achievement of individual and group goals. This chapter surveys the major conceptual aspects of the group and several group frames of reference that can be used to analyze group structure and group process. It should be noted that these structures and processes often overlap and represent to a large degree different ways of measuring group phenomena; however, as the literature represents all of the proposed concepts, we have attempted to clarify them in terms of their applicability to multimethod and other goal-oriented groups. In review of our own research with structured groups, we have found that when group issues are not given attention the normally high rates of change do not occur and the dropout rate is unusually high (Whitney and Rose, 1988). This chapter provides the theoretical framework within which attention to group matters is developed.

Group Structure Defined. Any structure represents an identifiable arrangement of elements at a given point in time. In a group, the structure contains elements that are interactive in nature or are products of interaction. Some group structure elements are the rules/norms governing the behavior of participants, the intensity and degree of involvement in self-disclosure, the prevailing emotional state of the group, the distribution of leadership functions among the members, the nature and distribution of distinct roles played by the members, and the degree of mutual attraction among members (cohesiveness). These elements refer to interactive or mutual phenomena, not to phenomena generated by an individual.

In some cases the element may be a product of an interaction, for example, the amount of common work achieved or the amount of mutual assistance given. The specific elements by which the entity is described depend on the theoretical justification of their relevance. A relationship must be demonstrated between the given structural element and the thrust of the theoretical approach. Each theory points to the relevance of a different set of elements. For example, in goal-oriented theories, only those elements that directly or indirectly impinge on goal attainment have relevance. In psychodynamic theories, those elements that contribute to deep and meaningful personal insight are relevant. It is because of this diversity of theory that so many different descriptions of elements of group structure are found in the literature.

Of course, many diverse sets of elements can be justified theoretically. For a given arrangement to be useful as well as theoretically meaningful, it must also be verifiable. That is, there should be some evidence outside of personal intuition that a given phenomenon is occurring. This assumption leads us to the third characteristic of group structure—it must be reliably observed and/or measured at some point in time.

In summary, group structure within a goal-oriented framework is a verifiable arrangement of predetermined elements characteristic of or resulting from the interaction of its members as measured at one point in time.

Group Process Defined. As noted in the preceding section, group structure is defined at a given point in time. Structure at the beginning of the group is likely to be quite different from that at the sixth session. The group structure is in part a result of the conditions existing at a given time. One description of the arrangement of elements does not typify the group in all circumstances. Thus, descriptions over time provide a better picture than any single description. Group process can be defined as the changes over time of the arrangement of predetermined elements of the interaction of members as measured at two or more different times in a given session. Process may be considered at multiple points within a given meeting or across meetings. In some forms of process analysis, every interactive act may be coded. A postsession questionnaire may be used to get a weekly picture of the group. Looking at the group at the beginning and at the end may reveal shifts in interaction patterns or other relevant group attributes. Access to the nuances of change depends primarily on a high frequency of observation and/ or measurement.

It is difficult to speak of a group structure or a group process in its totality. It is necessary to restrict the picture to one or a few elements, such as norm structure (and then often only one norm at a time) or group development. Each structure is a partial picture of the group at a point in time in terms of one set of related elements. Several structures may be described simultaneously, but in the absence of a comprehensive theory, a complete picture of *the* group structure or *the* group process cannot be obtained.

When a group is process oriented, the leader is concerned primarily with content of interaction over time. In addition, it is usually assumed that this content is described and discussed with the group members as the work of the group. When a group is goal oriented, the work comprises those interventions that lead achievement of goals. These may include process goals (in our terminology, group goals), such as increasing group cohesion or establishing protherapy norms.

Importance of Group Process and Group Structure. In examining these definitions, the reader may question why a group level concept is necessary. Why can one not look at the behavior of six people and describe how each behaves with respect to a given phenomenon, such as lateness, self-disclosure, patterns of communication, or attraction to the group? The major reason for positing a group-level concept is that shared opinions, values, and behaviors of group members mediate the behavior of each individual. Lateness would probably not remain a problem for George if all of the other members came on time and informally commented on his lateness. Of course, behavior is also a function of an individual's earlier learning history. Group phenomena merely influence in lawful ways whether previously learned behaviors or new behaviors are acceptable and desirable within the context of the group. Let us look at some group phenomena of concern in the multimethod approach and determine how these phenomena impinge on individual learning and goal attainment. Foremost is group cohesion.

Group Cohesion

A primary job of a group leader in the early phase of therapy is to facilitate group cohesion. Group cohesion is the degree to which members are attracted to one another, the program or group task, and the group leader (Lott and Lott, 1965). Cohesion is regarded as an essential attribute of groups because it appears to be correlated, under certain conditions, to productivity, participation in and out of the group, self-disclosure, risk taking, attendance, and other vital concerns (Stokes, 1983). Despite the diverse and fairly vague definitions, most practitioners regard this characteristic as a major group attribute. Yalom (1985, p. 48) hypothesizes that cohesion in group therapy is the analogue to relationship in individual therapy. It seems to reflect the relationship of members not only to the group leader but also to each other. As a result it is assumed to be one of the major curative factors in nondirective therapy. This hypothesis has found support in a number of studies on sensitivity groups (for example, Lieberman, Yalom, and Miles, 1973). Our own recent experience in more structured groups also tends to support the hypothesis.

Although cohesion is a group phenomenon, it is most often measured as an average of individual phenomena by asking the members about their attraction to the group and various elements of the group. In measuring group cohesion the practitioner must be careful to not attribute to the measurement all of the characteristics attributed to the more general concept. This particular definition has been selected because it can be readily measured by the postsession questionnaire and, in certain circumstances, by attendance and dropout data (see Chapter Five for detailed descriptions). Though not without limitations, attendance and dropout rates indicate a group-level dimension as people indicate their attraction behaviorally. The postsession questionnaire yields an average and a distribution of attitudes toward the group that can only approximate a group-level attribute. Thus, to catch the various dimensions of cohesion we recommend the use of multiple measures (see also Drescher, Burlingame, and Fuhriman, 1985, for a more detailed discussion of these issues).

Regardless of the type of group, it is essential in therapy to encourage the development of a high level of cohesion in the early phase of therapy. When that cohesion is threatened in the middle phases, it must be reestablished. As the group approaches termination it is usually necessary to help clients establish alternative social networks to the therapy group. This reduces the degree of dependence on the group once it has ended. Specifically, clients are encouraged to seek membership in alternate groups prior to termination. For those clients who have just begun to use therapy, a new group may be appropriate. For others, involvement in nontherapy groups or in relationships that have been neglected may be advisable. Open-ended groups are groups that new members enter and old members leave sporadically. The core group, those persons who remain in the group a significant length of time, provides the only cohesion in the group. Therefore, the group leader must make a special effort to prepare both the core group and the new member, as entry into the group may be difficult.

The Norm Structure

Norms constitute an important element of groups. Schopler and Galinsky (1985) define norms as rules that guide, control, or regulate proper and acceptable behavior of group members ("proper" and "acceptable" depend on a number of factors: as group expectations, agency policies and procedures, leader characteristics, problem composition among members, and more). They also believe that the sanctions, rewards, and penalties applied to members for adherence or nonadherence to rules help define the norms.

This definition is expanded by Belfer and Levendusky (1985), who emphasize that norms are behavioral rules that guide the interaction of the group and are established by the ongoing interpersonal process of the group. These authors also believe that leaders should build in "appropriate" norms, as some norms can be detrimental to positive outcome. In one example, there was a nonverbalized rule that members should not get too emotional or take group time to express personal feelings about another member. In a second example, a group of mothers agreed to arrive five to ten minutes before their meeting to exchange stories about their children. Rules may or may not be norms; only if rules are conformed to, can they be regarded as norms. Some norms are particularly important because they enhance or impede therapy outcome. For example, a stress management group agreed that at the second meeting, all members would reveal what situations made them anxious but not why the situations made them anxious. The reason for establishing this norm was that most members conformed to the norm. Moreover, those who failed to behave acceptably were criticized by the other group members, and those who conformed with the assumed norm received approval and reinforcement. Several other norms were noted: members were expected to arrive on time, to avoid criticism of peers at all costs, and not to socialize at the coffee break in the middle of the session. Thus, the norms of this group were the behaviors expected in response to explicit or implicit rules. To the degree that these norms could be verified by an observer or by the statements of the members themselves, and found relevant in terms of a relationship of the element to outcome, the group leader could design strategies to enhance or change them.

The norm process in the preceding example would be a description of how old norms changed and new norms evolved over time. For example, by the eighth meeting, members not only discussed what situations resulted in increased anxiety, but also revealed the self-defeating cognitions they hypothesized that seemed to exacerbate the anxiety. Most members arrived at sessions on time, and the group had done away with the coffee break and, instead, drank coffee throughout the meeting.

Development of Norms. How are norms established and how do they evolve? Sometimes simple rules defined by the leader are sufficient to establish norms. But this is often not the case. Sometimes a member with strong charismatic qualities models behaviors that are antithetical to the rules established by the formal group leader. In some instances, several people in the group have a well-learned pattern of behavior that cannot be overcome by a simple rule. For example, some people who are highly critical of others in all their interactions continue that behavior in the therapy group despite the rule of "looking first for positives." Others may be so frightened by self-disclosure that although it is expected, they cannot talk about the situations that bother them. Members also bring norms from other therapy groups. Members of previous encounter groups may push for entirely free interaction, spontaneous and totally unstructured, even though they originally were attracted to the limits inherent in a structured group.

Often, the rules are not clear or there are too many rules. Some rules (for example, expecting Hispanic men to talk openly about their problems) should not be proposed early in the group history. Some authors propose that deviation from protherapeutic rules established by the leader is one way the members can control the conditions of the group and successfully fight the leader. It is conceived as a form of resistance and a group process in its own right. To intervene in the norm structure, it is necessary to understand the etiology of a given norm and, on the basis of that understanding, to design an intervention approach. This and other strategies for intervening in the norm structure are discussed in Chapter Eleven.

Curative and Antitherapeutic Norms. It is possible to make a distinction between curative norms and antitherapeutic norms. Some mutually agreed-on behaviors, once established as norms in the group, are regarded in certain circumstances as curative factors: self-disclosure, feedback, socially appropriate behaviors, exchange of information and advice, respect and acceptance of others, and propagation of hope and security. As these are overt interactive behaviors, they can be established in part by the leader through modeling, encouragement, group exercises, and other structured activities. [Curative factors have been discussed in detail by Yalom (1985) and Bloch (1976). We identify only those curative factors that lend themselves readily to intervention. In some cases we have changed the description and the key terminology somewhat to meet our own theoretical orientation.]

Other norms tend to interfere with group formation or cohesiveness, for example, irregular attendance, frequent tardiness, pairing off, excessive interpersonal aggression, excessive dependence on the leader, dominance of interaction by a few members, general passivity in the interaction, and are regarded as antitherapeutic. Their presence requires the attention of the group and group leader. One norm that can be curative and antitherapeutic is self-disclosure.

Self-Disclosure. An exact definition of self-disclosure is elusive (Kaul and Bednar, 1985). Generally, it refers to the degree to which members influence each other to talk about the problems that are important to them. Flowers and Schwartz (1985) report that self-disclosure is increased when members are asked to specify in depth and in writing the disclosures they might make in the next session. Self-disclosure is even further increased if members are instructed to bring two written disclosures to the next group session with the alternative of disclosing either, both, or neither, depending on their feelings during that session. Yalom, Tinklenberg, and Giulula (1968) studied the Q-sorted statements of group members in twenty groups. They discovered that "being able to say what was bothering me instead of holding it in" was the second most important attribute for therapeutic progress, and "learning how to express my feelings" was fourth. "Expressing negative or positive feelings toward another member" was sixth.

Many people feel better after disclosing their problems to others with whom they are intimate. Of course, the key word here is "intimate." Without maximum group process, especially high cohesion, it is unlikely that the intimacy needed to reinforce the self-disclosure will exist. This would argue against too much self-disclosure, especially in beginning sessions when cohesion and intimacy have not had ample time to develop. If the member discloses information that is embarrassing and does not receive the support of the other members, emotional "breakdown" may occur or the person may drop out of treatment.

In behavioral groups, an additional benefit of high levels of self-disclosure is that clients describe problems of real concern rather than trivial problems. Thus, self-disclosure as a norm enhances assessment which, in turn, enhances the general quality of treatment.

A final observation on benefits of self-disclosure centers on improved communication skills. As members learn to verbally present their feelings and thoughts in an acceptable manner, they may be less likely to manifest them via symptomatic expression. Sometimes, it is simply a matter of learning descriptive feeling words and receiving "permission" or encouragement from the group to "try them out." Of course, subsequent reinforcement from the group strengthens not only the verbal skill, but the disclosing person's feeling of acceptance when not rejected or ridiculed.

The self-disclosure of group members can be enhanced by the self-disclosure of the group leader, as evidenced in studies on the dyadic relationship by Sermat and Smyth (1973); however, too much or too intimate self-disclosure by the group leader can lead to member distrust or the perception that the leader is using the group for his or her own therapy. Simonson and Bahr (1974) have shown that to be most effective, the leader should disclose private matters but not personal problems or conflicts.

In summary, it appears that one of the main benefits of self-disclosure is improved assessment, "getting feelings out" while being accepted as a worthwhile human being. A side benefit of others' self-disclosures (in groups) is finding that members realize that the "terrible" feelings they have are not unique. Moreover, the improved verbal skills resulting from their own self-disclosure and that of others should be of lasting value. Self-disclosure by reticent members can be enhanced by the self-disclosure of others in the group, including the group leader.

The Role Structure

Just as mutual expectations of behaviors may be regarded as norms, roles can be defined as unique expectations for individual behaviors by most group members. In some cases, these behaviors are characterized by a central theme such as "the critic," "the clown," and "the antagonist." Some roles may enhance the therapy process in that some people are more likely to perform such functions as providing negative feedback, which stimulates discussion of certain issues. In many cases, roles interfere with the achievement of therapy goals insofar as they become stereotypic demands on individuals or free people from the responsibility to perform certain behaviors. For example, one member is expected to joke about any demands made by the leader. If he fails to make such a joke, the group members are likely to comment on his reluctance. (For a further discussion of role theory, see Biddle and Thomas, 1966.)

Formal Roles. In most therapy groups usually two formal roles are assumed: group leader and client. The former, the helper, is high status; the latter, the person to be helped, is low status. As many clients are usually in low-status roles and situations, they must often rely on deviant behaviors to gain some semblance of control over their situations. Thus, an important function of group work is to increase the status of the members by letting them gradually assume the functions of higher-status roles.

Occasionally, a discussion leader, an observer, a recorder, or a secretary is designated by the group leader from among the members or is selected by the members themselves. These roles are usually associated with clearly defined behaviors, some of which were originally attributed to the group leader's role. Success is determined on the basis of the roleplayer's effectiveness in the performance of the prescribed behaviors associated with that role. Usually, formal training through modeling and rehearsal in the prescribed role behaviors is sufficient to ensure effective role performance. The use of multiple formal roles provides one vehicle by which the more influential behaviors can be distributed to the group members. To be most effective this distribution should be carried out with the members of the group. Formal roles are uncommon in adult therapy groups though they are used often in task groups such as committees.

Informal Roles. Informal roles seem to arise more commonly in therapy groups. Each role is characterized by certain identifiable behavioral patterns of a given person and others' behavioral expectations of that person. Examples of informal roles are the client who is the nurturer, reinforcing others for their participation and providing support in time of need, the person who annoys others across situations, the "informal leader" who assumes responsibility for making important decisions, the "disciplinarian" who takes it on herself to limit others when they make the slightest mistake. In general, however, analysis of the specific behaviors associated with each role, with a focus on how these behaviors are maintained through the roles of others, appears to result in useful interventions. For example, Alan responded to all critical feedback with anger. Fearing his anger, the members of the therapy group did not give him any critical feedback. Thus, Alan was disliked and often ignored. This appeared to be the case at home and at work. Alan controlled family, work, and therapy situations with his anger. The group maintained Alan's behavior, which interfered with group interaction and the establishment of sound working relationships. Alan's role impeded his use of the group and the use of the group by others. Although the situation may be viewed solely in terms of behavior, the role framework is an excellent way of linking behavior to what is going on in the group.

Positive roles can enhance change in others. Roles that provide a needed contrast to the more disruptive roles are models to others in the group. The informal leader may have to learn to share some authority but, in the long run, offers the group an opportunity to observe behavior worthy of emulation.

Roles are often identified by obtaining the perceptions of the members and the leader on questionnaires at the end of a session. Members are asked to characterize each other in terms of certain behaviors they can usually expect in various group situations. A role exists because a majority of the members agree that it should exist. Whether the role impedes or furthers the therapy process depends on the nature of interaction, assignment, completion, and cohesion in the group. Roles like norms can form the basis of a group discussion. The major focus of the group leader is on the way in which the group contributes to maintaining the various roles and the ways in which the group can help its members assume more effective roles.

Communication Structure

The communication structure comprises the various patterns of communication operating in the group. The answers to the following questions draw a picture of one unique pattern of communication: What is the frequency of participation of all members and the leader in the group? What are the prevailing themes of communication in the group? It should be noted that the only difference between norm structure and communication structure is that the latter is a special case of the former; that is, communication structures are norms concerning the content of communication. There is also a practical distinction. Norms are usually ascertained by looking at perceptions of the members as to their beliefs or opinions. The communication structure is more often ascertained by observation of group interaction.

A common pattern in discussion groups is the dominance of one or two people in and the withdrawal of others from group interaction. To attain individual therapy goals, it is frequently desirable to obtain broad participation. When some members discuss their problems, support others, and generate ideas while others rarely participate, the former profit more from the group than the latter. The avid participators become concerned with how the nonparticipators are judging their disclosures. Furthermore, where the discrepancy is large, the cohesion in the group and the reported satisfaction tend to be low.

A common theme in early sessions of groups of involuntary clients (for example, family violence groups and alcohol and drug abuse groups) is mutual denial of responsibility. Members in these groups tend to blame present and past family members for their problems. It is a group phenomenon rather than an individual one insofar as the members reinforce each other in their denial and the occasional self-disclosure is ignored or even criticized.

Another communication theme commonly encountered is "premature problem solving." These groups are characterized by frequent advice, limited evaluation of that advice, limited self-disclosure, and limited sharing of information about responses to that problem. This communication problem occurs most commonly at the beginning sessions when members are looking for quick answers.

Subgroup Structure

A special case of the communication structure is the subgroup structure, which partially determines who prefers to communicate with whom. In most groups we have found that it is easier for clients to communicate in groups of two and three. Subgroups are encouraged in the early phase through subgroup assignments and exercises. (Postsession evaluations have always rated these subgroup activities very high.) Wherever possible, we change the composition of subgroups from activity to activity to avoid establishing stable subgroups. "Pairing off" (Bion, 1959) is viewed as a group deterioration effect because it detracts from the cohesiveness of the larger groups. Pairing off is discussed later in this chapter. In summary, subgroups are useful tools in the treatment process unless the intensity of the relationships precludes relationships with the rest of the group and participation in the group.

Leadership Structure

Leadership is an essential dimension of group therapy. Groups are constantly guided or pushed in one direction or another, usually by the group leader. The role of leader and the functions of leadership can be distinguished. The functions are those behaviors that serve to move the group toward its goals (task function) or to enhance group cohesiveness (group maintenance). The group leader is responsible for seeing that goals are achieved and that the group is maintained in the process and for maintaining an appropriate balance between the two. To empower members, the leader usually provides them with the opportunity and the training to acquire leadership skills. These are social skills in their own right that enhance status outside the group.

If the group leader were the only leader of the group it would not be necessary to consider the leadership structure. The leader's activities would simply be included with interventions. The leader must seek ways in which members can assume leadership and must determine which members can take on such responsibility. Initially, in goal-oriented groups, the leader assumes most responsibilities. As the members observe the leader and as they become comfortable in the group, they are encouraged to share power with the leader. The leader works toward the broad distribution of leadership functions in the group.

In those therapy groups that have access to well-defined intervention strategies and a great deal of information (for example, stress management groups), there is a tendency for the group leaders to exercise a great deal of control through agendas and strict adherence to these agendas. After all they are experts, and there is some empirical support for the approach. Such leaders are often confronted by a high dropout rate (see, for example, Whitney and Rose, 1988).

At the other extreme, problems also arise when the leader abdicates all leadership functions. A deviant member of the group may assume the reins of power (see Redl, 1955; Bion, 1959), or someone with previous leadership experience, either professionally or in the group therapy setting, assumes this leadership. Rather than abdicate, leaders are most effective when they gradually shift responsibilities to the members.

Some members who assume leadership roles attempt to restructure the group to fit their image of therapy, an image that is often in conflict with that of the group leader and the original contract. (See Chapter Eleven.)

In summary, leadership comprises activities that a leader gradually shares with the group. The nature of that sharing depends on the characteristics and attitudes of the group members, but leadership sharing is a basic principle of good therapeutic practice and is interrelated to a curative factor, empowerment of the

client. Clients who actively share control of their therapy are most
likely to profit from the therapeutic experience.

Group Development

Group development encompasses the evolution of norms,
roles, cohesion, communication patterns, subgroups, and leadership over time. In that sense, group development is a metaprocess.
Common elements seem to run through most paradigms of group
development, which suggests that some phenomena are, at least in
part, functions of time. Our experience has led us to believe that
development is part of formal expectations. Group leaders should
be aware of group process insofar as the phase of therapy is one of
.nany conditions that may be eliciting certain behaviors viewed as
obstructionist or even constructive, such as the conflict phase. This
cognitive awareness normalizes the behavior. When conflicts persist
across phases, they are viewed in a different light. Unfortunately,
phase boundaries have not been adequately defined. Clinical
judgment and some paradigms provide the basis for that decision.
We have made a preliminary attempt to describe what we have
discovered to be common (but not universal) attributes of these
phases in Table 2. We draw heavily on the paradigm developed by
Sarri and Galinski (1985) in our clinical descriptions of the phases
and the attendant leadership activities.

In Table 2 the phases of development commonly found in
our structured groups are described in terms of the group processes
or structures characteristic of a given phase and the leader's most
common behaviors during those phases. We have selected those
leadership behaviors that also seem to contribute to a given phase
and, in a sense, participate in the evolution of the next phase.
Columns 2 and 3 represent only a sample of all possible structures
and leadership behaviors. The major phases are orientation,
preliminary work, conflict, resolution, secondary work, and termination, all described in Table 2. Failure to thoroughly orient
members to the leader, the program, and each other in the
orientation phase often results in low cohesion and limited
cooperation. Entry too early into the preliminary work phase
usually results in premature problem solving and superficial

Table 2. Group Development in a Structured Group.

Group phase	Leadership Behavior	Group Process
Orientation phase	Orients members to theory and approach Orients members to each other Introduces rules, promotes protherapeutic norms Encourages broad participation	Factual communication Limited self-disclosure High mutual anxiety Feedback limited and polite Norms loosely established Leadership functions controlled primarily by leader
Preliminary work phase	Stimulates self-disclosure Examines problem situations Teaches basic concepts Initiates roleplays Trains in effective feedback	Moderate self-disclosure Increase in cohesion Members' attention focused on leader Mutual search for clarification Participation increased somewhat Feedback descriptive Weak subgroups formed
Conflict phase	Examines nonproductive group processes Becomes more flexible Introduces cognitive exercises Examines cognitive distortions Initiates discussion of group problems	Homework completion rate drops Feedback highly critical Anger and withdrawal increased Goals reevaluated Cohesion diminished Roles challenged
Resolution phase	Introduces problem solving Assists members in assuming responsibility for therapy Encourages leadership in members Deals with complex situations Modifies program in concordance with requests agreed upon by group	Norms challenged by members Feedback constructive Self-disclosure increased Interaction broadly distributed and more task oriented New norms, roles, and communication patterns established Cohesion increases
Secondary work phase	Reduces own activity Encourages members to work on complex	Major leadership functions assumed Significant self-disclosure

Table 2. Group Development in a Structured Group, Cont'd.

Group phase	Leadership Behavior	Group Process

	problems
	Reduces frequency of
	    reinforcement
	Draws general principles
	    of change
		Interaction highly task
		    oriented
		Cohesiveness slightly
		    decreased

Termination
    phase
	Points to principles of
	    generalization
	Prepares for termination
	Increases activity slightly
	Summarizes progress
	Helps individuals to plan
	    posttherapy activity
		Plan for generalization
		Cohesion diminished
		Focus on personal
		    implication of
		    termination
		Focus on extragroup
		    activity

discussion of problems, which, in turn, can trigger the conflict phase, which when recognized can be dealt with in the group. This discussion initiates the resolution phase. Ignoring the conflict usually results in failure to go beyond the preliminary work phase. It is only when conflict and other deterioration effects have been identified and dealt with that the group enters the secondary work phase, in which important problems are dealt with. As the specified time approaches, or in open-ended groups as small subgroups achieve their major goals, the termination phase begins.

Phase length varies. It depends on leader behavior and the cohesion of the group. Some groups do not observe all phases. In other groups, conflict and resolution phases may be as short as a few minutes. When the conflict phase lasts longer than one meeting, the dropout rate often increases. If the group lasts seven or fewer weeks, the likelihood of a lengthy conflict phase, in our experience, is diminished (possibly because the leader has merely run through the agenda and failed to deal with important concerns). Groups meeting more than twelve sessions are likely to repeat the conflict and resolution phases. Also, we have noted that with inexperienced leaders far more often than with experienced leaders, conflict phases occur more frequently and last longer.

Emotional Group Processes

Many clinical observers have noted that although all group processes have an emotional component, some are more closely identified by their intense emotional character (Bion, 1959). Group emotionality can be defined as the mutual intense manifestation of affective responses in the group. It appears from clinical observations that if the emotionality is high and not dealt with, it interferes with other aspects of group life (Yalom, 1985). If emotionality remains low throughout the course of the group, the experience is often uninteresting and not very useful. Normally, emotionality peaks once or twice in every group. As part of group development, the first phase of group life, overt emotionality, is expected to be low even though a number of emotional stimuli are present, for example, ambiguity, questions on personal conduct, need to be liked, fear of excessive self-disclosure. As there is little self-disclosure in this phase, most clients are careful not to show others the intensity of their concerns. Later, intense emotional responses may be stimulated by blame, negative feedback, criticism, or even excessive praise. Emotionality can occur as a response to the fear of having to do something one does not want to do. These emotional responses are often the major target of insight therapies. In the multimethod approach, most group leaders assume these are concerns and deal with them simply by acknowledging their presence and pointing out that they are shared by most people in groups.

Bion (1959) points out three emotional processes that are the focus of the insight group therapist but have also been noted by group clinicians of other theoretical persuasions. We most often see them when the group is either too highly structured or unstructured and view them as group deterioration effects. The three processes are dependence on the leader, fight-or-flight, and pairing off. Bion (1959) notes that these processes interfere with the overt work of the group.

Dependence on the Leader. When leadership is not shared or accepted by the members of the group, the members often become dependent on the leader for decisions. Dependence on the leader, though an abstract concept, can be operationally defined as a group pattern of interaction in which decision making and responsibility are relegated to the group leader. The problem is that clients lose an opportunity to make decisions about their own behavior. Moreover, they do not have to take responsibility for failure: "My group leader made the decision; it's her fault that I failed."

Group Fight-or-Flight State. In the fight-or-flight emotional state, either members leave the field (withdraw from interaction or from the group) or they verbally attack each other or the group leader. This state interferes with effective group problem solving, it avoids discussion of the issue triggering this phenomenon, and works against mutual assistance and satisfying working relationships. The fight-or-flight state is characterized by an increase in sarcasm and generalized criticism toward each other and the leader.

Pairing Off. Occasionally, "pairing off" (Bion, 1959), defined as intense preferential interaction in pairs and triads of the group to the exclusion of attention to the group, is observed. While members or the leader try to make a point, these pairs and triads carry out their own private conversations, which may have little to do with the formal topic. Pairing off represents a substantial barrier to carrying out the work of the group. Complaints increase. The content is boring to some or too difficult to understand for others. Persistence of pairing off leads to group problems.

Group Problems

Group problems are group structures or processes that interfere with goal achievement or member satisfaction and are also referred to as group deterioration effects. Group problems may occur any time during group development but most frequently occur during the conflict phase. Group problems include situations in which the norms are basically antitherapeutic. (One is expected not to self-disclose. One is expected to put down others. One is expected to criticize the leader and/or the other members. One should come at least five to ten minutes late for a session and disrupt the meeting on entering the room.) Group problems occur when cohesion is too low or too high, roles are too stereotypic, communication is directed only toward the group leader and not among the members, decision making is a function primarily of the leader, and one or a few members dominate the interaction.

Rather than being liabilities, group problems, when dealt with, become therapeutic opportunities. In the resolution of group problems, problem-solving skills are acquired and practiced. The norm of "openness" is introduced. A shared problem is looked at and cooperatively solved, and relationships within the group are enhanced.

If resolution of group problems is an educationally valid experience, why would a group leader attempt to prevent them? Though valuable, the resolution of group problems is time consuming. If problems abound, the group may not carry out the work for which it was originally formed. Certainly, in a short-term group, preventative practices are necessary to preserve any possibility of therapy goal attainment. Prevention may not be as vital in long-term groups. In psychodynamically oriented groups, prevention may be undesirable, because resolution of group problems is the work of the group.

Basically, prevention strategies are good intervention approaches. When the attraction to the group is maintained at a high level by balancing of effective work and programming with adequate variation and challenge, the group leader ensures that all members participate equally, the leader runs well-planned meetings with reasonable and achieveable agendas, the leader makes judicious use of humor, then it is unlikely that many group problems will arise. Fortunately, none of us are perfect, and in the absence of perfection, someone or something is always overlooked. Group leaders, too, vary in mood, experience, and ability to handle complex group stimuli. So problems are inevitable and an approach to group problem solving is necessary. Although some general strategies have been covered in this chapter, in Chapter Twelve, we discuss intervention strategies commonly used for dealing with group problems.

Summary

Group structure and group process are defined. I review how and why group structures should be considered in group therapy. Structures include group cohesion, norms, roles, subgroups, and leadership. The changes in these structures over time, referred to as group development, are examined in detail. A number of group emotional processes—in particular, dependence on the leader, fight-or-flight, and pairing off—are defined and their relationship to group outcomes suggested. Finally, group problems and their prevention are discussed. We conclude that group structure and group process are essential components of any approach to group therapy. Failure to consider their impact eliminates environmental conditions that impinge dramatically on behavior.

THREE

Preparing for Group Therapy: Planning Treatment and Orienting Members

In preparing for group therapy two different sets of actions are required: (1) planning for the group; (2) orienting the members to the purpose, operating assumptions, and procedures of the group. Although preparation occurs largely prior to the first session, planning occurs throughout treatment.

Advance planning of general structures and specific details is a prominent feature of the multimethod approach. The group is organized by plan. The series of sessions is arranged in advance. Each session is individually designed on the basis of information from the previous session. Treatment procedures are selected and modified to the nature of the group and the needs of its members. Generalization strategies are drawn up in advance. The planning is based on the best available information accrued from the client in the pregroup interview, ongoing observations of the client in the group, and self-reports and postsession questionnaire responses during the early phases of treatment. The plan can be regarded as a base for the session-by-session preparation and ongoing decision making. It also provides an explanation to clients of what the group is all about, what will happen next, and what are the mutual expectations. As it is only a point of departure, the plan is flexible. It can be modified as new information is accrued.

In orientation, the clients are informed about the group in general and each procedure and meeting in particular. Clients are also informed of the potential advantages and risks associated with involvement in the group. In this chapter we discuss the planning and orientation processes and their implications in the multimethod group approach.

Planning

Planning a therapy group requires that decisions be made—many of which are discussed in this chapter. The first set of decisions concerns the central theme around which groups are organized. Usually, a theme is selected on the basis of a needs survey of the community or agency. Themes can be classified into two categories: The first and most common theme relates to a common presenting problem, such as parental difficulties with adolescent children. Some groups are characterized by their focus on general or vague complaints, such as group therapy for anxiety-related complaints. In the second type, the theme is a specific phase of treatment, for example, assessment or preparation for termination.

Groups with a Common Treatment Focus

Most groups are organized around a common theme such as control of anger, pain management, or coping with depression. Such focused groups tend to be short term (six to eighteen sessions) and have a fixed membership. Most of the groups discussed in this book are focused groups; however, groups such as those that train clients to manage stress are quite broad in the definition of their focus, as almost all clients seem to suffer some form of stress. As a result, some stress groups, especially if long term, may appear similar to the nonfocused group described in the next section.

Here I list types of groups and their themes that make use of the varied methods characteristic of the multimethod approach. Although the groups may be labeled assertiveness training, support, self-management, and so forth, the methods discussed in this book are used in these groups as well.

Assertiveness training for excessively shy or passive clients
Anger control groups for men who batter

Support groups and assertiveness training for wives of men
who batter
Stress management groups for highly stressed and excessively
self-demanding clients
Pain management groups for chronic pain patients
Self-management skill training groups for overweight
patients, smokers, and alcohol and drug abusers
Groups for anorexics and bulimics
Cognitive-behavioral groups for depressed patients
Group exposure for agoraphobics
Dating groups for young adults
Job interviewing and job preparation groups
Couples groups to improve communication skills
Support groups for the recently divorced

Groups with a General Focus

In groups formed without a common treatment focus, the
leader works with clients with diverse problems although the
common initial complaint may be general anxiety, low self-esteem,
and/or a sense of unfulfillment. Many groups advertised as group
therapy fall into this category. They tend to be long term (more than
eighteen sessions) and open-ended, that is, new members can be
admitted at any time. They tend to move from the general complaints to specific problems. Flowers and Schwartz (1985) describe
long-term, heterogeneous groups (that is, groups of people with
highly diverse presenting problems) in which they make effective
use of behavioral and group procedures. Such groups have unique
advantages and disadvantages, which are discussed later. These
long-term, heterogenous, open-ended groups are referred to and
exemplified throughout the book as are the homogeneous, thematic
groups.

Predominant Phase of Treatment

Once a theme is selected another decision the leader must
make is the phase of treatment on which the group will focus. Most

groups include all phases. In some special cases, as noted later, one phase of treatment is the focus.

Orientation Groups. Groups of men who batter tend to be orientation groups. Rather than postpone treatment, an open-ended orientation group is organized in which clients learn the conditions of treatment, the expectations, and the responsibility of the leaders. These groups provide some treatment while the members await assignment to a treatment group. For this reason, there are no limits on the size of the group and little attention is paid to increasing group cohesion. Clients may be trained in the roleplay skills necessary for the intervention phase of treatment. They may be introduced to the theory and have an opportunity to discuss it. Generally, people who participate in such groups become involved more readily in the treatment process and are more task oriented. Some assessment also occurs in the orientation group.

Assessment Groups. Clients who, on the basis of interviews, are difficult to place in specific treatment groups are referred to the short-term and often open-ended assessment group. Often, the mutual modeling process further clarifies the problem and the client's response so that referral to a focused group is possible. These groups are small, with three to eight members. Little attention is paid to increasing group cohesion, as the members will soon be assigned to another form of treatment. In our experience it is better to integrate the assessment group into an ongoing group, but for practical reasons this may not be possible.

Transition Groups. The transition group, usually found in psychiatric and correctional facilities, is geared toward preparing its members to leave the institution. The groups may last from two weeks to six months. Those groups lasting less than a month meet daily or several times a week. Multimethod transition groups focus on identifying and teaching those behaviors needed to survive in a particular environment. Such groups utilize social skill training extensively to help members, for example, to meet new friends, to get along with a probation officer, or to deal with peer pressure to commit delinquent acts. In addition, members may be taught noninteractive skills, for example, to budget, to use the telephone, and when and how to use social resources. In most groups, clients provide each other with mutual support about departure from the institution. Former institutional residents are invited to discuss their experiences. Considerable time is spent on systematic resolution of problems that the clients identify in their future environment. Homework, to be performed primarily when the member is on furlough, is encouraged. The size of the transition group varies from week to week depending on who is eligible to leave. Groups larger than nine are usually divided into subgroups to provide maximum individualization. One group of hospitalized patients preparing to leave the hospital discussed how to talk with a prospective landlady when renting and keeping a room, how to find and be a friend, how to get help in emergencies or crises, how to keep a budget, how to develop self-control concerning medication, and how to avoid the excessive use of alcohol and recreational drugs.

Maintenance Groups. Maintenance groups are usually time limited. The clients have already attended a series of sessions and now are meeting to reinforce or maintain the skills they have acquired. These groups usually meet as infrequently as once a month and are less structured than other groups described in this book. Most leadership functions are delegated to the clients. In general, the sessions focus on successes in maintaining behaviors learned in the group and evaluation of the problems that arise in the attempt to maintain. Many of the principles described in Chapter Twelve are incorporated into these groups.

Fixed Versus Flexible Membership

Regardless of the theme, the leader must determine whether the group should have a limited membership and limited duration or an open membership and indefinite duration.

Fixed-Membership Groups. In fixed-membership groups, clients begin and end together six to eighteen weeks later. The advantages of time-limited, fixed-membership groups are that the

clients go through the same phases of development, facilitating
planning; however, such a model requires that a sufficient number
of clients who meet the requirement of good composition (see later)
be available to start the group. As the major part of this chapter is
committed to describing the major characteristics of such a model,
we limit our discussion here. In the following subsections, we
present other, often overlapping, models of treatment, their goals,
advantages, and limitations, and their similarities to and differences
from the fixed-membership model.

Flexible-Membership Groups. Flexible-membership groups
or open-ended groups admit clients throughout the year. Clients
enter as they are referred and leave as goals are achieved. Usually,
such groups are limited in size. Most long-term group therapy
programs in agencies, institutions, halfway houses, group homes,
and transitional units are open-ended. Specific training groups,
such as social skill training or stress management training, rarely
fall into this category unless they are part of an institutional
program; however, we see no reason why they cannot be organized
along open-ended principles if the usual intake process yields
inadequate numbers.

The chief advantage of open-ended groups is that insufficient
recruitment is eliminated. In hospital pain clinics, pain groups are
organized with even as few as three clients, and clients are added when
they express an interest to their physician. Difficulties resulting from
the initial group composition can sometimes be corrected by adding
new individuals. Another potential advantage of open-ended groups
is that resistance to the treatment process has usually been worked
through by the initial clients when the new clients arrive. Group
leaders seldom have to deal with resistance of the group as a whole,
and the old clients serve as models to the incoming clients.

One disadvantage of the open-ended group is that incoming
clients perceive themselves as strangers in a world of friends. This is
not an easy role to play but it is a role that members will have to
play frequently in the real world. The leader can prepare both the
group and the new client for entry into the group. Specific orientation tasks can be developed by the group. Frequently, in the open-
ended group, the clients are in different phases of treatment. New

clients are concerned with getting to know others and feeling comfortable in the group. More experienced clients may be working on problems identified in previous meetings, and those about to terminate are focusing on generalization plans. To deal with this problem, the group leader may provide the opportunity for experienced clients to assume leadership responsibilities, for example, leading discussions, orienting new clients, and tutoring peers. If these skills have not been demonstrated in the group, they may be taught through modeling, rehearsal, and group feedback prior to the admission of new clients. New clients are rapidly integrated into the group through a pregroup orientation by an experienced member. Furthermore, to avoid creating low-status isolates, it is usually best to admit two or three new clients at a time.

In concluding this section, we note that most groups we deal with, and use as examples in this book, are organized with a central presenting problem as theme. Most groups go through all phases of treatment except maintenance and have a more or less fixed membership and fixed time frame. Nevertheless, all other variations are appropriate and useful for the specific reasons described.

Organization

The number of sessions, the duration of each session, minimum and maximum group size, and the number of leaders must be determined prior to recruitment. We refer to these as the organizational attributes of the group.

Group Size

The size of a group depends on its purpose. As individualization within the group context is highly valued, groups in which the multimethod approach is used usually contain five to ten clients (eight is the modal number). Groups of fewer than five clients seem to lack many of the beneficial group attributes discussed in Chapter One. Groups larger than ten make it difficult for all members to participate fully. Also, client satisfaction tends to increase up until there are six or seven clients and then to decline slightly. Most authors working with treatment groups also recommend a similar range (for example, Garvin, 1987; Yalom, 1985; Emmelkamp and Kuipers, 1985). Despite agreement with clinical observations, there is little empirical research to affirm this range.

There are clinical and practical (usually financial) reasons to modify this range. Larger groups of clients can also be treated successfully, provided that all the clients share a common problem, or two leaders are present and the group activities are frequently carried out in subgroups. The more homogeneous the group, the larger the group possible. Also, some groups do not make use of the group process. Groups that have more of a training or educational focus, rather than a group process-therapy focus, can be larger.

Group size tends to change over time. Illnesses, dropouts, and referrals to other services take their toll. If the change in number is too dramatic, group cohesion and satisfaction decrease. In some cases, the group leader may add new clients. (This topic is further discussed later in the chapter.)

Frequency of Group Sessions

Most groups discussed in this book are time limited, meeting about six to eighteen weeks. Regular weekly sessions are the general pattern primarily because of the personal or work schedules of the clients and the leader and not for any particular treatment rationale. Ideally, we prefer at least two and sometimes three meetings per week during the initial phase of treatment, gradually decreasing to once a week, once every two weeks, and eventually once a month for the remainder of the treatment year. We have been successful in keeping to schedule, except near the end of treatment, when bimonthly and monthly sessions have become somewhat more common. The frequency of meetings is gradually decreased on the basis of a maintenance-of-learning principle: When reinforcement is reasonably continuous, newly learned behaviors will rapidly fade away if reinforcement is terminated too abruptly (Goldstein, Heller, and Sechrest, 1966). If it is assumed that the group is a source of reinforcement, then it is important that there be many meetings at the beginning to incorporate the desired behaviors into the client's repertoire as quickly as possible, and that in later phases, there be fewer meetings to maintain the behaviors.

The exact number of sessions depends on the purpose of the group, the complexity and intensity of the presenting problem, the duration of each session, group composition, and certain practical limitations, such as costs, availability of leaders, and schedules of participants. For heterogeneous groups, fourteen to twenty-four sessions are usually required to meet the wide variety of treatment goals. For example, in groups of men who batter, the program has been extended to more than twenty-six weekly sessions. In groups in which the goals are quite similar and highly specific skills are presented, as in a dating group for young adults, eight sessions have been sufficient for the majority of clients. When an even more specific goal is pursued, still fewer sessions may suffice. For example, a number of mothers associated with a community center wanted to learn to set limits for their preadolescent children. Four sessions were sufficient to provide information and discuss the situations that required reinforcement for achievement or limits. Even within this limited time frame, clients were able to practice at home and report to the group.

In summary, for most homogeneous groups, eight to twelve sessions are sufficient to attain treatment goals. To treat social anxiety, D'Alelio and Murray (1981) demonstrated that eight two-hour sessions were significantly more effective than four two-hour sessions. Would twelve be better yet?

As mentioned earlier, the open-ended groups have no set duration. When the group leader or the client provides evidence that goals have been attained and a plan for generalization made (see Chapter Twelve), the client may terminate. Of course, in such groups, termination of a given individual may also occur against the advice of the group leader when the client is no longer attracted to the group. In the open-ended groups with which we have worked, the average number of sessions per client is usually twenty-four, with each session lasting two hours. Long-term behavior group therapy is advocated by a number of authors. Belfer and Levendusky (1985) have utilized unlimited sessions for agoraphobia; others have utilized long-term therapy for bulimia (White and Boskind-White, 1981) and for depression and sexual dysfunction (McGovern and Jensen, 1985). As mentioned earlier, Flowers and Schwartz (1985) utilized long-term groups for the treatment of diverse problems in heterogeneous groups. In these groups, a specific number of sessions is set. Most of these authors combine insight and relationship enhancement approaches with behavior therapy. Although there is no research to back up this extended cost of treatment, in our experience we have, along with the previously mentioned authors, found that where there are a wide range of presenting problems, more than twelve or even sixteen sessions is advisable. Furthermore, clients who have experienced recent loss or trauma may need a grieving period before they can be task oriented. During this grieving period, the leader is supportive and encourages the members to support each other. Before all group leaders shift to long-term therapy more research is needed on who needs long-term therapy and for whom eight to twelve weeks are sufficient. When required, treatment can be extended to include a pretreatment or orientation group, the regular group, and a maintenance group. Thus, those persons who require additional sessions can more readily obtain them, and those who require fewer sessions can more easily stop treatment.

Duration of Sessions

Most group sessions in the multimethod approach last one and one-half to two hours. This length appears sufficient to allow all members to participate, for one group exercise to be carried out, and for everyone to present and deal with at least one problem. Some groups have asked for more time per session and we have extended those sessions to two and one-half hours; however, there is considerable variation from agency to agency and even within the same agency. Sessions range from one to three hours for such practical reasons as the availability of a room or the schedule of the leader. Hand, Lamontagne, and Marks (1974) advocate three-hour sessions for group exposure because of the time it takes to prepare, go out into the community, and then process the experience. They have even used five-hour sessions. We have noted no differences in outcome in our own experience or in research findings; however, after the longer sessions, clients have complained of fatigue. And, after the short sessions, clients commented frequently, on postgroup evaluations, that there was not enough time to do what they wanted.

Some groups are organized on a completely different time basis. For example, some stress management groups meet three consecutive Saturdays, six to seven hours per day. Some leaders have organized weekend sessions, as long as ten hours a day, for treatment groups. In institutions, transitional groups meet from one to three hours daily from the onset until termination, which is usually about three to six weeks later. In general, intensive daily programs are avoided. As homework is an important part of this approach, marathon and daily meetings would restrict the frequency and relevancy with which homework assignments can be given.

Number of Group Leaders

As the number of group leaders in any one group increases, so does the cost to the client and/or to the agency. There is no consistent evidence that two group leaders are more effective than one, provided that all group leaders are experienced. Although in most cases one group leader is adequate and less costly, there appears to be consistent preference on the part of practitioners to have a co-leader. Most practitioners feel there is more support, they learn more, and it is more fun. There are also several situations that call for more than one group leader (compare with discussions by Middleman, 1980, and Galinsky and Schopler, 1980, for other types of groups).

1. If the second group leader is a trainee.
2. If both group leaders are leading a new type of group for the first or second time.
3. If the second group leader is a supervisor of the first.
4. If the second group leader alternates with the first as observer (however, having an observer is cheaper).
5. If specific skills are necessary to lead the group, and these skills are split between the group leaders.
6. If the group contains more than eight members (although it is usually better to have two small groups rather than a group as large as ten).
7. If one group leader is unlikely to be able to remain with the

group until the end (usually one group leader is slowly phased in while the other is phased out).

8. If the clients are highly active or aggressive and control is a major problem initially (for example, with men who batter).

9. If it is desirable to have models of both sexes, as in marital counseling groups (some leaders advocate male and female co-leaders in all mixed groups).

Co-leaders sometimes create problems for themselves and the group by competing with each other, by dominating the group interaction, and by frequently amplifying and repeating what the other says. Thus, careful self-monitoring is needed; the group is asked to comment on the roles of both leaders on the postsession questionnaire. If the problems persist, a supervisor or consultant should be called in to help the pair systematically problem solve the issue.

Agency Auspices

Under what auspices will the group be formed? In what setting will the sessions take place?

Though not all social agencies provide group treatment facilities for clients, the examples in this book are drawn from therapeutic, health, socioeducational, industrial, recreational, and welfare organizations as well as private practice. Hospitals and health clinics have sponsored groups on pain management, stress management, weight loss and other eating disorders, smoking cessation, and alcohol and drug abuse for both outpatients and inpatients. In industrial settings, stress management training, assertiveness training, alcohol abuse groups, Smoke-enders, and weight control groups have been established. Family service clinics have sponsored all the previously mentioned groups, as well as groups for couples, men who batter, victims of men who batter, and incest victims. People who have recently experienced stressful events may join self-help groups that eventually became structured groups guided by leaders. In mental hospitals, social skill training groups, relaxation training groups, stress management groups, drug and alcohol abuse groups, and transitional groups have all been established. And almost all of the previously mentioned groups have been observed in private practice.

The importance of agency auspices to the group is not trivial. Agencies have a purpose in organizing a group program. They justify their existence through the services they render. The group leader is responsible for helping the agency to clarify those purposes (Garvin, 1987, pp. 35-36) and to relate to the group these purposes. One family service agency's purpose was to provide young adults with the opportunity to meet each other. The purpose of the members was to obtain inexpensive therapy for their interpersonal conflicts. Although the group leader was qualified to offer the therapy, he had to interpret to the group the agency's purpose and help them either to renegotiate the purpose with the agency or to go elsewhere for the help.

For space, staff, budget, and similar concerns, agencies often regulate length, duration, number of leaders, and other organizational aspects of the group. Many agencies even restrict the theoretical framework within which the therapist can work or the types of intervention that can be used. Some agencies encourage, whereas others discourage, data collection for various reasons. The advent of computers and the increased demand for agency accountability pressure agencies to do more data collection. The leader, before organizing the group, must be aware of the agency-determined parameters and, if necessary, attempt to modify those that interfere with the achievement of treatment goals. Even groups organized under cooperative private practices are governed by some considerations. Private practices are also governed by profitability. Because of their greater efficiency, groups may increase profits.

Fees

The determination of fees for group therapy is complex. It might be assumed that the cost to join an eight-person group should be one-eighth that of individual therapy. Only the therapist's fee per hour is approximately one-eighth, and usually groups meet almost twice as long as clients in individual treatment. Moreover, the administrative costs per person are almost the same, as each person is billed separately, records are kept on each individual as well as the group, and a large room is required for the meeting. Short-term groups often incur some publicity costs for advertisements and fliers. Preparation costs for therapists in structured group work are almost the same as for individual treatment, per person, because of the complexity of the group. Therapist costs are doubled if co-therapists are used. Even if only one leader is used, the cost per person for group therapy is approximately one-half to one-third that of individual treatment. Because many insurance companies do not cover group therapy, many therapists avoid groups, even if they might be the indicated form of treatment.

In social agencies, fees are usually determined on a sliding scale, whereas in private practice, the entire cost is charged, although some practitioners are beginning to use reduced fees to attract low-income clients.

The fee is normally collected prior to the sessions in short-term therapy or is collected in two half-payments if it is more than the individual can handle at one time. This decreases clients' tendency to drop out for trivial reasons. In long-term groups, people sometimes pay in advance of each session, although we prefer that payment be made in advance of 4-week modules to encourage regular attendance. Advanced payment reduces billing and collection costs and the savings can be passed on to the consumer as a fee reduction.

We have experimented with fee rebates for success in treatment. Although this practice motivates clients to make verbal statements of success, we have rarely seen any evidence of unusual gains. Moreover, except for staff on salary, it could be a negative motivator for the therapist.

Setting

In most cases, the setting for a given group is within the building housing the sponsoring agency or private practice. There are, however, exceptions. Groups have met, at least for special sessions, in restaurants, bars, and other recreational settings, depending on the focus of the group. The principles involved in these natural settings are twofold: simulate as nearly as possible the setting in which the problems occur (see Chapter Twelve for the rationale behind this principle) and find as attractive a setting as possible to increase the cohesiveness of the group. When these two principles are in conflict, we begin to increase attractiveness which is later faded to simulate the real world.

Although it is desirable to have adequate space, recreational equipment, audiovisual aids, comfortable chairs that move, and other facilities, some group programs have been carried out with only a few of these amenities. In our opinion, such facilities may enhance but are not necessary for a successful outcome. In most cases, group leaders are able to take advantage of the facilities made available to them (or struggled for). At least for the first few meetings, it is indeed helpful to have a regular place to meet and be safe from interruptions. Careful directions (and a map) to the meeting place will alleviate some of the initial anxiety. In later sessions, variation in the setting to more nearly simulate the real world is recommended to enhance the likelihood of generalization.

Recruitment and Selection

A group cannot form if clients are unaware of its existence. The program must be publicized and potential clients recruited.

Recruitment

In one family service agency, the group leader learned from the staff that there was no program available for women who were shy and withdrawn. Many of the women had been placed on a waitlist because their problem was not considered high priority. After discussions with the director and colleagues and their eventual concurrence, she designed a small brochure that described the kinds of groups that these women might find useful. She was allotted fifteen minutes at a staff meeting to explain the program and to answer questions about it. At that time she distributed the brochure to the agency staff, who shared it with appropriate clients, mailed copies to women on the waitlist, and also placed an ad in the local weekly. She was able to obtain free spots on public service and commercial

radio stations. In addition, the director arranged an interview
with a writer in the local paper. This article drew the largest
number of referrals. Within several weeks, a sufficient number
of clients were interested and the group leader could begin the
selection process.

In the preceding example, several techniques were used to
recruit clients: brochure mailings; radio, television, and newspaper
advertising; and a feature article in the newspaper. It was especially
important to negotiate with staff and director because without their
support for the new program, the recruitment process would never
have been started. The cost of the publicity was minimal, the paper
for the four-page brochure being the most expensive item; however,
if the time expended by the group leader were taken into account,
the overall costs for the group would rise considerably.

Different types of groups require different types of recruitment programs. Staff for a family service agency program for men
who batter spoke and showed a film to police, who were familiar
with such problems, addressed an agency serving the victims of
these men, and sent a program brochure to agencies who came into
contact with such men but who did not have the facilities or
expertise to deal with them. A program for drug abusers was
advertised similarly. A marital communication improvement group
program sent literature to a large mailing list of graduate students
and faculty at a major university (see Edleson, Witkin, and Rose,
1979, for a detailed description of an elaborate and highly successful
recruitment program).

There are programs that require little or no recruitment. The
waitlist for some agencies is so long that groups appear to be the
only way to serve the diverse needs of these long-waiting clients.

Selection

Not all clients who express interest in a program are suitable
candidates. Once the list of potential clients is generated, the process
of selection begins. Prior to treatment the group leader usually
interviews the client and, occasionally, significant persons in the
client's life. The purpose of these interviews is to answer four basic

questions: Is treatment necessary? Is group treatment appropriate? If appropriate, what kind of group would work best for the potential member? What should be the composition of the group? (These interviews also play a major role in orientation and assessment. The orientation function is discussed later. The assessment function is discussed further in the next two chapters.) In this section, we focus on the function of the interview in organization of the group; however, these three functions often overlap. The group leader attempts to elicit from each person involved with the client at least some of the client's behavioral attributes and to focus on specific incidents in which they are manifested. These interviews are usually brief, aimed at obtaining background information and descriptions of problem situations and their causes, and geared toward the interactive pattern of the client with others. An example of the pregroup interview is found in Chapter Four.

To determine whether an individual should be placed in a group at all, the purposes of the groups available must be reviewed. If an individual describes himself as someone having difficulty managing the day-to-day hassles without anxiety or stress, a stress management group may be appropriate, unless the client is showing delusionary behavior or heavy depression. Parents who complain that they do not know how to handle their adolescents' recent rebellious behavior might find help in a parent training group. The clients themselves may request a specific type of group. Once they learn what the group is all about, admission to such a group would be almost automatic. There are also certain practical considerations in a recommendation for treatment. Are adequate alternate resources available? Is there a danger that treatment will create an additional handicap if, as a result, the client is labeled "a troublemaker" or "sick"? Is there an appropriate group available to which the client can be assigned, or must the client be waitlisted? Can the client wait (for example, the potentially suicidal person) or would immediate individual treatment be more appropriate? Are other facilities available to the client? Only with knowledge of community agency resources and the goals of the client can these questions be fully answered.

A general guideline that can be used in deciding to place a

client in a group is "the absence of behavior so bizarre as to frighten others, and no wide differences that are personally or culturally beyond acceptance" (Klein, 1972, p. 60). Although it may be possible to have an entire group of clients who occasionally hallucinate, one client who hallucinates may be far too threatening to the other clients. Similarly, a group of passive clients with a limited repertoire of assertive skills may be startled and frightened by a highly aggressive client, who might be better off in another group.

Mandatory Clients

Up to now, we have assumed that all clients come to a program of their own free will. This is sometimes not the case. Some clients, such as men who batter and sexual abusers of children, may be court mandated. Other clients may join the group to accede to the demands of significant persons in their life, for example, the wife who threatens her husband with immediate departure if he does not enter an anger control program, or the adult child who threatens to terminate the relationship with his aged father if the father does not seek help for his alcoholism. These clients often resent joining the group. Thus, their personal attraction to other members and the group as a whole is usually low, which reduces the general group cohesion.

Group leaders who indicate that they understand clients' feelings, who solve small problems with the clients, who provide the group with helpful information in an area of concern, who are able to enhance the cohesiveness of the group, and who provide opportunities for all members to participate often capture the reluctant and poorly motivated client. In a project dealing with men who batter, Saunders and Hanusa (1986) found that although the dropout rate was greater than 60 percent from the time of first contact to the time of the first meeting, it decreased to 7 percent once the group began, even though the majority of clients were court mandated. The strategies mentioned earlier were those that the leaders used to increase the clients' motivation.

Composition

The composition of the group is determined by the group leader on the basis of presession interviews and tests. Though the research in this area is limited, we have extrapolated several model compositions from this research, as well as from recent theory and clinical experience.

Festinger (1954) points out that when motivated to evaluate their opinions and abilities and when no objective standard exists, people tend to compare themselves with those who are similar rather than different. The inference for grouping is that although the members of a group may differ in some characteristics, each member needs to find someone in the group who is not too different in social skills, social background, or presenting problem. On this basis, it might be assumed that a group composed entirely of clients with exactly the same presenting problem, for example, aggression toward others, would be ideal. Our clinical experience shows us that groups of this nature, indeed, are quite cohesive; however, since the cohesiveness is based on similarities in the very problem areas the group leader is trying to alter, considerable resistance, mutually reinforced, is generated toward the group leader and against acceptance of the treatment contract. Clinical experience and sociopsychological theory suggest, then, a somewhat more complex basis for grouping than similar or dissimilar behavioral manifestations. It is useful to form groups on the basis of a broad range of behavioral attributes and skills.

Inclusion of a Model

As discussed in Chapter One, modeling is a major tool in intervention. Although the group leader may serve as a model, clients are far more effective in this capacity. Often, in heterogeneous groups, clients with behavioral strengths in one area serve as models for clients with behavioral strengths in another area. In homogeneous groups, occasionally, models without major target problems may have to be placed in the group primarily for modeling effect rather than for their own treatment. These are often members of earlier groups; however, the model-client needs some reason to be in the group, perhaps for maintenance. The ideal model is slightly older, slightly more intelligent, and slightly more competent in the target area, although not necessarily in all areas (Bandura, 1977b).

Gender

Most adult groups are composed of persons of both sexes. Many problems encountered by clients in the real world involve members of the opposite sex and, therefore, an environment that reflects the real world is a desirable therapeutic condition. Occasionally, however, clients may, initially, need the comfort found in a same-sex group. In such cases, all-women or all-men groups may be formed, and members of the opposite sex added later. In one assertiveness training group that consisted mostly of secretaries, male employees were later added so as to simulate more nearly the real world. In mixed groups where members of one sex feel uncomfortable in dealing with a certain issue in the presence of the opposite sex, this issue is addressed in the group. Of course, some themes tend to attract more clients of one sex than another. Also, we often depend on referrals from others who see certain problems as uniquely male or female and may refer clients of only one sex. We generally avoid, for the reasons mentioned earlier, forming a group in which only one member is male or female and the remaining members of the opposite sex. Stress, assertiveness, and depression groups tend to attract many more women than men and occasionally no men at all. (This may result from the unwillingness of most men to examine their thoughts and feelings, especially in public.) Thus, we often end up with all-male or all-female groups even though it was not the intent. Many same-sex groups are organized by plan: women with premenstrual syndrome; assertiveness training for the second phase of a woman's consciousness-raising group; men who batter; female victims of male violence.

Sometimes problems arise when the group members are not of the same sex as the leader. Since the leader may be a major model for the group, a model of one sex may be a problem for clients of the other. Moreover, the group members may feel that no official really understands them. For women in particular, the man in power may be readily interpreted as one more symbol of their powerlessness. Therefore, we advocate female leaders for all-female groups, male leaders for all-male groups, and male and female co-leaders for mixed groups. If such arrangements are not possible, the issue of sex should be discussed early in the history of the group. Sometimes, in mixed groups, men dominate the interaction, giving women less opportunity to participate. Initially, leaders must be sensitive to this possibility and deal with it as a group issue should it arise.

Race

We do what we can to combine applicants of different races in the same group; however, we avoid forming groups with only one client of a given racial group for fear of isolating that client. If one client is isolated because another member drops out, we discuss this issue in the group. Occasionally, if necessary, we add a member to provide support for the isolate.

Although it is not the primary purpose of therapy groups to deal with cross-racial issues, these issues so permeate our culture that they provide therapy groups with an opportunity in cross-racial problem solving. Many clients' racial attitudes are intertwined with other psychological and behavioral problems and must be dealt with whether the group is of one or mixed races, before progress in other areas can be made. Group cohesion depends on high interpersonal attraction. Racial conflict or bias would impede cohesion. Mixed groups initially have lower cohesion than same-race groups; however, the lower cohesion is well worth the natural laboratory provided for dealing with racial conflict and the underlying behavioral and cognitive patterns. The race of the leader is an issue. There are many more white therapists. Where possible, it is preferable to have co-leaders of different races. If this is not possible, the race issue must be dealt with in the group.

Socioeconomic Status

Race is often, though not always, linked to socioeconomic status. To obtain a diversity of perspectives on problem situations and to improve the acceptability of the group to lower-status individuals, we include people of a variety of socioeconomic backgrounds in the group. In one study, we found that in groups combining middle class parents and lower or lower middle class parents, the rate of learning of the lower class parents was almost double that found in groups of only lower class parents (Rose, 1974). The rate of improvement of the middle class parents remained the same. Unfortunately, this socioeconomic mixture is not always possible because of the location of the agency, the purpose of the agency, or the nature of the private practice, which may serve only people in the middle or higher socioeconomic classes.

General Principles

We try to form broadly diverse groups in terms of sex, race, socioeconomic background, and similarity in general presenting problem. However, we avoid isolating individuals in groups. For example, we added one more man to a seven-person pain management group that initially had only one man. One of the women in the group was Hispanic, as was the man just added. Two of the women had college training; the rest had a high school education or less. This was a balanced composition.

It is not always possible to obtain such a balanced composition. In fact, sometimes we find ourselves fortunate to have enough members to start a group. If peculiarities exist in the composition, the diversity of the group is pointed out and valued by the leader. Problems (for example, use of sexist language or racial prejudgments or a person feeling isolated or excluded) that arise because of the composition are discussed.

Orientation

The results of pregroup planning must be communicated to clients. They are conveyed to potential clients through posters, advertisements, letters, news stories, and word of mouth. Further information is shared with the clients in pregroup interviews and the early sessions.

In the pregroup interview, the client is given details about the group program, how it might be of help, the types of clients that might be in the group, and the general activities of the group. At the end of the interview, the client should know, at least generally, what to expect and what is expected of her or him. Occasionally, videotapes are used in the pregroup interview or in an orientation session; during this session former members may describe their experiences in similar groups.

Additional information about rules, therapist expectations, and the range of goals that can be achieved in such groups is shared. The group therapist may anticipate a problem and suggest steps the client may take to remedy the problem or at least bring it to the attention of the therapist and/or the group. Some clients are disappointed in the initial relationships or the content of the group. Others are concerned about the pace. Occasionally, conflict may arise in the group. Clients are encouraged to talk about their fears in relation to the group; some of these fears may be easily dispelled with understanding and information. Other fears may be of a nature that the group may not be appropriate.

One concern of clients and therapeutic staff in particular has been abuse of confidentiality. It has been my experience that if this issue and its consequences are discussed in the first session, breach of confidence simply does not occur. Yalom (1985, p. 292) describes a similar experience. We share this with our clients.

Other misconceptions that clients may have are often revealed in the pregroup interviews or in the orientation session. For example, some clients think that the group may be extremely large and they might have little opportunity to participate. Some think they will be embarrassed if they are not immediately open. Others think they will be forced to do things they would rather not do. In addressing clients' concern over the second-class status of being in a group, I tell them about studies in which clients were assigned at random to either group or individual treatment. At the end of treatment, members in both conditions thought they were lucky; the outcome was the same, but the group members claimed they had more fun (Tallant, Rose, and Tolman, 1989). Thus, the therapist uses examples to dispel misconceptions. In orientation sessions, previous group members tell about typical meetings and the range of responses made without criticism or sarcasm. Most of these ideas are incorporated into the treatment contract.

The treatment contract is a statement, usually in writing, of the general responsibilities of the members, the group leader, and the agency for a certain period. It usually specifies goals and commonly used procedures as well as mutual expectations. One important condition of a group treatment contract is that the members agree to help one another. The treatment contract differs from a contingency contract (see Chapter Seven) in that the latter specifies a more narrow relationship between expected member behavior and the reinforcement that follows. The treatment contract is broader in scope and covers a longer period. Exhibit 1 is an example of a treatment contract for a stress management training group.

A number of authors have pointed out the relevance of the contract to group treatment. Belfer and Levendusky (1985) suggest that it is critical in beginning any psychotherapy group. Rice and Rutan (1981) point out that insofar as it establishes the boundaries of the group, it is a component of group structure. There is evidence to support the contention that clear knowledge about treatment and agreement to participate are prerequisites for success in treatment (Hoehn-Saric and others, 1964). Ausubel (1963) provides evidence that success in learning is linked to advance knowledge about what one is to learn. It also appears that knowledge of the parameters of a situation reduces anxiety about that situation. It is for these reasons that a treatment contract is a major strategy in orientation of structured groups.

The contract, however, is not static. As relationships between members are established, as their negotiation skills are enhanced, and as their early expectations are clarified, the contracts receive greater input from the members. The contract increasingly reflects the members' opinions of what they can learn from the group. Moreover, detail and structure are added to the contract. Not every detail can be clarified at the first meeting. An attempt to do so may overwhelm the clients. The group leader must successively structure the contract in a step-by-step process as the members experience growing success and satisfaction with the approach.

Exhibit 1. Treatment Contract.

I understand that the stress management group will meet weekly for ten sessions on Wednesday nights from 7:00 to 9:00 P.M. to focus on problems in dealing with stress. The leader will provide information on stress and means of stress management and the members will relate that information to their own stress responses.

I. Member
   A. I will pay a fee of $_____ for participation in all of the group sessions.
   B. I will attend each session if at all possible. If not I will call the leader.
   C. I will arrive on time and stay for the complete session.
   D. I will bring problems of concern to the group meetings and be prepared to discuss them.
   E. If I agree to certain home assignments, I will show evidence of the work I have done on those assignments.
   F. I will allow data accumulated during the group to be used for research and/or educational purposes, with protection of confidentiality ensured, and I will allow the group leader(s) or a representative of the agency to contact me in the future, by mail or phone, for follow-up. In return, I will receive a lifetime membership in the Stress Management Alumni Program (SMAP), which qualifies me to assist (if desired) in future groups.

II. Group Leader
   A. I will begin and end each session on time.
   B. I will help members clarify their problems in such a way that something can be done about them.
   C. I will help members identify personal and other resources and make use of them in dealing with their problems.
   D. I will provide members with the procedures that offer the best chance of effective and efficient resolution of problems presented in the group.
   E. I will provide information about stress and stress management strategies.
   F. I will involve all members in the group discussions.
   G. I will respect the confidentiality of members' communications.

| Group Member | Date |

| Group Leader | Date |

For some clients, such as those who are pressured or court ordered to attend, the treatment contract may be more specific and too demanding of the members and they, as a result, may be unwilling to participate. For these clients, a contract may be informal and extremely general, in stark contrast to the contract in Exhibit 1. The expectations from the members may be minimal. The clients may be asked only to observe and to participate when they are willing. The only expectation is that they not be disruptive. They are made aware of the group leader's long-term expectations, but initially the members are asked to do nothing to advance those therapeutic goals. Vinter (1974) refers to this as a preliminary treatment contract. The preliminary treatment contract in our experience is useful primarily with highly resistant members. Although the contract in Exhibit 2 is a written contract, often preliminary contracts are verbal agreements.

Exhibit 2. A Preliminary Treatment Contract.

I agree to attend at least two meetings of the anger control group. I understand that I will not be expected to participate but that I can participate if I choose. I agree to evaluate my decision with the group leader after the second session.

The preliminary contract demands little of the client but it serves as an initial contact; eventually, a more treatment-oriented contract may be appropriate. The client is also freer to drop out after an initial but brief experience.

Summary

The major steps in prestructuring group therapy are planning for and orienting the client to treatment. Decisions that must be made before the group is organized and the factors to be considered in these decisions are indicated. Examples are provided of groups organized around themes, such as depression, stress, and family violence. Other groups are organized with respect to the phase of problem solving, for example, orientation and maintenance groups. Group membership can be either fixed or open-ended.

The rationale behind setting for group size, frequency, meeting length, and number of leaders, and the influence of agency auspices and group settings on leader activity and group structure are discussed. Tentative criteria are established for recruitment and selection of group members. Group composition is examined in terms of need for a model, race, sex, similarity of members, and other factors. Finally, specific strategies are outlined for orienting members to the philosophy and practices of group therapy. Orientation to treatment is an important part of this approach as it clarifies the parameters of the approach and reveals and corrects misconceptions. Orientation also serves to enhance motivation and begins to establish the values and theory of the approach. Orientation usually occurs in a pregroup interview or in special groups established for that purpose. As part of orientation, special attention is given to the use of treatment contracts. Two types of contract are distinguished: a highly structured contract for clients clearly interested in committing themselves to the group and a preliminary treatment contract for those who want to look and see whether the group is for them. The need for adequate information for both planning and orientation is emphasized throughout.

FOUR

Assessment in Groups: Identifying Clients' Problems and Resources

Assessment is central to all problem-solving and cognitive-behavioral approaches. Without adequate assessment intervention is meaningless. In group therapy, assessment has many purposes; some purposes overlap those of individual therapy, whereas others are unique to the group context. In this chapter, these purposes are discussed and the major strategies of assessment presented.

Purposes of Assessment

The major purpose of assessment for individuals in small group treatment is to describe the problem in a way that indicates the most appropriate intervention. To achieve that purpose, situational analysis is used.

Two other purposes of assessment, to determine whether a client can utilize small group treatment to resolve the problem(s) and, if so, to ascertain the type of group that can best serve the client, were discussed in Chapter Three. A fourth purpose of assessment, to evaluate progress during and after intervention, is covered in Chapter Five.

Assessment is designed initially to characterize situations clients view as problematic, the coping responses they presently use, and behavioral and cognitive skills and other resources they have at their disposal.

Here we describe how situational and resource analysis contributes to treatment planning, the various ways in which information is collected to make a situational analysis, and, unique to training and therapy, how the group is used in the process of individual data collection and situational analysis. Within the group, the leader searches for common characteristics among members' situations and determines how the member may serve as a model, source of information, or coach for other members in the group. We also describe strategies for determining the individual's resources for and impediments to achieving individual treatment goals. The employment of these situations in evaluation and research is discussed in Chapter Five.

It should be noted that though the focus of the pregroup interviews and the early group sessions is primarily but not exclusively assessment, assessment is a process that continues throughout treatment. Initially, determining the appropriate group and individual target problems is the function of assessment. Later, ongoing assessment is used to facilitate decisions on modification of the treatment focus. Finally, assessment shifts to evaluation of the ongoing progress and outcomes for individuals and the group.

The components of situational analysis are artificially separated for purposes of examination. Although not the only information gathered, as we shall observe in later sections of this chapter, the foundation of the assessment process is the overt and covert behavior of the clients in a situation. Let us look first at situation responses that clients have complained about in groups and how these situations were analyzed for purposes of group treatment.

Situational Analysis

In situational analysis in groups, the leader helps the clients look at problematic situations in such a way that a plan can be developed for their resolution. Situational analysis consists of determining the general problem as the client perceives it, and helping her or him to redefine that problem in terms of situations. The background of the problem, specific situations that exemplify that problem, the client's behavior and/or responses to that specific situation, the consequences of that situation response, and the relative importance of the problem to the client must be considered. Also included in a situational analysis is an estimate of the level of satisfaction of the client with his or her responses to previous or similar occurrences of that situation. Finally, the analysis is complete only if the resources of the client for dealing with that problem are ascertained. The following descriptions illustrate most of these components of situational analysis:

I guess I worry a lot. I've been a worrier since I've been a kid [general problem and background]. For example, yesterday, when I was alone in my bedroom and felt a headache coming on [situation], I worried that my health might suddenly be lost and then I'd lose my job and my friends [cognitive responses]. Then my anxiety level boils over [immediate consequences]. Of course, the more I worry, the less attention I seem to be able to pay either to the job or my friends [long-term consequences]. I really am unhappy with the way I worry all the time [dissatisfaction with responses].

Even though I am lonely most of the time and would like to meet people, I guess I don't do much to help myself [general problem]. For example, just this evening my brother called me to come for dinner, Friday. He said there would be some interesting new people there [situation]. The idea of meeting all those people scared the hell out of me [affective response], so I lied to him and told him I would have to work that night [verbal response]. I guess I'll never meet people that way [indicates dissatisfaction]. But the people in this group have told me I'm a pleasant person and an interesting one too [resources], so maybe this is something I can work on.

Sure, I have trouble controlling my temper [general problem]. My dad was that way too [background]. But, jeez, sometimes my wife Shirley really pushes my button with all her nagging. Thursday, when she told me to take the garbage out for the third time [situation], I thought "there she goes again" [cognitive response], then I really got teed off [affective response] and I let her have it [physical response]. She called the cops [consequence] and I'm out on my own again [long-term consequence]. I guess I shouldn't have done it [dissatisfaction with response], but I just lose it sometimes.

When clients complain about a problem, they often are concerned with the environmental conditions. The focus of the leader is on the response over which the client has some control, as shown in the preceding examples. In the assessment process, the locus of the problem is established on the basis of the responses or the absence of certain responses of the client. Either the desired behavior is absent or of low frequency (for example, in a lonely client who does not reach out to others even with the help of relatives) or an undesirable or excessive behavior manifests itself (such as a mood change in the face of criticism). Group treatment usually involves modification of the habitual, but often ineffectual, responses to or perceptions of the situation itself. The usual procedures are direct demonstration of and practice in the target behavior. It may also be possible to change the consequences of both the previous and the new desired responses as a means of acquiring new sets of behaviors. For this reason, in assessment, the general problem as perceived by the client, the situations in which the problem is manifested, the responses of the client to the situation, and the immediate and long-term consequences of responses for the client are carefully examined. Although it is difficult to separate the behavior from its situation and its consequences, we briefly examine the situations most commonly brought up at the group sessions.

The General Problem

One client in a pain management group complains that he has frequent pain at periodic intervals over which he has little or no control. His physician has thus far been unable to prescribe medication that provides him with much relief. He panics and tightens up when the pain first begins because he claims he knows it is going to be unendurable. Another client in a stress management group is upset because no one in her family pays attention to her even though she is frequently nervous and unable to get out of the house. Despite her children's words to the contrary, she "knows" she is hated. She almost always feels "upset." A client in a parent group does not know how to handle a rebellious teenage son. A client in a group for violent men claims that if his wife did not nag him, he would not lose control the way he has been doing lately.

In each of these examples, the client presented early in treatment a brief and sometimes complex and inconsistent picture of the problem as she or he perceived it. Such a general picture suggests few intervention strategies that can be employed to help the client resolve the problem. To determine whether and how the client can be helped, the observable components of the specific situations linked to the problems must be identified. General formulation of the problem can be considered a useful first step toward situational analysis. But dwelling on it results in continued complaining, self-pity, blaming of others, and avoidance of responsibility. It is only when the client perceives improvement that the client feels treatment is successful.

The Situation Response

The preceding examples illustrated a number of responses— evaluative, verbal, and motor—that the client could change. The appropriateness of a given response is dictated by the conditions of the situation. One purpose of assessment in the early phases of treatment is to help clients to analyze systematically the components of a situation as well as their response to that situation. Clients usually need to be trained in such analysis. One group of elderly clients who complained of generalized anxiety were presented with the following examples for analysis and then asked to develop their own examples.

For years, I have had trouble getting along with my family. Things seem to be getting worse recently. I'm begin-ning to think that everyone in my family dislikes me [back-ground and general statement of problem as initially formulated by client]. For example, last Tuesday my daughter came to the house with dried apricots, which I usually like [situation]. I asked her what she had done to me that she needed to bring apricots [cognitive and verbal response]. She got upset with me and left [consequence], which proves my point [evaluation].

I have a problem with the neighbors and I have had it for years. They are always dropping in on me when I don't want to see anybody [background and general problem]. Just this morning, Mrs. Gell stopped in for a moment at the worse possible time. She didn't even knock [situation]. I thought "there she is again, oh no!" [cognitive response]. I offered her a cup of coffee and some freshly baked coffee cake, which she accepted. I was so nervous and upset [affective response] that I dropped the coffee pot [behavioral response].

My problem is just this nervousness. I can't think of any situations because everything seems to make me nervous [general problem]. Was there a recent event that particularly upset me? Oh, yes, like last night. I saw that something or someone had knocked off the garbage can lid [situation]. I thought it might have been a burglar or, worse, a rat. Then I thought maybe I forgot to put it on, and that was worse yet, because I was losing my mind [cognitive responses]. My heart was beating so fast I thought the neighbors could hear it [affective response]. My mind kept going on like that so I couldn't sleep [consequence].

In these examples, the clients have identified recurring situations to which they responded with inappropriate behaviors or cognitions. Each situation is related to a general problem. Each situation is considered important to the client who described it. Each situation is highly specific in terms of time, place, persons, and event. For each event, we note the responses of the clients: verbal, cognitive, and affective. Finally, each client appears to be dissatisfied with his or her response. The goal of treatment would be either to help them to modify their responses to or their evaluation of the situation *or* to help them change or avoid the situation. The appropriate strategies cannot be determined without a careful description of the components of the situations that are experienced as problematic and the client's responses to it.

Clients rarely, at least in the initial phases of treatment, describe problems in sufficiently specific terms. When a new situation is introduced, the previously mentioned information (background, event, place, persons, responses, satisfaction, importance) is elicited in early sessions by the group leader and later by other clients. Specific cases similar to those used here are presented to the group and discussed as a means of acquainting the members with the criteria. The problem may not be perceived in the same way by the leader and the client. Many of the clients described in the examples initially blamed others for their problems. In some cases, they distorted or misinterpreted the actions of others. Eventually, the group is helpful in pointing this out and in suggesting how the problem might be redefined or how situations might be evaluated differently. Such redefinition is enhanced as the client repeatedly identifies to the group the concrete elements of the situations constituting the problem.

Interactive and Noninteractive Situations. Two types of situations stand out by virtue of their implications for differential treatment in groups: interactive and noninteractive. An interactive situation is an event that involves talking to, working with, or, in other ways communicating with people. Most situations worked on in group treatment are interactive in nature, as it is this interaction that can most readily be simulated in the small group and that can be altered by modeling, cognitive restructuring, and other procedures commonly applied in the multimethod approach. In groups that focus on excessive eating, poor study habits, alcohol and drug intake, lack of exercise, and similar behaviors whose modification requires extensive "self-control" on the part of the client, the purpose of situational analysis is to determine the conditions under which the target behaviors occur. (In noninteractive situations, rather than *situation,* the term *antecedent conditions* is often used; see, for example, Cormier and Cormier, 1985, p. 185).

As was pointed out in the previous chapter, we have found it useful (though not necessary) to form groups of clients with similar types of problem situations. Such commonality serves to make the intervention process in groups more efficient both because of mutual modeling of self-disclosure and because a wealth of alternative responses is made available to each group member. The group leader can also devote more time to a shared situation, since it is relevant to almost all members of the group. All of the examples in the preceding section involved situations shared by some or all of the group members.

In-Group Situations. One of the advantages of the group is that problematic and stressful interactive situations arise within the normal interaction of the group that provide a natural laboratory for working on a common problem. Let us look at two examples.

In one group, Gary disagreed with Peter, who assumed it was a personal attack. As a result, Peter became sullen for the rest of the session. The usual enthusiasm of the members seemed dampened after this exchange.

In another group, Anne claimed she was disappointed in Clarice because she had not said very much in the group while everyone else told of their problems quite openly. Anne announced that it was not fair that some do all the self-disclosure. The other members agreed with Anne, except for Donna who came to Clarice's defense and said that everyone had the right to talk as little or as much as they wanted. In both groups, the leaders helped the members to examine the situations, in terms of the situation response consequences, from the perspective of each member as means of learning the vocabulary, of learning how to do a situational analysis, and of helping them to solve a real group problem.

Because these situations are directly observed by all the members and the group leader, a great deal of reliable information is made available. Such problematic responses to intragroup events are often typical of the client in the extragroup events and therefore highly relevant. Most other situations brought before the group rely solely on the self-report of the client with the problem. In-group situations provide a natural setting for reanalysis and formulation of more effective responses to them, and a continuous opportunity to practice those new responses.

Chained Situations. Thus far we have discussed situations as if they were isolated events; however, situations often occur in a sequence, as in the following example:

> Larry was distressed because he had "caved in" to his sixteen-year-old son, Lex. Lex had received a ticket for speeding the week before and Larry told him he couldn't use the car for a week. His son began to beg him for the car for Saturday night when he had a big date [situation 1]. Larry said he felt guilty, but he stuck to the limit. Then Lex said that Larry was a rotten father and that he was going to leave home, which caused Larry's wife to cry [situation 2]. Larry told Lex he could go on the date, but only if he got in by midnight. Larry thought that he had become a weak and ineffectual father.

In this example as in most other situations, the group must examine not only each isolated incident, but the entire sequence of events, to obtain an accurate picture of the relevance of the given situation to the given client. The description of the situation is not complete until the client's responses to the events are examined. In this example, overt behavioral responses, cognitive responses, and affective responses can be identified. Let us look more closely at each type of response.

Responses to Problematic Situations

In any given event the response of the person experiencing the event is crucial in defining whether the situation is indeed problematic. As observed in the earlier examples, there are many different kinds of responses. Obviously, if the client perceives that she or he has not handled the situation appropriately, or if the individual has labeled the situation problematic for historical or intuitive reasons, or if the situation creates stress, panic, and feelings of failure, incompetence, guilt, or intense anxiety, the situation can be assumed to be problematic. This does not deny the contribution of often objective circumstances to creation of the problem. Both the characteristics of the event and the responses are necessary objects of scrutiny in the assessment process.

To train clients to formulate behavioral responses, case examples, group discussion, and group exercises are used in which situational and behavioral response specificity is modeled and reinforced by the leader. Furthermore, if a client makes a broad or general statement, the group leader usually asks for a specific example.

Eric: I guess my problem is that I tend to be a nervous person.

Group Leader: How does a nervous person act? That is, what does a nervous person do or say when he or she is experiencing nervousness. What is he thinking? What is she feeling?

Eric: I guess when he's shaking and he's feeling tightness in his head and stomach.

Pamela: And when she's having trouble breathing even though she isn't exercising.

John: I don't know about the rest of you but I sweat a lot even though it's cold. And I clench my teeth until my jaws hurt.

Group Leader: I think these are some pretty good indications. They seem to vary from person to person. Now Eric, can you think of a recent situation in which you felt or acted in some of these ways?

Eric: Now that you mentioned it, when I was sitting on the bus coming here. The person next to me took more than his share of the seat and he smelled of garlic, which I hate. I thought how awful it was to have to ride the crowded bus every day. My head began to hurt, I began to feel angry, then tense all over. My hands were clammy too. I can feel it all now, too. I got up and stood even though I was tired, just to get out of the cramped seat. I felt so nervous it was difficult for me to breathe.

The questions asked by the leader moved the client from a general to a more specific statement of the problem and delineation of the different responses typical in problematic situations. In this example, three types of responses are identified: overt motor and verbal, cognitive, and affective. It is necessary to make such a distinction because the intervention strategy depends on the predominant type of response.

Overt Behavior. In many of the examples cited earlier, the responses were either overt behaviors or cognitions. In some instances the response may have also been emotional. In every event, the overt behavior could be specifically described and observed. In almost all instances, the behavior was a response to a given situation. The behaviors were often inappropriate or maladaptive in that the responses failed to resolve the problem or reduce the stress inherent in the situation or to maximize the probability of achievement of the client's goals. For example, when Per was asked by his employer to do something he did not want to do, he often argued with the boss; after a few arguments, he lost his job. He needed to learn to reduce the frequency of arguing and to increase the frequency of other more adaptive responses to disagreement. When asked to lend his car or money to others, Arlon (who wanted to refuse) was unable to refuse in a decisive manner. Much assessment is aimed at identifying and spelling out those behaviors that become the target of change as well as the conditions under which those behaviors might best occur. These behaviors are defined in highly specific terms that lend themselves to observation and monitoring. The responses of both Per and Arlon were verbal responses.

Cognitions. Cognitions have been described as thoughts, beliefs, images, conceptual schemes, values, evaluations, expectations, and silent self-instructions or self-statements. These are all examples of private or covert events; often they are responses to internal or external situations. Some are general guidelines to overt or other private responses. Cognitions may be associated with anxiety or stress. Either the cognition is identified by asking the client to describe it in writing or aloud or it is deduced from other behaviors or statements. We are particularly concerned with cognitions as responses to situations or recurring thoughts across situations. In an earlier example in this chapter, one client had the repeating thought he might die. In another, the client responded to a difficult situation by silently predicting his absolute failure to achieve his goal. In a third situation, a client evaluated himself as a "total loss." All of these are examples of cognitions requiring the attention of the group and leader. Because of their private nature, cognitions are difficult to ascertain reliably. Moreover, many clients have difficulty even recalling their cognitions. Nevertheless, as cognitions often impinge on the resolution of problematic situations, it is important to explore their presence as a response to problematic situations with the clients.

Some clients are not readily able to identify their thinking in response to a given situation. For them, training in cognition perception and expression is an important prerequisite for assessment and treatment. To train them to formulate and look at their cognitions, a group leader may use this exercise.

After an initial orientation by the group leader as to what are thoughts or cognitions the clients are instructed to respond to a series of situations by writing down what they would think if they were the target persons in the following situations (designed primarily for an anxiety management group):

1. You find yourself listening to a highly aggressive and loud person of the opposite sex who is telling offensive jokes about your gender.
2. A person whom you dislike at work or in an organization to which you belong asks you for help on a project over an extended period. You have the time available and necessary skills but you do not want to work with the person.
3. A person with whom you have little contact compliments you effusively about your activities and personality to a group of other people, some of whom you know quite well.
4. You finally have mapped out your plan of work for the week. You think you can now catch up. Suddenly you begin to feel ill. You are sure you are getting the flu.

The clients then present aloud their written cognitions and affective responses. They give feedback to each other as to the level of effectiveness of each of the cognitions in helping the individual to cope with the stressful situation.

Other exercises have been developed to help clients to practice their competency in identifying cognitions. Meichenbaum (1976) has suggested a range of tasks that may be used in assessing a client's cognitions: imagery exercises, tasks during which internal dialogues are verbalized, and projective techniques using pictures of people interacting. Meichenbaum's suggested use of imagery focuses on the client's recalling a critical incident and running it through his or her mind "like a movie." While imagining an incident, Meichenbaum helps the client focus on reporting his or her cognitions as the event occurred. In the same manner, the client's cognitive strengths may be assessed by "running through" situations in which the client succeeded in some way.

In a similar vein, Meichenbaum has suggested the use of behavioral tasks for assessing cognitive behavior. Much like the roleplay tests to be described, the client is asked to engage in a problematic behavior, in a real-life or a simulated setting. The difference here is that the client is asked, either during the event or immediately afterward, what she said to herself during the event as well as what physiological events (for example, faster heartbeat, tight stomach, sweaty palms, dry lips, head pain, increased breathing rate) occurred.

Occasionally, clients identify a given cognition as occurring constantly or across so many situations that its relationship to specific situational cues is unclear. For example, one client stated that "in all situations in which I find it difficult to do what is asked of me, I think to myself I'll never get it done." This is usually dealt with by asking the client to discuss the most recent occurrence of the response and the situational attributes that occurred at that time. Repetition of this analysis often yields identifiable components that precede or covary with the response. Thus, patterns of self-defeating cognitions may be discovered that interfere with or enhance the client's functioning in many diverse situations.

Not all cognitions can be identified as actual covert statements. A person may act in such a way that the observer might extrapolate from his words and other behavior a given cognitive theme. For example, a client who never expresses his opinion to others when they disagree with him nor sets limits on his adolescent children might indicate by his behavior that he wants to be approved of and loved by every significant adult with whom he interacts (Ellis, 1974). The group may point out in a given situation how that or another assumption might be operating across a number of situations and how the given assumption seems to color the choice of actions the client might take. Ellis (1974) provides the practitioner with a number of similar personal themes that the group therapist might use as guidelines for their formulation. Many of these themes are discussed in Chapter Nine.

Affective Responses. Affective responses refer to emotional reactions to or in a given situation. They are identified by the statement the client makes. For example, "I felt awful when he said that," "I was really angry when he pushed me down," "I was depressed sitting at home all alone yesterday," "I was excited when our team won the ball game." The distinction between cognitive and affective statements is not always clear, since a cognitive statement is often used to describe an affect. For example, in response to the group leader's question "How do you feel about that," the client responds "I feel awful." The statement "I feel awful" is a cognitive evaluation of the client's perception of her affective state. Affective responses can also at times be identified from nonverbal cues. Excitement, depression, joy, fatigue, and disgust may often be interpreted from facial expression, body posture, and other nonverbal cues during the group interaction. Yet, group leaders vary in their skill in identifying these cues. It is often helpful to check these cues with the client and the other group members to see whether the client indeed feels the same affective response as perceived by the group leader. "Elsie, you've been quiet and you seem really down for the last fifteen minutes. I wonder if you were upset by the critical comments that others made to you. Would you say this is accurate or am I way off base, Elsie?"

Some of the major targets of change may be the inadequate manifestation of appropriate affect in critical situations. Ross is

upset with the way his children bicker in loud and violent tones of
voice. He tries to be calm and friendly at all times even though when
the bickering begins, he feels his body tightening up and he has
terrible headaches. Often, however, other clients may suffer from
excessive affective responding to relatively trivial situations. If
anyone asks Terry to do anything, she becomes immediately annoyed and tearful.

We review the potential targets of change as overt behavior or
covert cognitions and affective responses to carefully described
situations. For purposes of analysis, the situation and its responses
have been separated; in practice, they are usually inseparable.

Critical Moment

The interface between the interactive situation and the
response is called the critical moment. It is that instant in the
situation when the client has perceived the concomitant situational
events but has not yet responded. Al describes a recent encounter:
"At the moment that my wife said I was drinking, I felt an electric
shock of anger go through my body and I smacked her." The critical
moment occurred when Al heard his wife's comments but before he
hit her. The critical moment is important because it is that point
when the client can do (think and/or feel) something other than
what she or he actually did (thought and/or felt).

In any complicated event or sequence of interactions, many
critical moments often occur. For example, when Alexi, a member
of a parents group, described how, when she saw her teenage
daughter leave the house in ragged cut-off sweat pants (critical
moment 1), she became violently angry and yelled "get back in the
house." When her daughter began to scream at her and call her a
witch (critical moment 2), Alexi grounded her for a month. It is
important for Alexi to determine at which critical moment in the
event she wants to work on her responses; otherwise she may go
back and forth between the two. Of course, she can work on the
immediate situations surrounding all critical moments but one at a
time, so she still must select which one she will do first. If the group
leader and/or members do not agree that a given moment is the
most critical, they discuss it. But the client whose situations are

being discussed is the final arbiter of his or her own critical moment. In the evaluation of various alternative responses, clients often shift from one critical moment to another, if in the given event the critical moment of concern is not precisely defined. We will discuss the implications of the critical moment in treatment throughout the intervention chapters.

In training clients to use the critical moment concept, we present them with a number of examples. Afterward, the clients are given several situations and responses and are asked to identify the critical moments. An excerpt from a commonly used list follows.

After hearing my father tell me that he had given up drinking forever, because of his liver problem, I discovered him in the kitchen getting a beer. I became furious and yelled at him. [The critical moment is that point when the subject saw the father taking the beer.]

Laurie is the most popular secretary among the staff. When she asked me to the staff party, I was so frightened I told her my mother was coming that weekend so I wouldn't be going. [The critical moment was that point when Laurie asked the client to go to the staff party.]

My customer canceled his order, and when I asked why, he said it was none of my business. I was very upset, but I couldn't think of anything to say. [There are two critical moments in this situation: when the customer canceled his order and when the customer said it was none of the client's business.]

In the discussion that follows such a list, more than one critical moment is identified in several situations. The group leader would point out that the client is ultimately responsible for determining what was most important to her or him; however, it is also possible to work on each of the situations immediately preceding each of the critical moments one at a time. Once the clients can identify, with reasonable accuracy, the critical moments in a wide variety of situations and the responses to the problematic situations, they begin to look at and evaluate the potential immediate and long-term consequences of the responses.

Immediate Consequences

A given situation and the client's response have both immediate and long-term consequences for the client. Alexi's violent responses to her daughter's clothing and other typical teenage behavior of which she does not approve result in her daughter losing control and a series of undesirable responses on both their parts. The long-range effects, were the pattern to persist, would be damage to the relationship and continued unacceptable behavior on the part of both parent and child.

Reinforcement theory maintains that the pattern of immediate consequences to a series of similar events may influence the frequency or nature of the client's response pattern to that event. As a result, rearranging the consequences may become the major focus of intervention for some clients. For example, when Nolan complains, as he does constantly, about various small annoyances in the house, everyone tries to explain why they do what they do. In a group analysis of the event, it was agreed that this attention appears to maintain his complaining behavior. It was recommended that he suggest to his wife and brother-in-law that they not respond to his complaints. The group members also agreed to ignore his complaints. If he wanted something done differently, he would write it down and the family would discuss it systematically.

Having identified a series of problematic situations, the critical moment, and the client's responses to those situations, another group exercise similar to those described earlier can be introduced to the clients. Using lists of situations described in earlier sections, the leader asks clients to identify and evaluate the immediate consequences of using the given response described in the situation. As the clients become accomplished in identifying potential consequences, they learn to identify resources in their environment that might serve either as reinforcing consequences or as additional tools to help the client achieve his or her goals.

Long-Term Consequences

Group Leader: Supposing Nolan continues to complain to his wife, friends, fellow group members, what do you view as the long-term consequences of this behavior?

Clem: They are certainly going to be annoyed with him. I would avoid him after a while.

Anneke: You got to show me something else. It's just boring that's all, and who wants to be bored?

Elsie: I think it would be awfully difficult to stay married in those circumstances.

In this example, the group leader has helped the members to examine the long-term consequences of the behavior of one member of their group. Such an analysis serves as a form of confrontation of the client with the effects of his or her behavior on others. To determine whether a situation-response pattern is worth the investment of therapeutic time, evaluation of the potential long-term consequences is essential. Often the client may feel that such consequences are not sufficiently negative and may choose another type of situation to work on. Jerry, who was a member of a group of moderately depressed and anxious clients, told the other members that he was repeatedly annoyed by his grocer, who continued to joke with him even though he was often in a bad mood. Jerry generally ignored the grocer. When asked what were the long-term consequences of his "ignoring" and "upset" behavior, Jerry decided that it really did not matter much and he would not use group time to work on that situation. Furthermore, Jerry was not dissatisfied with his response, so there was no reason to learn another response. Later, if Jerry changed his mind, he was free to reintroduce the situation for further consideration.

Client Satisfaction with Responses

Thus, in every situational analysis, it is important to ask members not only what they perceive to be the long-term consequences of a given situation, but also whether they are dissatisfied with their usual response to their problem situations. (Often, satisfaction and long-term consequences are closely linked.) Occasionally, a client brings to the group a situation response with which she or he is satisfied. The problem as they perceive it is in the situation or the actions of others. It is usually best to reinforce the client for finding what they feel is the best action possible at that time, and then go on to another situation or another client (as we see in the following example). Otherwise, a great deal of time is spent looking at alternatives that the client is not motivated to accept. Frequently, the client returns with the same situation the next week, admitting to less satisfaction than the previous week. It is at that moment that it becomes effective to spend time developing the situation.

Harvey: I have this problem situation, see, in which I have to deal with this obnoxious client. He never talks. He always shouts. And complains, you should hear him complain. My price is always too high. And he hates me. I know he does. Yet he always comes just to me. Yesterday, it was the same old thing. I said to him, Carl, you always shout and yell at me. But in the end you make the purchase. Can't we deal with each other like gentlemen? And you know what he said? "You aren't a gentleman."

Gladys: Are you really dissatisfied with your response? It sounds to me as if you know what you're doing and feel pretty good about it. I get the feeling you want him to do something different.

Harvey: I guess you're right. I wouldn't do anything different. Just the way I did it.

Tom (Group Leader):   It seems to me to be a tough situation, and it's great that you handled it to your satisfaction. Do you have another situation that was a little more difficult for you?

Harvey: I guess not this week.

Tom: No problem, but keep track during the week and see what comes up. What about you, Gladys, do you have a situation in which you were dissatisfied with your response?

Not all situations that clients bring into the group represent situations that have already occurred. Increasingly, as treatment progresses, clients bring to the group situations that they must handle in the immediate future. The client indicates that she or he either does not know what to do or has some ideas but wants the group's feedback: Marietta, an unmarried twenty-year-old woman, states, "Next week I must visit my mother. I have to tell her I'm pregnant, and I just don't know how to approach her."

The Response Pattern

Most of the situations described earlier are not simple, isolated situations that are problematic to the client. Rather, they often reveal a pattern of responses to stressful situations. These patterns are frequently dysfunctional. For example, Candice responds to almost all situations in which she seeks help by worrying before seeking that help. As a result, she seldom gets the help she needs until a crisis occurs. Where a response is part of a general pattern, the situations associated with that pattern become even more important to deal with. Part of assessment involves drawing the larger pattern for the client. Usually, this occurs after a client has presented a number of situations for consideration in the group. The group provides a useful resource for discovering and presenting patterns to each other.

Resources and Impediments to Treatment

Problem situations do not occur in a vacuum. Personal characteristics, persons with whom the client has frequent contact, physical attributes, and potential reinforcers all impinge on the strategies that will eventually be employed. Sometimes these characteristics of the client or of his or her environment serve as potential resources available to the client; at other times, they may act as impediments to the effective use of therapy.

One determines these resources through testing, interviewing, and observing as the group progresses. The leader of one group asked the members to list all the possible aspects of their lives that might help them to solve the problem they had identified. The leader then asked them to list those aspects that might prevent them from solving the problem. Although an entire session was devoted to discussion of the results of this exercise, the group leader and the clients had a much clearer picture of what resources they could draw

on and what barriers they must face, in relation not only to the
immediate problem but also to future problems.

Potential Reinforcers

An important strategy of intervention described in this book
is reinforcement. As a result, one of the most important resources a
client has is interest or skill in participating in events that serve as
self-reinforcers for the performance of desired behaviors. Another
reinforcer is attention of a spouse, relatives, friends, or the group
leader. To obtain a list of these reinforcers for each client, a
reinforcement survey schedule is administered to clients in the
pregroup interview or at the first meeting. Although a number of
schedules are available, we most commonly use the following
reinforcement survey:

> If you could be with whomever you wanted, name the three
> persons you would most like to be with.
> If you could eat anything you wanted, name the three foods
> you would most like to eat.
> If you could play any game or sport you wanted, name three
> games or sports you would play.
> If you had $50.00 and could buy whatever you wanted, what
> three things might you buy?
> If you could go wherever you wanted in this general area, to
> what three places would you go?
> If you could do whatever you wanted at work, what three
> things would you do?
> If you could do whatever you wanted in the group, what
> three things would you do?

The clients first fill in the survey, and then each client
presents a summary of the events, persons, foods, and so forth that
they like best to find common reinforcers. By sharing their lists,
clients are reminded of individuals or objects that may be added to
their lists. Furthermore, common interests may serve as group
reinforcement. Many of the clients we work with have access to a
limited number of reinforcers. This limitation may be a barrier to

treatment. In that case, a part of treatment might initially be expansion of the list.

Social Attributes

Every client comes to treatment with a number of social and other skills, interests, personal characteristics, and unique knowledge or information that may enhance or interfere with the achievement of treatment goals. The behavioral and cognitive attributes that are not direct targets of change may be used as resources in treatment. For example, Delbert is skilled at roleplaying. Helena makes cautious but thoughtful suggestions when asked. LouLou listens attentively to the other clients when they are complaining. Greg can effectively empathize with the feelings of frustration experienced by other members of the group. These skills may facilitate group interaction as well as enhance the individual's own treatment. They also may function as a source of recognition and reinforcement from the other group members or leader, even though such skills are not the primary targets of intervention. Further enhancement of these skills may be one of the side benefits of the group experience. Lewinsohn and his associates (Lewinsohn, Weinstein, and Alper, 1970; Lewinsohn, Sullivan, and Grosscup, 1980) make extensive use of this approach in the treatment of depression individually and in groups. To assess clients' resources, they have developed two scales to assess changes in the intensity of activities.

Physical Attributes

The client may come to the group with major physical impairments (for example, difficulty hearing, a heart condition), athletic skills, required medications, limits on particular activities, all of which either facilitate relationships, separate her or him from others, focus attention on the client, or in some other way influence the progress of treatment. The group leader usually requests information about such attributes from the client. Physical limitations in particular may be closely linked to self-defeating cognitions. Helen Jean, who has difficulty hearing others, feels disliked and unwanted. In the group, the members pointed out that they ignore her because she does not seem to listen to them. They wondered if she would not feel more well liked if she wore her hearing aid. They also discussed whether this may have been a problem in other groups to which she belonged. Such characteristics often are embedded in problematic situations and limit the types of response.

It is helpful to have a medical clearance and knowledge of physical restraints. The group leader should be aware of any medication that clients are taking. Some medications may interact with even such innocent activities as relaxation training to create surprising side effects (see Everly and Rosenfeld, 1981, pp. 112–113, for more detail). Other medications may cause fatigue or hyperactivity. Obviously, the formulation of treatment goals must take the effects of such medications into consideration.

Social Support Networks

The client's environment may contain persons who can enhance the achievement of treatment goals. For example, a cooperative spouse, a close family, interested friends, a support group, and an active church group may enhance treatment. Where such resources are lacking, they may need to be developed before effective treatment can begin.

Spouses, parents, siblings, and significant others may also interfere with the achievement of change. Some spouses may be unwilling to reward the same behavior being reinforced in the group. Friends may attempt to maintain the very behaviors the group is working to eliminate. Some significant others remain passive and leave everything up to the group. Various support networks may be in conflict with each other. Providers of support may be in conflict with the recipient. Support may come with a demand for change. Support may be viewed as interference or even nagging.

In assessment, such potential support networks must at least be ascertained and, where possible, agreed on by the client and the significant others included in goal setting and treatment. In our experience, the greater the involvement of family members, the greater the likelihood of success with adolescents (Rose and others, 1971). Yet, Tallant, Rose, and Tolman (1989) found that the persons on the waitlist who showed the greatest improvement in stress reduction without professional help were those having the least extensive social support networks. Perhaps the social networks do not necessarily provide only social support. They may also seek to control the client or even to support his or her resistance to change as a means of protecting their status quo.

Despite these problems, it becomes clear that either the group or significant others should provide a source of social support and that as the group approaches termination, the extragroup networks increase in importance. Clients, however, must be taught how to deal with such problems as nagging, demands for change, and conflict. To determine the focus of network building and use, social support networks are assessed at the beginning and end of treatment through interviews and, sometimes, the Social Support Questionnaire (Schaefer, Coyne, and Lazarus, 1981). This questionnaire seeks the client's perception of the number of others he or she can turn to in time of need and the degree of satisfaction with the available support.

Physical Resources

The eventual resolution of some situational problems may lie in the availability of adequate financial resources to the client. Eligibility for welfare or other agency programs may also be of value in problem solving. Ready access to day care may be instrumental in the treatment of situational problems related to more general problems, such as divorce adjustment or agoraphobia. In assessment, the availability of such resources must be determined insofar as they impinge on situational problem solving. Some of these resources, for example, day care, may be related to the supportiveness of social networks. In one group, a woman wanted to work on harassment by her employer. If she were fired or she quit, there would be an immediate loss of income for her and her child. Training her to use assertiveness in confronting her employer had no impact until she knew that her child could be taken care of by an aunt living in the same neighborhood, were she to look for an alternative position.

Motivation

Clients differ dramatically in their willingness to use treatment. Evidence of motivation lies in the performance of homework, promptness, degree of openness and self-disclosure, attendance, and helpfulness to others. Obviously, this attitude is essential to help any client effectively. In the absence of high motivation, strategies for stimulating motivation must be employed. First, however, the leader must assess the level of motivation. To determine the level, each client's perceptions of the long-term consequences of present patterns of behavior are examined. Clarity as to the long-term consequences and concern about them can be considered one index of motivation. Motivation is also weighed by asking the clients to indicate, on a five-point scale, how dissatisfied they are with their responses to each identified situation. Ratings are then discussed in the group. Clients who are not very dissatisfied with a given response are unlikely to work very hard to change it. Moreover, if the clients are not dissatisfied with responses to any situation, it may be assumed that motivation for this form of treatment at that time is generally low.

A third indicator of motivation is the willingness of the client to take a risk. As discussed earlier, each client examines the risk involved in any set of alternative responses. If the client is not well motivated, he would be expected to persistently choose the low-risk strategies. A fourth indicator of low motivation is persistent blaming of others for one's problems. Although, initially, most clients fail to assume responsibility for their part in interactive problems, the poorly motivated client continues to blame others.

Fortunately, the level of motivation is not static. With most clients it tends to increase over time. As others in the group identify clearly problematic situations, as the program becomes attractive, as the reinforcers become of greater interest, and as the relationships with peers and the group leader are enhanced, motivation often increases. However, in those instances where motivation remains low, each of the previously mentioned indices can be worked on separately:

Sean was considered poorly motivated because he rarely brought up situations he wanted to work on, he often came late and left early, and he blamed others for all his problems. The other group members expressed their annoyance with Sean and asked him why he needed to be there. Sean said his wife would have divorced him if he had not sought help. At least in the group he didn't have to do anything. The members said that he was wasting their time because they were not helping him and he certainly had nothing to offer them. Sean said he had not realized that he was imposing on them and that he guessed it would be fairer if he quit. The group leader agreed but offered him the option of figuring out how he might better use the group and remain a contributing member. The group offered him several suggestions before resuming the regular agenda. A subgroup offered to meet with him during the week to help him complete the assignments. At the following meeting, Sean arrived on time with his diary. The other members applauded his efforts and welcomed him to the group.

During another group meeting, following a suggestion by Kanfer and Gaelick (1986, p. 296), members were encouraged to imagine and discuss what life would be like if their behavior patterns were altered. As an additional means of enhancing motivation, they discussed what life would be like if they did not change at all.

In summary a continuing estimate of motivation is included in the assessment of each client. If the impetus for working toward treatment goals and remaining in the group appears to be decreased, these deficiencies in motivation can be dealt with as part of the treatment approach.

Resource or Impediment?

As in the case of social support, no one resource is always an advantage or a disadvantage in facilitating change. For example, a high level of intelligence may result in greater ease in understanding the concepts that must be grasped to analyze situations or to make use of sophisticated cognitive strategies. This same level of intelligence may cause clients to become excessively critical and unaccepting of the treatment process. Enthusiasm, though a desirable characteristic in a client, in excess may result in the same client's closing out more taciturn clients in the group discussion. Within the context of specific situations, each attribute must be considered in light of its contribution to the achievement of treatment goals and as to whether it should be encouraged or ignored.

Assessment focuses on the situation, the client's response to that situation, and the resources the client has available to deal with the situation. Most clients are not prepared in the early phase of treatment to discuss situations in this manner and often must first be trained in the assumptions and procedures of situational analysis. In addition to discussion in the pregroup interview, group procedures are used to accrue the information necessary to develop the analysis to a point where it can be used for planning intervention. Many of the data-enhancing techniques to be described make systematic use of the unique characteristics of the group.

Tools Used to Identify Problematic Situations

To identify problematic situations, a number of overlapping group strategies are used, including structured group interviewing, group discussion, diaries, case studies, assessment roleplays, and behavioral checklists. These strategies may be employed to train members in identifying appropriate and inappropriate responses to situations. In this section, we discuss how the clients are trained in the use of these procedures and are taught their function in the data-gathering process.

Structured Group Interviews

In pregroup interviews and early group sessions, clients are asked to describe situations in which they were unhappy or dissatisfied with their responses. Often, this technique alone is sufficient in providing a wide range of situations that require only further specification in the group. Before this, the group leader may present examples from his or her own experience or from previous group members.

Often, the clients initially provide excessively general or vague descriptions of the problem situations. In the following example, the group leader distributed lists of criteria (Exhibit 3) to the members of an anger management group.

Exhibit 3. Criteria for Problem Situations.

Describe in two or three sentences the background of the situation.

Describe the relationship of the situation to the general problem.

Describe the degree to which the situation is important to you.

Is this a one-shot or recurring situation?

Describe a recent concrete example of a situation with a definite beginning and end; include the location and the persons involved. Describe what happened.

Describe your responses (what you did, what you said, what you thought, and what you felt).

Would that same response be appropriate under any other set of conditions? Describe them.

Describe what you perceive to be the consequences of your responses to yourself and others.

Describe the degree to which you were satisfied with your responses.

Having received these criteria and having been provided with an example, the clients, working in pairs, described situations that met the criteria. (This analysis may also be offered as a homework assignment.) Let us examine a specific presentation.

Stanley: My situation is that I don't like to be told what to do by anybody, especially my wife.

Tom (looking at his handout): Tell us about a recent event.

Stanley: Last week my wife told me to take a short cut which I knew was much longer. I really fumed.

Group Leader: Who's got another question? Look at your handouts, if you want.

Calvin: Let's see, you told us who was involved. But when and
where did it happen?

Stanley: It happened Tuesday when I was driving my wife to the
bowling alley the way I always do on Tuesday night. It ruined the
whole evening for me.

Group Leader: Anything else we need to know?

Barry: What was your response? I mean what do you mean by "I
fumed" and what was the critical moment as you see it?

Stanley: Well, the critical moment was when she told *me* how to
get to the bowling alley. I guess the critical moment was just after
that. And my response was something like "I've driven this a
thousand times, I know how to get there." I felt really angry. I also
thought "where does she get off telling me where to go?"

Barry: What was the result of your responding in that way?

Stanley: Well she just shut up and pouted the whole evening.
Both our games were ruined. She's got to learn to keep from bossing
me around.

Group Leader: I guess we all have to learn something from this
situation. I wonder what you think you might have to learn?

Stanley: I don't know. At least, I'm not sure.

Barry: I wonder if you are really dissatisfied with your response. It
sounds to me like you really don't want to change anything about it.

Stanley: That's not exactly right. My big mouth gets me into a lot
of trouble. Besides I really don't like losing control like that.

Although this type of dialogue is carried on until clients can
effectively present problem situations, the procedure is used only as
long as the clients are unable to interview each other without cues.
Eventually, the handouts are eliminated and replaced with occa-

sional verbal cues by the group leader and, ultimately, the cues are eliminated entirely. Thus, the clients are provided the opportunity not only to help each other to develop useful situations, but also to learn to become involved in group discussion.

Keeping a Diary

Although, by questioning each other, clients are trained to correctly formulate problematic events, they are asked to keep a diary of situations in which they are satisfied or dissatisfied with their responses. Situations to which their responses were satisfying afford an opportunity for reinforcement, whereas dissatisfying responses indicate potential targets of change. Even when the client is satisfied with a given response to a situation, the group leader or members may disagree, pointing to another potential target of change for the client. The diary contents are discussed at the beginning of every session.

To train the clients in the use of diaries, model diaries are presented and discussed and an exercise is given in which part of a diary situation is described and the group members are asked to fill in the rest. The members may use the statements in Exhibit 3 to help them complete the fictional diary situation. Afterward, members pair off, and partners evaluate each other's diary situation in the light of the criteria in the handout (Exhibit 3).

Not all clients are literate or sufficiently disciplined to keep a diary. In some cases, we ask clients to dictate their situations to tape recorders. In some groups, the partners call and interview each other between sessions about their situations.

We have also been able to increase the likelihood of diary keeping by asking clients to describe only two situations (in the beginning) each week: (1) a problematic situation in which the client was dissatisfied with her response and (2) a problematic situation in which the client was satisfied with her response. The latter provides an opportunity for reinforcement. The exercise also provides an occasion for clients to differentiate between a situation that can be worked on and one that does not lend itself to work in practicing new responses.

Self-Monitoring

Clients often are asked to self-monitor certain behaviors to ascertain the frequency and the situations in which the behaviors usually occur. For example, in one stop-smoking group, members monitored the frequency of smoking and situations in which they smoked. Social skill group clients monitored occasions on which they successfully and unsuccessfully responded to pressure from their peers by standing up for their own position. A group of recently divorced clients monitored, on a scale of 1 to 10, their level of depression three times a day and at certain critical moments; they also monitored the number of times they thought about their previous marriage.

In a stress management group, the clients monitored the level of stress experienced after each "hassle" experienced in the course of a day. Conformity to requests for self-monitoring is not always forthcoming, and such requests must be planned carefully. Self-monitoring is also used as an evaluation strategy, and for this reason is discussed in somewhat more detail in Chapter Five. Principles for increasing the probability of success in monitoring are discussed in Chapter Thirteen.

The Case-Study Technique

When clients are reluctant to bring up or unable to conceptualize a problematic situation, we commonly present them with a case study, a short description of a (fictional) client who is experiencing difficulties similar to those of the other clients in the group. The group leader usually develops the case around a common problem he or she thinks is shared by a number of group members. But the leader is careful to ensure that the case is not identical to that of anyone in the group. Clients are asked in what ways they are similar to and different from the subject of the case study. They are asked to be as specific as possible. The following brief transcript (taken from a group for depressed patients) shows how a case study might be used.

Val (married, age 41, no children) is an extremely tense man. He has few outside interests except for watching TV and reading an occasional mystery. Outside of work, his contacts are few. His wife tries to get him out of the house, but he shows no interest in anything. He describes life as flat and sometimes oppressive. His relationship to his wife has suffered in recent months because of his increasing passivity. He demands a great deal of himself, and although others think he is successful, he rarely meets his own standards. Lately he has been having trouble concentrating, especially at home. He neither receives nor gives much praise, but when he does receive praise, he usually rejects it. He describes himself as an unhappy person who never gets angry.

Group Leader: You have all read Val's self description. I would like each of you to write down how you are different from Val and, if you wish, how you are similar to Val.

Donald (after a few moments):   I guess I'm different in lots of ways. First, I'm doing something about my problem by coming here. [Others nod in agreement.] Second, I hate TV, and I have a number of interests, including mysteries. I especially like going out to restaurants. I also get angry easily. I do get a bit down and I am a bit tense, and I guess I don't see as many people as I'd like.

Juanita: First, I don't have a wife. [Everyone laughs.] I don't have trouble concentrating usually, although I do have a lot of thoughts running through my mind. More than I like. I don't mind TV, Donald, just some programs. I feel angry lots of times, but I rarely express it. I guess I don't praise much either. And I do demand a lot of myself. Like Donald and I guess everyone here, I sure have my down moods, but those little pills help. Dick and I have the same problem. We use those little pills a lot.

Dick: Yeah, but the doctor is reducing them, I think. Besides they don't help much. Except for the TV, which I don't watch much any more, you could have almost been describing me. Oh, and I don't have a wife, well, anymore, either. But like Donald and everyone else here, I'm trying to do something about my problem. I force myself to do things. But it hasn't been working lately, especially with all the pressure on my job. He didn't mention sleeping. I hardly sleep a wink at night.

As we see in these examples, the clients have little or no difficulty comparing themselves with a fictional case; however, these same clients had difficulty discussing themselves or keeping a diary in the previous session. The case study is a valuable step in encouraging clients in the early phases of treatment to self-disclose. It is possible to make the cases much more complicated by including the fictional client's thoughts and feelings in the situation as well. In this way, the clients can practice comparing their own cognitions with those of the case and each other. In general, this exercise is used in the first or second session.

Roleplaying

Case studies, diaries, and interviews (either group or individual) may not be sufficient to reveal what the client actually says or how she or he physically reacts. Less costly and less intrusive than observations, roleplaying provides a great deal of information about a client's responses to various problematic situations. In this technique, a client presents to the group a description of a situation that he found problematic in the course of the week and recorded in his diary. The client is asked to roleplay the actual response as closely as possible to the actual situation. The responses may be recorded and eventually coded along predetermined criteria. An example of one situation and its presentation to the client follows:

Group Leader: Max, that was a difficult situation. I wonder if it wouldn't be clearer though if you roleplayed it for us. I'll play the part of the salesman. Tell me a little bit more about him.

Max: Well, he's hardnosed. You know the type. He kept coming on strong. I had other things to do but he kept saying he wouldn't leave unless I gave him an order, even a small order. What finally got to me was when he said I was wasting his time.

Group Leader: OK, I think I've got it. Why don't you start.

Max (in the roleplay):   Sorry, Ed, I'm not interested.

Group Leader: C'mon, Max, just a small order.

Max: Ed, we don't need any. Come back in six months.

Group Leader: What kind of friend are you? I'm just asking for a small order. You guys could carry that and nobody would know the difference, and I wouldn't be wasting my time here.

Max: You son-of-a-bitch, get out of here. [That's what I really said. I just exploded and threw him out of the office, and now I may end up in a lawsuit.]

Group Leader: And this is the kind of thing that happens to you from time to time when pressure is put on you.

The group leader gets a better picture of Max's affect from the roleplay than from his telling of the situation. Moreover, the group leader can go on to question the client about his cognitive responses as well. Some clients may be reluctant to roleplay. Often, through the example and encouragement of other clients, the reluctant client attempts roleplaying. If not, the client is permitted to wait until she feels ready.

A more systematic procedure is the use of standardized behavioral roleplay tests, which usually consist of six to eighteen items. These tests may be given prior to treatment only for purposes of assessment or prior to and after for purposes of evaluation of change. Some practitioners use small samples of the situations throughout treatment. Roleplay tests and their use, development, and coding are presented in Chapter Five.

Tests and Inventories

Tests and inventories are used primarily for evaluation; however, they can also be used to identify components of the problem and general patterns or characteristics of the client. Easier to code than roleplays, tests and inventories are often preferred by practitioners. Unfortunately, most focus primarily on general responses rather than on a response to a specific situation. Nevertheless, they do suggest inappropriate responses and behavioral deficiencies. To be useful, such pretreatment tests should be coded immediately and reviewed with the group. Because tests and inventories are covered in great detail in Chapter Five, they are not discussed further here.

In-Group Observations

Informal observations of the interaction often indicate many problematic situations that can be treated in the group. Usually, the leader keeps track of the problems each person presents in the group and records those with similar problems. The leader notes the typical responses of each person to these situations. Observations of problem situations that occur within the group are also recorded; however, as the leader must attend to so many actions at the same time, the recording is usually delayed until after the meeting. To correct this problem, a few group leaders employ an observer who does the recording. Alternatively, a different group member can be assigned the role of observer each week, especially if the observation system is simple. Unfortunately, systematic observation in extra-group situations is costly and intrusive, so its use is limited except in institutional settings. Other uses of observation for evaluation purposes are discussed in Chapter Five.

Toward a List of Problem Situations

All of the major information-gathering techniques used in situational analysis contribute to the development and tracking of all situations (1) obtained in interviews, (2) evolving out of group discussion, (3) recorded in diaries, and (4) extrapolated from roleplays, observations, situational checklists, and other tests. In this way, a list of problematic situations is accrued for each person in the group. These are eventually organized into common themes if such can be identified. The lists change as the group progresses and become the focus of most of the therapy. In short-term training programs, the lists may be restricted to those problems shared by most group members. In general, only a few situations can be handled at a meeting. The more the situations overlap, the more situations relevant to each client that can be handled. Now that we have described the essential ingredients of situational analysis, a question still remains: Is there room for a more general diagnostic approach within this assessment strategy?

Diagnostic Approach

Although our emphasis throughout this chapter has been on conducting a thorough situational analysis of concrete situations and behaviors that define a given problem and formulating a concrete description of the resources available to the client and impediments to successful treatment, client problems can be organized in the form of diagnostic classifications. Many inventories and other paper-and-pencil tests lend themselves readily to such diagnostic statements. One of the most common systems used currently is the *Diagnostic and Statistical Manual of Mental Disorders,* third edition, revised (DSM-III-R, American Psychiatric Association, 1987). The DSM-III-R consists, for the most part, of detailed descriptions of a variety of mental and psychological disorders divided into sixteen major classes and numerous subclasses. It provides basically an atheoretical framework. DSM-III-R (1987) also has a multiaxial system that includes descriptions of mental disorders, physical disorders and conditions, severity of psychosocial stressors, and global assessment of functioning. This biopsychosocial system ensures the use of the information in planning treatment and predicting outcome. Although the DSM-III is considerably more reliable than the DSM-II, except for mental retardation, the interjudge correlations are not yet very impressive. As new results come in, perhaps DSM-III-R may prove to be more reliable than DSM-III.

Even though the interjudge reliability is low and DSM-III and DSM-III-R retain their bias toward the medical model, the practitioner can use the diagnostic system in the assessment process in several ways. First, diagnostic categories help relate the client to a wealth of clinical and research information. Some but by no means all of the diagnostic categories provide help in determining the specific treatment modalities (Nelson and Barlow, 1981). For example, diagnosis of phobic disorders suggests that clients would profit both from modeling and from direct confrontation with the phobic objects. Often, no one behavior provides sufficient information to describe a problem. The diagnostic category at least suggests other specific behaviors to look at (Taylor, 1983). These are behaviors that often covary with the initially apparent behavior within a given diagnostic category. Because the resources available to group leaders are often limited, insufficient information may be available to arrive at a supportable diagnosis. As treatment progresses and information, especially on interaction with clients, is directly observed, a more substantial diagnosis can be made. A nontrivial matter is that those leaders cooperating with other agencies and/or receiving funds from insurance programs may be required to have diagnoses for their clients. Familiarity with the DSM-III-R is certainly an advantage to the group leader and ultimately should aid in the treatment of the clients.

Summary

After the major purposes of assessment are set forth, the essential components of a situational analysis and its relevance to the group assessment and treatment process are described. Strategies employed to facilitate group members in helping each other to develop situational analyses are examined. The major components are the situation, the critical moment, the responses (behavioral, cognitive, and affective), the long- and short-term consequences, and the resources for and impediments to treatment. To evaluate and determine appropriate treatment goals, the physical attributes and limitations and the motivation of the client must also be considered. At one point in the assessment process, for each member in the group, the leader prepares a list of carefully described problem situations, the client's responses to the situations, and the consequences of continuing those responses.

Numerous strategies for employing the group in the assessment process are outlined. These strategies include the group interviews, training procedures and exercises followed by group discussion, use of subgroups to facilitate analysis of more problems at the same time, and extragroup assignments. The product of these assessment techniques is an assessment statement for each client and the group as a whole. On the basis of the assessment statement, goals can be established and intervention strategies planned.

FIVE

Measuring and Evaluating Individual Achievements and Group Process

with Richard M. Tolman

Most of the assessment information discussed in the previous chapter was obtained in interaction of each member with the group leader and the other members. Assessment data are collected with a variety of measurement instruments, some of which are described in this chapter. In general, if collected prior to treatment, data can be used by the group leader to determine the types of situation with which the client has difficulty coping and to establish appropriate goals. Furthermore, these instruments can be used to evaluate the effectiveness of group intervention. Although research generally supports the use of groups (see, for example, Bednar and Kaul, 1985, Toseland and Siporin, 1986), the issue of the effectiveness of any particular group must still be addressed. The first part of this chapter focuses on those techniques for measuring change in individuals that are used both to enrich assessment and to evaluate outcome in groups. The second part of the chapter focuses on measurement strategies that can be applied to evaluation of group phenomena. In the third part, research designs used to evaluate change in either individual or group attributes are examined. The

Note: This chapter was coauthored by Sheldon D. Rose and Richard M. Tolman.

emphasis throughout the chapter is on evaluation by practitioners rather than researchers. Although in practice such evaluation is usually less rigorous than that in experimental studies, we describe techniques that can be readily utilized by group leaders in their own practice.

Purposes of Evaluation

Evaluation serves a number of purposes. First, evaluation guides intervention on an ongoing basis. The group leader determines whether or not progress is being made toward individual goals. Second, evaluation enables the group leader and client to decide the extent to which the goals of intervention have been achieved. Some evaluation designs enable the group leader to determine whether the group intervention itself likely caused the client's improvement. Finally, systematic evaluation strategies assist the group leader in determining how the information gathered from one individual or the group as a whole can be used to guide subsequent interventions with other groups.

The evaluation process can be divided into two major activities: choosing appropriate measures of the targets of change and choosing an appropriate evaluation design.

Measurement with Individuals

Group leaders can use a number of procedures to evaluate their practice. The most common are self-rating checklists and inventories, roleplay tests, self-monitoring, extragroup observations by others, and goal attainment scaling. We discuss each with respect to their use in small group evaluation. In-group observational methods and postsession questionnaires are covered at the end of this Chapter.

Self-Rating Checklists

Implementation. Self-rating checklists are paper-and-pencil instruments that the clients fill out. These instruments enable the client to report systematically on a specific target problem or on a general problem area. The checklist used depends on the theme of the group or on the target problem the client has identified. Although for most groups the same checklist is used for each member, to facilitate intragroup and intergroup comparison, often an individual is given a checklist specific to him or her.

We have utilized some standard self-rating checklists with specific themes. For clients complaining of stress, the Profile of Mood States (POMS) (McNair, Lorr, and Droppleman, 1971) is used to ascertain mood changes. The Hassles Inventory (Kanner, Coyne, Schaefer, and Lazarus, 1981) is used to determine intensity and breadth of stressful events. The Gambrill and Richey (1975) Assertion Inventory or the Rathus (1972) checklist is administered to unassertive individuals. Depressed individuals are given the Beck Depression Inventory (BDI) (Beck, Mendelson, Mock, and Erbaugh, 1961). One very common checklist used to evaluate group treatment of problems related to anxiety is the State–Trait Anxiety Inventory (Spielberger, Gorsuch, and Lushene, 1970). In groups for men who batter, the Conflict Tactics Scale (Straus, 1979) has been used along with the Novaco (1976) Anger Scale, the Attitudes Toward Women Scale (Spence and Helmreich, 1978), the BDI, and the Psychological Maltreatment of Women Inventory (Tolman and Rose, 1989). In pain management groups we use the Sickness Impact Profile (Bergner, Bobbitt, and Pollard, 1976) and the POMS to evaluate outcome. In our parent training groups, both parents and adolescent children complete the Interaction (Conflict) Behavior Questionnaire (Prinz and Kent, 1978), which provides scores on parents' evaluation of the adult–adolescent interaction and of the adolescents' evaluation of the parents' behavior. Obviously, a large range of tests are available to the practitioner. Those used in our groups represent only a small sample. Hudson (1982) has published a set of checklists many of which can be used for clients in groups. These have received extensive evaluation for reliability and validity. The reader is also referred to Walls, Werner, Bacon, and Zane (1977) as a resource. In these publications, the tests are evaluated in terms of reliability, validity, and sensitivity to change. Levitt and Reid (1981) have listed and evaluated the "rapid-assessment instruments" available to the practitioner.

Advantages and Disadvantages. Several disadvantages characterize the use of self-report checklists. Members may give socially desirable answers or may fall into a response set, that is, they may indiscriminately answer items in a similar manner, for example, always toward the middle or always toward an extreme of the scale. If the checklist is used more than once, for example, before and after group treatment, the second administration may be affected by the first.

Despite these and other limitations, checklists are often the best way to access certain evaluation information. First, checklists are cost effective and convenient, that is, the client can report information quickly and systematically. Second, some checklists have been carefully studied and have established reliability, validity, and norms for interpreting responses to the checklists. Third, clients may be willing to indicate more information on a checklist than they would disclose in the group or in an interview with the leader.

Roleplay Tests

Implementation. Although, ideally, observation of interactive behavior in the real world should be used to obtain information about the client, it rarely is, because of the practical difficulties. One possible substitute that we have drawn on is the roleplay test. Roleplay tests simulate clients' real-life problem situations. The tester presents the client with descriptions of situations (generally six to twenty-four in total), one at a time. The tester asks the client to imagine herself in the situation and respond. Roleplays are often videotaped or audiotaped to facilitate evaluation of the client's responses. The client's responses are evaluated according to some criterion, for example, the social appropriateness or the probable effectiveness of the response. Using the results of the roleplay test, the group leader determines the types of situations difficult for the client. In addition, the group leader can compare the results of a pregroup roleplay test with the results of a later one to evaluate the client's progress.

Roleplay tests are used most effectively when the target response is (at least in part) a response to an interactive situation. Most targets of change in groups fall into this category. The roleplay test is especially suitable to determine how clients deal with people in authority or people who impose on them, interact with people they would like to know better, ask others for help, request their rights, socialize informally, deal with interviews, respond to racist or sexist remarks, express feelings appropriately, or receive and give feedback.

Group leaders may draw situations from a number of existing standardized roleplay tests for different populations. Berger (1976) designed a test for evaluating social skills unique to the institutionalized elderly; Rosenthal (1978), for evaluating social skills of delinquent female adolescents; Delange (1976), for evaluating assertiveness in women; Bates (1978), for evaluating social interaction among mildly retarded adults; Schinke (1975), for evaluating the social skills of self-referred outpatients; and Clark (1975), for evaluating the social skills of Vietnam vets. Recently, we developed a similar test for social skills in men who batter (Rose, Scobie, Saunders, and Hanusa, 1989). Most of these particular tests have precoded scoring systems and have been designed following the methodological steps recommended by Goldfried and D'Zurilla (1969).

Variations. Some variations expand the information gathered from a roleplay test. After the client's response, the tester might ask the client to describe his or her affective and cognitive responses to the situation. For example, clients may be asked to imagine themselves in and rate the level of distress they feel in various situations. In this way, an index of the client's anxiety in the situations can be developed. Clients can also be asked to rate their satisfaction with their response. The satisfaction data are used to estimate whether the client perceives the situation to be problematic.

The tests may be used in the standard form or may be modified to serve a particular purpose. For example, clients may be asked to read all of the situations for their problem area in advance of the test and then select those that are most relevant to them. In permitting a choice, standardization of content is lost, but the level of relevance to the client is increased. When we have used both choice and standardized items, we have found that choice items are more sensitive to before–after differences. A completely different but promising approach was used by Carson and Deschner (1987), who asked clients (men who batter) to view six videotaped vignettes and indicate how they felt and what coping skills they would use in the situations.

Although often administered before and after treatment, roleplay tests can be administered during treatment sessions. After the test, the group provides the individual with feedback as a form of group intervention. In this way, ongoing evaluation data are also collected. If pre–post individualized measurement is too time-consuming, the in-group procedure may save time.

Limitations. Roleplay tests have major limitations. Roleplay skill can be confounded with the behavioral skills the test is designed to measure. The extent to which improvement on skills in a roleplay test reflects changes in real-life performance is unclear and has not been empirically established. For this reason, other tests should be used to evaluate outcome in addition to roleplay tests (see Bellack, Hersen, and Turner, 1976, for criticism of roleplay tests).

Example of a Roleplay Test Item. A more vivid picture of a roleplay test can be obtained by focusing on one item of a test we recently developed (Rose, Scobie, Saunders, and Hanusa, 1989) to evaluate the outcome of groups for men who batter. The following situation is presented to the client.

You decided on a used car that you want. You have thought it through very carefully. The price is right and the condition seems pretty good. Your partner states in no uncertain terms that she does not want that car. She doesn't like the color and she prefers automatic. What are you likely to do or say?

These responses are tape-recorded and coded for appropriateness on a scale from 1 to 7 (with 1 most appropriate and 7 least appropriate). The scores had originally been determined by judges and are available for each item in a coding manual. Items similar to those in the manual are scored similarly. The score is reduced if the client uses sarcasm or a disinterested tone of voice. Note these examples from the coding manual:

1	A.	Take a deep breath, think positive thoughts, and say, "Honey, we've been looking for a reasonably priced car for a long time. This is a good deal and we really need one, so please let's talk about this before you make a hasty decision."
2	B.	Tell your partner your feelings are hurt and ask if you can reach a compromise.
2	C.	Look her straight in the eye and firmly explain that you both have been looking for a car for a long time and need one desperately. Tell her you would like to get a car that both of you can agree on, so maybe you should talk about this some more.
3	D.	"I don't think you understand what I am saying, let me explain one more time."
4	E.	Say nothing in support of or against the situation that is upsetting you; just clam up and sit on it.
4	F.	Go along with your partner; then tell her of your dissatisfaction with the outcome the next day.
5	G.	Scream at her, "I can't believe you are judging whether or not we should buy this car on the color of the paint. That is the most idiotic thing I have ever heard."
5	H.	Simply glare at her and walk away.
6	I.	Threaten partner (verbally) if she does not agree to buy the car.
6	J.	Say to your partner, "You better cut this shit out or you'll be sorry."
7	K.	Grab your partner, shake her, and tell her that you are sick of her complaining.

Self-Monitoring

Self-monitoring, observation of one's own overt behavior or covert behavior (thoughts or feelings) requires that the client record his or her behavior at specified intervals or under specific conditions in a systematic manner (Eisler, 1976). If it is carried out systematically and evidence of reliability exists, the results of self-monitoring may be used to evaluate the progress and outcome of group treatment. Overt behaviors are self-monitored especially when the frequency of a given behavior indicates the severity of the problem. For example, in parent groups, parents are asked to count their praise responses to their children's behavior. In social skill groups, clients are asked to count the number of people they have approached in a week. In anger control groups, clients count episodes of their verbal and physical abuse of others. Some overt behaviors monitored by group members in self-control groups are eating, consumption of alcoholic beverages, and hours spent gambling.

In groups, self-monitoring is especially useful where external observational methods do not provide the personal data necessary to assess cognitive behavior. For example, clients in self-control groups often count, in addition to actual episodes of eating, their urges to eat high-calorie foods. They may also record their overt and covert responses to the urges. Some parents in parent training groups record the frequency and intensity of anger that they experience either periodically or during stressful situations. Others have kept track of "self-put-downs."

Exhibit 4 is a self-monitoring form used in a therapy group. Members were asked to keep track of their stress four times daily by recording the average level of stress (with 1 as the lowest possible response and 10 as the highest possible response) experienced during a time period. They carried the cards with them.

Self-monitoring is a behavior in its own right with which the client has had limited experience. As a result it must usually be shaped as any other behavior. Failure in self-monitoring is often due to inadequate definition of the monitored behavior, to high expectations in the early phase of therapy, and to inadequate training in monitoring. Because of its unique structure, the group lends itself to efficient training of clients in self-monitoring. The

Exhibit 4. Self-Monitoring Card.

	Sun	Mon	Tue	Wed	Thur	Fri	Sat
8 A.M.	5	forgot	4	3	3	4	3
12 P.M.	6	5	4	5	8#	7	4
4 P.M.	5	6	9#	6	9##	3	5
8 P.M.	8*	8*	3	3	7!	3	2

Comments: *Visiting mother-in-law. #Boss in bad mood and ##he yelled at me. !Kept thinking about it.

group leader can model the process of self-observation. For example, one leader told the group that he was monitoring his urges to make puns and pointed out the number of times he failed to resist the urge. The members were then encouraged to provide each other with diverse examples. In addition, the group setting provided the opportunity to practice self-observation and receive ample feedback from peers as to the efficacy of the self-monitoring. Clients can also work in pairs to see that the behavior being monitored is adequately defined. Ample peer reinforcement exists for those who monitor carefully. The group also lends itself to the monitoring of self-observations. Since all members must report publicly to the group the results of their observations, there is pressure to carry out the assignment and to be as accurate as possible in the recording. Some group leaders provide incentives for monitoring by reserving a certain portion of group time for those who have successfully completed their ongoing monitoring assignments.

Evaluation by Others

Most of the data collection procedures discussed thus far depend on self-report or self-observation. Dependence entirely on self-report data has a number of limitations. It gives rise to such problems as the social-desirability and other response sets which threaten the reliability and validity of the measurement process.

Significant others in the client's life can also monitor the client's behavior. Direct observation of the client in extragroup situations, unfortunately, is quite costly and quite difficult; however, simple observation systems have been used in institutional settings. In these cases, staff, family, or school personnel have been trained to look for highly specific target behaviors, such as cooperation with others, approach responses to others, put-downs, reinforcing statements, overt indications of mood swings, and anger responses. These behaviors are counted or rated by the observers. Because of its cost, the need for careful definition, and the demand for careful and extensive observer training, direct observation of adult behavior is rarely used outside of institutional settings where groups take place; however, some applications are possible. Lewinsohn (1974) used home observations of depressed patients to evaluate the effectiveness of treatment. Mash, Terdal, and Anderson (1973) described a response-class matrix procedure for recording parent-child interactions in the home. These were coordinated with treatment, which made it acceptable to the clients. For further information about the uses and pitfalls of observations in evaluation and assessment the reader is referred to Mash and Terdal (1976, pp. 261–342).

A somewhat simpler and less costly procedure used to obtain extragroup impressions of clients' progress is problem cards. This technique was proposed by Goodman (1969) and further developed by Flowers (1979), who applied it to trainees in a group. On each of two cards, a client briefly describes a problem she or he is currently experiencing. The client also names someone who could judge the client's improvement in that area. The raters could be family members, friends, or any other person whom the client feels comfortable asking for a rating. Whenever possible, the client should work out his or her own contract with the rater. Group members often need to be trained to negotiate a contract.

At times, significant others may fill out rating scales or practitioner-designed scales to determine progress of group members. For example, in groups of men who batter, it is critical to ask the men's partners if violence is continuing. A standardized instrument, for example, the Conflict Tactics Scale (Straus, 1979), on which the partner indicates the frequency and severity of physical abuse, may be used.

Goal attainment scaling is also commonly used to measure

attainment of individual as well as group goals. This procedure is discussed in detail with examples in Chapter Six.

Collection of Group Data

A major characteristic of the multimethod approach is its reliance on data in defining group structures and processes and in determining whether or not a problem exists. As part of the assessment process, information is gathered that provides group leaders with a basis on which to determine the major attributes of the group as a whole.

The purpose of group data collection is to identify the dimensions of group structures, group processes, and group problems. Insofar as these attributes interfere with the achievement of individual treatment goals, they are formulated in such a way that the group leader can eventually act on the information. It should be noted that many group data collection procedures give us information on individuals' responses to the group. As such, these data also facilitate individual assessment.

Many different procedures are used to collect data in small groups. To obtain descriptions of most structures and processes, data are collected on a regular basis for the duration of the group. Because these data collection procedures are used primarily by practitioners, we discuss here only those instruments that are minimally intrusive in the treatment process and relatively inexpensive to administer. These include the postsession questionnaire, in-group observation, attendance and promptness rates, and rates of extragroup task completion. Even though the purpose of these procedures is to collect information about the group, some of these procedures use the individual client as the source of information.

Postsession Questionnaires

Postsession questionnaires are administered to all members at the end of every session. They have two major purposes: to determine how members evaluate the various components of each session and to give the practitioner an idea of how well various perceived factors are operating in the group. No one questionnaire is appropriate for every group. The postsession questionnaire to be described was developed for a general therapy group for which we had hypothesized specific curative factors. We wanted to see whether these were perceived by the clients as well. We were also interested in eliciting more comments as to what should be done differently in the group to meet the needs of its members more closely. This questionnaire is sufficiently general to serve as a point of departure for other groups.

Specifically, in this questionnaire, we attempted to estimate the emotionality of the group members, the degree of perceived self-disclosure, the cohesion of the group, the feeling of control, specific actions of the leader that were liked and those the clients would change, the degree of clients' insight into their own areas for change, and clients' satisfaction with the entire experience. A leader may also seek information about other aspects of a group, necessitating other questions. The client is provided not only with the question but also the rationale behind the question. The order of questions is random.

The first question was asked to determine how emotional the group was perceived to be by its members. It is generally thought that goal-oriented groups are highly rational. We found that this is not always the case. Because emotionality may be related to cohesiveness, high rationality may not even be desirable. To code this question, we calculated the ratio of emotional words to nonemotional words.

1. Circle the words that best describe how you felt at various times throughout today's session? . . . interested . . . flat . . . emotional . . . angry . . . happy . . . down . . . upset . . . sober . . . rational . . . excited . . . calm . . . bored . . . sad . . .

Question 2 was asked to estimate the degree to which the clients perceived themselves to be in control of their own treatment. If clients did not feel in control, the leader would be required to give the issue serious attention.

2. To what degree do you feel you were in control of your own training in today's session? (Circle the number that best indicates your degree of control.)

    1 _____ 2 _____ 3 _____ 4 _____ 5 _____ 6 _____ 7

    not at all   completely

Question 3 was asked to determine what members thought the leader could do differently. When we asked this as an unstructured question, we obtained very little response. By providing cues, as in the following example, the response increased.

3. Check all the things the leader could do differently to improve the quality of the group sessions.
    (a)   Talk less
    (b)   Share more of himself or herself
    (c)   Allow group members to talk more
    (d)   Not allow group members to talk so much
    (e)   Put more emphasis on group exercises
    (f)   Stick closer to the schedule
    (g)   Schedule less rigidly
    (h)   Be more supportive
    (i)   Change nothing
    (j)   Change something, but I don't know what
    (k)   Other (write out) _____
           _____

Question 4 was asked to help the clients verbalize publicly what they perceived they could change in the group to help themselves. It could also be used to indicate willingness to self-disclose.

4. Circle all the things you could do to improve the quality of your own learning experience.
    (a)   Share more of myself with others
    (b)   Be more sympathetic/supportive of others
    (c)   Do my homework more consistently
    (d)   Listen more attentively
    (e)   Participate more actively

(f)   Participate a little less
(g)   Take more responsibility for my own change
(h)   Disclose a little more about my own problems
(i)   Do nothing, I have no suggestion
(j)   Do something, but I'm not sure what
(k)   Other (write out)_____

_____

Question 5 was asked to determine satisfaction with the entire experience. It serves as a comparison with other studies and is a sensitive indicator of change in the group. (Some group leaders prefer the word *useful* to the word *satisfied;* in earlier versions these words were highly correlated.)

5. In general, how satisfied were you with today's experience in the group? (Check one.)
    (a)   Highly dissatisfied
    (b)   Moderately dissatisfied
    (c)   Somewhat more dissatisfied than satisfied
    (d)   Neither particularly satisfied or dissatisfied
    (e)   Somewhat more satisfied than dissatisfied
    (f)   Moderately satisfied
    (g)   Highly satisfied

Questions 6 and 7 were used to learn which procedures the group found useful or not so useful. For prompts, the participants are reminded to look at the session agenda. The procedures used that day could also be listed with the questions.

6. Which procedures or exercises used today did you find particularly helpful (look at the session agenda to remind you what we did today)?
7. Which procedures or exercises used today were not very helpful or were annoying?

Question 8 was asked to estimate the cohesion of the group. In our experience, cohesion is highly correlated with outcome.

8. How close were the members to each other in today's session?

1 _____ 2 _____ 3 _____ 4 _____ 5 _____ 6 _____ 7

   not at a little   moderately   close   very

   all close close   close   close

Question 9 was asked to determine members' perceptions of the degree of self-disclosure in the group.

9. How important was the content of the self-disclosures in today's session?

1 _____ 2 _____ 3 _____ 4 _____ 5 _____ 6 _____ 7

   trivial slightly   moderately   important   very

         important   important   important

We can measure many dimensions of the group experience by asking clients questions. The danger is that too many questions can be asked. Members rapidly become satiated if they must answer more than a dozen questions each week. In our most recent groups, we have used ten questions. There should be a strong justification for each question used.

Although satisfaction ratings are relatively easy to compile and to code, they, as all subjective rating scales, are subject to rating errors, for example, individual patterned differences in use of the scale (response sets), individual differences in expressing satisfaction, and absence of a fixed zero on the scale. Nevertheless, a dramatic change in the average member rating provides information that can be used along with other information to estimate covert characteristics of the group and its members.

One major problem with the preceding data is that the mean or median for all individuals in the group is often relied on as the indicator of a group phenomenon. From a conceptual point of view, the average does not exactly characterize group or interactive phenomena. The range or standard deviation, an index of agreement of members, and stereotypical patterns in the data might suggest other interpretations that might be conceptually more consistent with our definition of a group attribute. That is, an average of 4 calculated on the basis of a range extending from 1 to 7 has a completely different meaning than an average of 4 calculated on a range of 3 to 5. In one group we found a bimodal response of 1 and 2 and 6 and 7, which represented another group problem. The data must be interpreted carefully and the average should be only one statistical attribute considered.

In-Group Observational Tools

Data are also collected through direct observation. The observational tools can be simple or complex. Because the simple systems have proved quite useful and require minimum observer training, we recommend them for regular clinical use. The observers are often colleagues who want to learn the group method; by observing, they have a function in the group. Students who wish to learn about the treatment method may also be employed as observers. Occasionally, especially when simple techniques are used, group members may serve on a rotating basis as observers.

The most frequently used simple observational tool is the fixed-interval system. This system provides the frequency of participation of each member and the leader, from which can be calculated the distribution of participation among members and the ratio of member-to-leader participation. We find that these data correlate highly with outcome in assertiveness training groups (Rose, 1981). Every ten seconds, the name of the person who is speaking is recorded, as shown in Table 3 (the initials rather than the entire name are recorded in the table). The "X" is used to indicate silence. Other letters may be used to indicate that two people are talking at the same time, or the members are divided into subgroups, or the given participant is roleplaying.

Recording the name of each speaker is another simple method of measuring participation. Usually, a pie (circle) is drawn, with pieces (segments) of the pie, representing the members and leader(s) of the group in the order in which they are seated. Each time a person speaks, it is tallied in the appropriate piece of the pie. Generally, no consideration is given to the length of time a person speaks, although some group leaders instruct observers to add to the tally every twenty seconds if the person continues to speak.

The first simple method (Table 3) estimates the length of

Table 3. Fixed-Interval Recording.

1. SL	11. TD	21. SL	31. BR
2. MA	12. MA	22. TD	32. BR
3. NA	13. MA	23. MA	33. BR
4. TR	14. RN	24. TR	34. NA
5. SL	15. MA	25. TR	35. NA
6. TD	16. RN	26. MA	36. SL
7. TD	17. RN	27. RN	37. NA
8. TD	18. MA	28. RN	38. SL
9. SL	19. RN	29. RN	39. SL
10. X	20. SL	30. RN	40. SL

Total	SL 9	BR 3	TR 3	MA 7	NA 4	TD 5	RN 8	X 1
Percentage	22.5	7.5	7.5	17.5	10.0	12.5	20.0	2.5

LEADER = 30.0%   MEMBER = 67.5%   SILENCE = 2.5%

time each person in the group is speaking. The second provides the group leader with a better estimate of the frequency with which low-frequency or short-response speakers speak.

If, in the fixed-interval system, the observer is also asked to indicate whom the speaker is addressing (with the group being the default category), a new dimension is added, as we see in Table 4 (in which fictional data are used). Even this simple addition requires considerably more training before reliable observations can be made.

The major use of observers has been in observation of individuals rather than of groups. For example, observers have collected data on participation in roleplaying, off-task behavior, positive reinforcement or praise, and criticism or other negative categories. The specific category to be observed depends on the

Table 4. Record of Speakers and Addressees.

1. SL-GRP	5. TD-NA	9. SL-MA	13. BR-GRP
2. MA-GRP	6. MA-GRP	10. TD-GRP	14. BR-GRP
3. NA-MA	7. MA-GRP	11. MA-GRP	15. BR-NA
4. TR-NA	8. RN-MA	12. TR-MA	16. NA-BR

To group = 8(50%)   To MA(leader) = 4(25%)   To NA = 3(18%)
To BR = 1(6%)

leader's preassessment of frequently appearing behaviors in the group. If, for example, the group leader has noted informally that there is too much off-task behavior, systematic observation of on-task and off-task behavior for several meetings may be useful. The observers would be trained to identify off-task behavior and then record with a stopwatch all behavior that is off-task. With this method, a group indicator of off-task behavior is obtained, but the individual who is off-task is not indicated. It is possible to use the system illustrated in Table 3 and circle whether a given communication is on-task. The same structure can be used for any of the following observations of specific behaviors.

Another behavior commonly observed is interruption of others, especially in groups in which aggressive and shy clients are mixed. If one person is speaking and another begins, the act of the second is regarded as an interruption. The initials of the interrupter, or a code letter, is recorded for every interruption.

In a parent training group formed in part to increase positive reinforcing behavior, all responses in the group discussion were classified by two observers as positive reinforcement (+), punishment (-), or neither (0). Although we found that after two hours of training, the rate of observer agreement was low (.35), the general trend indicating an increase was the same for both observers. It was clear that even with a simple category system, more training was required.

The category put-downs was observed in a stress management group, all the members of which had recently had heart attacks. Most were professional people. The clients served as observers. After discussion of the definition of a put-down, clients recorded all statements they perceived as put-downs. They also recorded statements made by themselves that they regarded as put-downs. The totals and the discrepancies between self-perceptions and others' perceptions were discussed at the end of the session with respect to treatment goals and impact on group interaction.

Other more sophisticated (and hence more costly) observational methods in which multiple categories are observed may also be used to classify the content of the interaction. A commonly used method is the Hill (1965) Interaction Matrix Analysis system. Toseland, Rossiter, Peak, and Hill (1988) describe the use of this system in evaluating the significance of self-help support groups for caregivers of the elderly. Piper, Montvila, and McGihon (1979) described the use of a modified version of the Hill Interaction Matrix in research on group therapy. The reader is also referred to Mash and Terdal (1976, pp. 261–352) for other ideas concerning the use of various observation systems. As it is usually too costly for the practitioner to train people to carry out and interpret these observations in the typical clinical group program, a more detailed discussion is not included here.

Rate of Task Completion

The rate of task completion refers to the percentage of tasks negotiated and agreed on at one session and completed by the next. Since each client negotiates separate sets of tasks, the group rate is estimated as the average individual rate of completion. This rate has been shown to correlate highly and significantly with behavioral change, as indicated by the findings on a roleplay test with adults in assertiveness training groups. The rate of task completion has been used as an index of ongoing productivity (Rose, 1981) because the extragroup task was developed during the previous meeting. Only if the assignment is actually carried out, can it be considered an indicator of positive productivity. A low weekly rate of extragroup task completion is a major group problem and requires group consideration as soon as it is detected.

One way to determine the rate is to ask members at the beginning of each session what tasks they assigned themselves and which of these tasks were they able to complete partially or totally. The group leader must determine the score to be given to partial completion. Usually, the rate of completion is calculated as if all assignments were of the same importance or relevance to the outcome. One problem with this index is that all tasks are not equal in terms of level of difficulty or time required to perform. An assertive task such as "talking to a new person on four different days" might be far more important, more time consuming, and more difficult than "writing down a stressful situation that you recently experienced." Some group leaders give more weight to behavioral tasks because of their greater relevance to behavioral change in ascertaining weekly productivity. Despite the limitations, all tasks are considered equal in ascertaining productivity because of the arbitrariness often involved in weighing. (Specific tasks and other assignments, as well as strategies for obtaining compliance with those assignments, are discussed in Chapter Twelve.)

Attendance and Promptness

It is assumed that the more time spent in the treatment situation, the greater the opportunity for learning. Group attendance is measured as either the percentage of members attending a given meeting or the percentage of total minutes attended. For example, if a meeting of a four-person group is sixty minutes long, and one person is ten minutes late, another leaves five minutes early, and a third is absent, then the attendance rate would be (240 - 5 - 10 - 60)/240 = .69. The general formula is $R = (MT - t - AT)/MT$, where R is the percentage of minutes all members are present in the group, M is the number of members in the group, T is the length of the meeting in minutes, t is the total number of minutes arriving late or leaving early for all members, and A is the number of persons absent.

This measure is useful primarily if attendance is voluntary, although even in groups with involuntary clients, such as family violence groups, irregular attendance is a strong indicator of low cohesion or disinterest. Resistance may also be indicated by a high rate of lateness. In addition, such important reasons as illness of the client or a family member and extreme weather conditions may influence interpretation of the data.

Evaluation of Group Data

As in the preceding example, the group data must be interpreted by the group leader and the group members, who may or may not agree that a given group pattern is a problem. Examination of group data and discussion of their meaning are important parts of group treatment.

Once they have been collected, the data are first reviewed by the group leader and then shown to the members of the group, often in graphic form. Figure 1 summarizes graphically the data collected at the beginning of the eighth session of a fourteen-session anger management group.

In the example in Figure 1, at the beginning of the fifth session, the leader had noted that the task completion rate was low and that satisfaction at the previous session was also low. Once a group problem is hypothesized, the group leader has a number of options, which are discussed in Chapter 12. In the example in Figure 1, she merely asked what the members thought the data meant. It should be noted that differences are often quite dramatic as in this example and provide an excellent opportunity to initiate a discussion about what is happening in the group.

Summary of Group Measurement and Evaluation

In determining group structures and group problems, group data such as postsession questionnaires, observations, attendance and promptness rates, and extragroup task completion rates have been found to be helpful. In this chapter, we reviewed these instruments and examined how the data can be used and interpreted in the ongoing group treatment process. Usually, data are collected at every session or in a sequence of sessions to show how group and individual phenomena change over time. Moreover, these data can form the basis for evaluation of the effectiveness of group intervention strategies.

Figure 1. Average Satisfaction and Task Completion Rates.

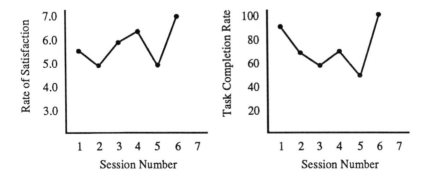

Evaluation Design

Group leaders design their evaluation efforts on the basis of the questions they want answered. Evaluation data can be used to guide intervention on an ongoing basis, provided that data are collected throughout treatment. To measure the change that has occurred from the beginning to the end of treatment, baseline data must be gathered. The baseline comprises observations (measurements) made prior to intervention. When examined together with observations taken after intervention, they allow one to draw conclusions about the direction and magnitude of the change. Contrast this situation with one in which data are collected only at the completion of intervention. Measuring the level of a target problem at the completion of intervention helps to determine whether the problem is at an acceptable level. To judge whether the treatment itself, as opposed to some other factor, accounted for improvement, a more complex design must be used. Brief descriptions of designs that practitioners can use to answer evaluation questions follow.

Case-Study Designs

Those designs that are used to evaluate the success of an intervention are characterized by Bloom and Fischer (1982) as case-study designs. Although readily implemented, case-study designs are generally inadequate for deciding whether the group intervention is the *cause* of a positive change. The easiest case-study design for the practitioner to implement is the pre–post design.

Pre–Post Design. In the pre–post design, data are gathered prior to the start and then again at the completion of intervention. This design allows one to make a judgment about the magnitude and the direction of change. The group leader might better use a pre–post and follow-up design to determine whether changes obtained at posttest are maintained at follow-up.

Because only a single measurement is taken before and after intervention (and possibly at follow-up), confidence in the inferences drawn from pre–post measurements is limited. Each measurement may be subject to influence from many factors (for example, a worse day than usual, a headache, an unclear instruction). Nevertheless, the pre-post design is the easiest to carry out, and if replicated by many practitioners, it can also make a contribution to knowledge. The effectiveness of the pre-post design can be improved by taking multiple measurements in the baseline phase and throughout intervention.

AB Design. In an AB design, repeated measurements are taken throughout the baseline (A) phase and the intervention (B) phase. Thus, the leader can make judgments about the magnitude and direction of change with greater confidence than with the pre-post design. In addition, when multiple measures are taken throughout the intervention phase, the leader can determine if the intervention is proceeding successfully. Adjustment in techniques may occur as a result of this information.

Although the AB design provides useful information, causal inferences cannot be made about the role of the group in bringing about the changes the client experiences. Maybe an uncontrolled event occurring concomitantly with intervention produced the change. Campbell and Stanley (1963) refer to this as a threat to validity due to history. For example, one client improved dramatically from the pre- to the posttest. It was learned that his previously separated parents had reconciled during the course of group treatment. The improvement may have occurred because of the extragroup situation.

Despite this limitation, the AB design is practical for group treatment. The threats to internal validity are reduced when the design is used in a group setting. When measures are taken on several group members and change occurs, it is less likely that the positive change is attributable to factors other than the group, especially if change occurs at a similar point in time, that is, following baseline. It is not likely that improvement would occur simultaneously for several group members if the group intervention did not have some role in the change. Moreover, if the same type of group is used for different clients, the outcomes can be compared to decide who can best use the given treatment. Finally, if, when the same treatment is used with similar clients, the results are comparable, confidence in the method is increased.

B-only. Sometimes, because of a need to intervene quickly or because of other practical constraints, the group leader is not able to collect baseline information. Measurement can still be useful. Repeated measurements made after the start of intervention could not be compared with a baseline but would indicate whether improvements were occurring. Even a single measurement made at the conclusion of the group can be used to help decide whether treatment can be terminated or whether further treatment is advisable. It can be improved somewhat by a retrospective report showing whether the new data represented an improvement. For example, in a group of men who batter, it was clear that initial reports of frequency of abuse were not accurate because of the characteristic denial of the members. It was only after trust in the leaders had developed that the reports on the frequency of abuse became more accurate. (This conclusion is based on interviews with significant others.) Therefore, it may be necessary to elicit retrospective baseline reports when the cohesion of the group is high.

Experimental Time-Series Designs

Though used less frequently by practitioners because of the controls required, experimental time-series designs provide us with greater confidence in the assumed cause of the changes. Several single-system designs allow many threats to internal validity to be ruled out. Such designs enable the group leader to infer that the group intervention was responsible for change in target problems; however, these designs are often difficult to implement, and certainly no practitioner is likely to use them in all cases. At times, a leader may choose a design that allows for causal inference; these types are characterized as experimental (Bloom and Fischer, 1982). We only briefly summarize these designs here, as they are rarely used in clinical practice. In the ABAB, or reversal or withdrawal design, treatment is initiated and then withdrawn to examine its effect on the target behavior. Because of the objection to withdrawal of a successful intervention, clients and practitioners alike often object to this design. In the multiple-baseline design, intervention is initiated in phases across behaviors, clients, or settings. If behavior changes occur beyond each baseline after the initiation of intervention, then confidence is increased that the intervention is responsible for the changes. The major objection to this design is the dependency of data. That is, working on one target behavior will in all probability influence a nontarget behavior in the same person. This is less of an objection across clients and settings. Another criticism is that the results are difficult to interpret if, in one of the conditions, changes do not occur in the predicted direction. I (Rose, 1978) used a multiple-baseline design to test the effectiveness of group contingencies for increasing compliance to extragroup tasks. In four groups, the introduction of contingencies resulted in small to large increases; in one group, there was a major drop. Thus, the results are ambiguous. Analysis of the unique conditions in the group that did not increase led to some interesting hypotheses.

Edleson, Miller, Stone, and Chapman (1985) used a multiple-baseline design to evaluate the success of a cognitive-behavioral approach in nine men who battered. Seven of the men reported cessation of violence over a thirteen-month follow-up period. As in the two studies described earlier, the multiple-baseline design, similar to the ABAB design, focused on fairly specific, narrow-range behaviors. The following design can be used with more complex behavior that must be shaped.

The changing criterion design (Hartmann and Hall, 1976) requires successively more difficult levels of performance for access to reinforcement. If a certain behavioral level is repeatedly achieved, then that level becomes the baseline for the next level until the final goal is achieved. When changes occur in this stepwise manner, confidence that the intervention (reinforcement) is responsible for the change is increased. This design has been used to reduce the number of cigarettes smoked (Hartmann and Hall, 1976) and appears to be especially useful in other high-frequency behaviors that require self-management. Although promising, this procedure has not, to our knowledge, been used to evaluate outcome in groups.

These designs and others are further discussed elsewhere

(Barlow, Hayes, and Nelson, 1984; Jayaratne and Levy, 1979; Bloom and Fischer, 1982). Control group experimental designs have not been discussed here because they are rarely if ever used by practitioners in the normal course of evaluating practice; however, should practitioners wish to examine the causes of change in their groups and have the resources and time to devote to research, some of the previously mentioned texts have excellent chapters on control group designs.

A Case in Point

This discussion focuses on evaluation procedures used in an ongoing group for clients who complained of general depression, particularly low activity levels, sleeplessness, and moodiness. Most members in this group were referred by physicians. Several were self-referrals. These clients attended primarily for problems related to difficulties in managing their depressed moods, yet their concrete problems were quite diverse and in many cases quite serious.

Although the tests and measures used in this group were different from those used for other types of groups, the evaluation program was not atypical. Before the first meeting, each member was interviewed to establish preliminary goals, which were used in goal attainment scaling. After the interview, each person completed three paper-and-pencil checklists: Beck's Depression Inventory (see Beck and others, 1961), the Profile of Mood States (McNair, Lorr, and Droppleman, 1971), and the Pleasant Events Schedule (Mac-Phillamy and Lewinsohn, 1974) on which the client checks off all the pleasant events in his or her life. One goal of treatment was to increase pleasant events. Members were also requested to record, three times daily, their mood on a scale from 1 to 10 and any critical events. The specific goal for one person involved lowering his BDI score and increasing his self-reported recreational activity and vigor subscale on the POMs. Another client aimed at increasing communication with friends at work and his BDI score. He also wanted to reduce the intensity of his self-reported depression on the daily depression report. A third person, in addition to decreasing the indicators of depression, wanted to increase her assertiveness toward a colleague who always imposed on her. The remaining goals were similar.

Finally, both at termination and three months after the group program, all members repeated the checklists and were interviewed in the group to determine the degree to which each of the goals was achieved and maintained.

The research design used for most of the goals on the checklists was a pre-post follow-up design without a control group. Because several other groups had been sponsored by the agency using the same sources of data, the design might more accurately be referred to as a replicated pre-post follow-up design. The cost of the evaluation activities was equal to two sessions or eight hours of professional time. This averaged out to one hour per group member beyond the six professional hours per person for ten sessions. Included in this cost were preparation, interviews, administration and coding of the checklists, and review of the measures to determine degree of goal achievement.

Conclusions

Although useful, the evaluation program just described incurred considerable expenditure of effort and time. The thrust of this chapter has been that failure to design such a program is by far the most costly approach. Without evaluation, we cannot estimate our progress, our failures, and our successes. In designing specific measurement efforts in a practice situation, the cost in time, effort, and intrusiveness to the client must be weighed against the benefits expected. When this is done, in our experience, the cost/benefit ratio is favorable.

The emphasis in this chapter has been on quantitative techniques; however, we do not advocate the exclusive use of measurement data in evaluating groups. Quantitative evaluation can supplement such nonquantitative evaluation as subjective impressions of group process, underlying motives, and cognitive and affective responses of clients to ongoing group stimuli. Quantitative data can correct the perpetuation of unfounded hunches and personal biases or expectations. Often, we are confronted with data that argue against what we "felt" was the outcome. Our clients, when asked to measure problem behaviors, often find that the problems they felt were quite extreme occurred much less often than they had believed. The next step at such a juncture is not to dismiss intuition or data but rather to use the incongruity to spur rethinking or deeper probing. Other times, data serve as satisfying confirmation of our intuitive hypotheses.

Three issues in group evaluation are discussed. The first, individual tests and measures, includes self-report checklists, role-playing, self-monitoring, extragroup observations, and problem cards. The second issue is collection of those data that facilitate judgments on group events, including extragroup observations and postsession questionnaires. Third, evaluation designs are used to evaluate the significance of the changes that occur. Advantages and limitations of each type of design are noted. Examples are used to illustrate the implementation of these methods. We noted that both quantitative and nonquantitative methods have a role in evaluation.

Evaluation cannot take place until goals are established and interventions implemented. At first glance it appears that our discussion of evaluation is out of place; however, measurement is closely linked to both assessment and evaluation, and a discussion of measurement would not be complete without a discussion of evaluation. Moreover planning for evaluation occurs in the assessment and measurement phases of treatment.

SIX

Setting Individual
and Group Goals

Madeline has not spoken for several weeks to her daughter, who lives in her house. The immediate goal for which she is preparing in the therapy group is to approach her daughter and ask her to sit down and talk about the differences between them. She wants to achieve this by the end of the week. Her long-term goal is to establish a more open and mutually trusting relationship with her daughter.

In this chapter, we distinguish between short- and long-term goals and note their relationship to each other and to the intervention process. The purposes of goal setting within the multimethod approach are clarified, and the principles of goal formulation are established. In addition, orientation of the client to the goal-setting process is explained, criteria for effective goal setting are established, training in appropriate goal formulation is illustrated, and identification and selection of group goals are examined. Let us first define what goals are and consider the distinction between short- and long-term goals.

Long-Term and Short-Term Goals

In group therapy, a goal is defined as a set of related behavioral, cognitive, and/or affective responses under specified conditions that a client aspires to perform within a specified time frame. An example of a behavioral goal would be asking a friend, within a set time, for help at work. One cognitive goal might be to be able to respond at the end of a given time to difficult situations with the statement, "If I analyze the steps carefully and take one step at a time, I can do it." The client who aims, within a given time frame, to be less upset (angry) with his children when they disobey him or to express his feelings to his wife when he is upset by all the pressure put on him at work, is working toward an affective goal. Occasionally, elements of all three goal types are operative. In most groups individual goals, such as those just described, are formulated with clients to establish the parameters of intervention. In this chapter, we distinguish between short-term (immediate) goals and long-term goals. In general, short-term goals are achieved within days or weeks. Long-term goals require more time, sometimes the length of treatment. Long-term goals tend to be more complex, to cover more situations, and to be somewhat more general than short-term goals. Short-term goals tend to be subgoals leading toward long-term goals. A distinction can also be made between individual and common treatment goals. All of the goals mentioned thus far are individual treatment goals. To the degree they are shared by other persons in the group, they can be considered common goals. The commonality of goals in groups is usually established at the level of long-term goals, not short-term goals. Group goals, which are defined later in this chapter, are distinct from common goals because they involve interaction of the clients.

Individual Goals

The formulation of goals for and by clients in groups has a number of purposes. First, it provides the basis for evaluating outcome of treatment by each group member. They can ascertain whether each of their goals has been partially or completely attained by the end of treatment. Second, goals set by a client reflect what that client perceives as a problem requiring attention. Individual determination of goals restrains the leader and other group members from imposing their perceptions on an individual. Third, in setting goals, both members and the leader discover areas of harmony and of difference. They can hypothesize where each can be of help to the other and where there are common concerns. Fourth, goals provide structure for treatment. Goals often indicate the best possible means of preparing clients to achieve their goals. They help leaders to focus their endeavors. Fifth, in formulating goals, clients and the leader may discover that the group is not appropriate for an individual, and a referral may be in order, or that the group should be supplemented, for example, with financial aid or dietary counseling. Sixth, as Lloyd (1983) and Locke, Shaw, Saari, and Latham (1981) have demonstrated, the process of setting goals is therapeutic in its own right, provided the client is actively involved.

The final purpose of goal setting is to link the approach to the problem-solving process. The first step in problem solving, problem formulation, is described in Chapter Three. Only until the problem is formulated in terms of situations and the client's responses to those situations, can goals be established.

Characteristics of a Well-Formulated Goal. To examine the characteristics of a well-formulated goal, let us look at several examples.

Greg told the other group members that he has to talk to his boss today. When he arrives at his office, he experiences the usual vague sense of discomfort. His goal is to tell himself that he should take a deep breath, relax, and think about the good work he has done so far for the company. Then he will look his boss in the eyes and, in a firm voice, speak about greater involvement of personnel at lower levels in the planning process. Greg's long-term goal is to talk without undue anxiety to his boss on a regular basis about his concerns with the business.

Mr. McHarol stated that he would like very much to meet Ms. Luann, who works at his office. He would like to get to know her much better and ultimately to take her out. His short-term goal by the end of next week is to talk to Ms. Luann at least once in the course of the week. When he approaches Ms. Luann he will remind himself to take one step at a time, to comment on the weather, and to ask her how she likes it at the office.

Mrs. Clanrahan explained to the group that she has not left the house except to attend the group meetings for a month. Her short-term goal by the end of the week is to go shopping once with Mrs. Galaway, another member of the group, at the mall near Mrs. Clanrahan's house.

Once the problem situation is formulated, it is necessary to establish the specific behaviors to be carried out or the cognitions to be altered to cope more effectively with the situation. Each short-term goal in the preceding examples involves one situation. Eventually, goals are set that involve two or more similar situations.

The preceding short-term goals present certain common characteristics. Each goal is defined in terms of a situation and the responses (at a given moment in time) that the client would like to make when a similar situation arises. "When I am faced with a decision and I begin to get anxious because I do not know immediately what to do, I will first relax, sit down and analyze the situation with paper and pencil, and then finally list and evaluate all possible solutions to the problem." The situation and responses are described in highly specific terms. Although, initially, goals are formulated for specific situations, eventually the goals pertain to recurring situations. For example, Mr. Rivers has difficulty refusing his son-in-law's requests to borrow money. Therefore, as a short-term goal, the next time he is asked by his son-in-law to lend him money, Mr. Rivers will refuse him in a clear, friendly, but firm voice. The long-term goal for Mr. Rivers is that when anyone wants to borrow money or in any other way impose on him, he will refuse in a clear, friendly, but firm voice.

The time within which the goal should be achieved should be explicit, as should the statement of what the client intends to do or think: "I will attain the stated goal by the end of treatment [by the end of the week, within the next three weeks]."

In summary, a goal describes a new or adaptive set of behaviors to be achieved by a given client under specific conditions and within a specific time.

Principles of Initial Goal Formulation. Seven principles, discussed here in brief, must be taken into consideration in the formulation of goals.

1. *The goal should be important to the client.* All too often, because of the pressure to formulate something, clients state trivial goals. Of course, the group leader does not always know what is trivial and what is important. In a parent training group, a client set a goal of developing skills to facilitate the picking up of toys. The nonparent leader thought that this goal was relatively unimportant, until the parents in the group pointed out the number of pieces in various puzzles, erector sets, and other toys and the amount of time required to pick up those toys. At the very least, the client should be asked whether a given goal is important and why.

2. *The goal must be realistic.* Although a goal should challenge the client, it should not be so difficult that even with training it is not achievable in the stated period. It is probably unrealistic for a client to expect that by the end of short-term treatment, she will eliminate all anxiety in the face of several phobic objects. It would be more realistic for her to expect that by the end of short-term treatment, she will be able to face the most restrictive phobic objects and to function with a reduced level of anxiety. At the beginning of treatment, clients are better off setting small goals, so that they can achieve some success before moving on. If daring goals are set at the beginning, the client may encounter more failure than success and be disheartened.

How realistic a goal is depends, at least in part, on the personal and environmental resources available for, and the barriers to, achieving the goal, as well as the potential long- and short-term consequences of the proposed responses.

3. *The goal should be a change in behavior, affect, and/or cognition for the person with the problem, not for others in the client's life.* Clients often want to change significant others in their lives rather than themselves, because they blame these others for their suffering; for example, the client who sets as his goal that his wife will be more understanding when he comes home exhausted at the end of a hard day's work or the client who wants her boss to be more flexible about time off. In most cases, it is the attempt to change others that is the major source of the client's unhappiness or sense of failure. The group is encouraged to discuss the difficulties involved in changing others. Examples are employed to enhance the group discussion. This step is not easy but must be taken if change

is to be achieved. Many clients have a pattern of blaming others for their difficulties. The goal-setting process may reveal these patterns, and the assumption of responsibility for his or her own difficulties may become the client's goal.

Of course, some clients find themselves in devastating circumstances over which they have little or no direct control. While environmental change strategies are being considered, attitudinal- or cognitive-change goals should also be contemplated. In one parenting group, a single parent with three children was locked into the income provided by the welfare program. The agency provided the babysitter and bus money that enabled her to attend the sessions. Many of her problems were associated with her financial limitations and time-consuming attempts to supplement her income. Her goals in the group for parenting had to reflect this particular limiting circumstance.

4. *The risks of goal achievement must be explained to the client.* The client should be made aware of the potential risks involved should a given goal be achieved and must decide whether she or he is willing to accept the risk. The client should be asked to compare the risks of continuing the present pattern of responses with the risks that might be encountered after carrying out the goal responses. In a group of female victims of their partners' abuse, one woman decided that her goal was to tell her husband face-to-face that she was going to leave him. In an evaluation of the risk involved, she decided that it would be better to leave him a letter, even though she would have more self-respect if she confronted him in person.

5. *The goal is limited by the general group purpose.* Individual treatment goals are restricted to a large degree by the general group purpose to which the members agreed on joining the group. For example, in a group organized for the purpose of helping parents develop better child management skills, one member set the individual goal of improving her relationship with her husband, or improving her depressed affect. Unless the members unanimously agreed, the goal would have to be modified to conform to the group's general purpose. For example, an appropriate goal may be, for her and her husband as a couple, to coordinate their parenting efforts to provide their children with the best

possible parenting. The goal may be sufficiently important to the client that a referral to alternative treatment would be appropriate. This restriction is less applicable to a group labeled "group therapy" or "group counseling," since no general purpose exists in such groups. As pointed out in Chapter Two, too much diversity in goals, at least in short-term groups, limits the time spent on each. This may not be a major problem in long-term treatment.

Goal formulation in groups is restricted not only by the group purpose, but also by the search for common concerns. In short-term groups, it is difficult to help people with diverse problems achieve their goals. The group leader seeks common goals. For example, the leader of an assertiveness training group found that most of the members were interested in increasing refusal responses when they were imposed on by others. Another leader became aware that all the parents in a child management group wanted to learn to deal more effectively with the physically aggressive behavior of their children when they were angry, tired, or frustrated by parental refusal. Because the preceding groups met for only six and eight weeks, respectively, the focus made it possible to involve everyone intensely even in the short time available. In longer-term groups (eighteen or more sessions) greater diversity in goals can be permitted and planned for.

6. *Long-term goals are initially broken down into short-term goals.* When the long-term goal is complex, is too general, or involves multiple situations, it is helpful to formulate it in subgoals or short-term goals. For example, Jerry's long-term goal is to make new friends. His short-term goals might be, first, to learn approach statements; second, to learn minimal conversational skills; and, third, to learn to express feelings appropriately. After a few short-term goals have been achieved, the more general goal can be reconsidered.

7. *Short-term goals evolve into long-term goals.* Most of the criteria point to highly specific short-term goals. As the group progresses and as clients demonstrate ability to formulate concrete goals, more general goals can be tolerated and should, in fact, be encouraged. After achieving some success in reducing the frequency with which he tried to change his wife's behavior, Richard agreed to the goal of taking greater responsibility for his own difficulties and

placing less blame on others in general. Virginia, who had learned to ask for help from members of the group when she needed it and to talk to people at work more frequently, formulated the long-term goal of establishing more comfortable and more effective social and work relationships in general. Thus, goal formulation moves from the specific to the general, from the short term to the long term, and from isolated situations to different types of situations.

Training in Goal Formulation. Correctly formulated goals clearly indicate the form of intervention necessary to train the client in the desired behavior or cognition. Let us examine several ways in which this training is carried out.

As in all procedures, the clients are made aware of the importance of setting treatment goals. They are then presented with the criteria of a well-formulated goal and are trained, through models and exercises, to meet these criteria. The following example illustrates how a leader might handle a situation:

We have discussed many different problems that you have been experiencing. It is often helpful to focus on several of the more resolvable ones. Therefore, at this point in treatment, we will take a few moments to set goals for ourselves. It is interesting to note that the mere setting of goals often helps us to get started on working on our problems. What we are going to do is to help each other set goals on the basis of these criteria:

Is it *feasible*, that is, can I achieve the goal with training in the time available?

Is it *important*, that is, if I achieve the goal, will my life improve significantly?

Can the group help me to achieve the goal? [You may not be able to answer this question. I (leader) will be the consultant in the beginning.]

Is the goal sufficiently specific that it indicates the training needed to achieve it?

Is there a specific time frame within which the goal should be achieved? (By next week, within two weeks, by the end of this program?)

Six procedures are commonly used to train clients to meet these criteria.

1. The group leader describes to the clients a number of situations (such as those described earlier) for which he or she models correctly formulated goals.
2. The group leader provides one problem situation to the members—a case study—for which the clients must "brainstorm" as many goals as possible and afterward evaluate together which goal best meets the criteria.
3. The group leader lists all the situations described earlier and asks the members to state what they would do if they were in those situations.
4. The group leader provides a list of improperly formulated goals and asks the group members to evaluate them.
5. The group leader writes the problem statements voiced by the clients thus far on separate cards and places the cards in a pile. Each client then picks a situation and formulates a reasonable goal according to the previously mentioned criteria. Other members evaluate the goal and make alternative suggestions.
6. As homework, pairs of clients are instructed to formulate appropriate goals for each other with respect to already stated problem situations. The homework is discussed in the group at the next session. (Actually, all of these procedures could be assigned as homework, thus saving in-group time for other purposes.)

Not all of these exercises are required to train clients in the end criteria. As soon as clients have demonstrated in the exercises that they have learned the criteria for correct goal formulation, they will formulate treatment goals for their own problem situations. There are a number of ways to arrive at individualized goals. First, the group leader can ask clients to describe to the group those responses they feel are the best responses in a given situation. Occasionally, especially if inadequate time is available in a given

group meeting, the leader may assign the homework described
earlier in procedure 6. When a given client has a set of responses she
or he would like to achieve in a given set of circumstances, the
leader can ask the client and the group to evaluate them in terms of
the established criteria.

If the client has no clear idea as to what to do in response to a
given problem situation, the leader can use brainstorming (Osborne, 1963) to generate suggestions for actions or cognitions that
might remedy the situation. Even when the client comes up with his
or her own ideas, the group may still brainstorm to widen the range
of ideas available to the client.

Goal Attainment Scaling. Goal attainment scaling is a
practical technique used to evaluate client progress (Kiresuk and
Garwick, 1979). Unlike standardized measures described in Chapter
Six, goal attainment scales are devised by the group leader and the
members. Goals are specified for each individual, and then for each
goal, a scale is developed. Each goal describes the most favorable to
least favorable outcomes that can be expected as a result of
intervention. Generally, the midpoint of a 5-point scale is the
"expected" outcome. The outcomes may be behaviors, thoughts,
feelings, or changes in environment. Table 5 illustrates one possible
format of a goal attainment scale. In most groups, clients have three
to five such scales.

Goal attainment scales have several advantages. They focus
specifically on the individual. They provide specific criteria on
which to determine whether a client has improved or deteriorated.
Because changes are quantified, the rating scales offer some degree
of intra- and extragroup comparability. In addition, it is possible to
involve the entire group in the process of establishing goals. In our
experience, it is difficult to develop goal attainment scales until the
third or fourth week, when the language of goal setting is well
developed and the clients are willing to self-disclose.

Of course, the practitioner should be aware of the threats to
both reliability and validity. Adequate formulation of goals
requires extensive training of group leaders. Serious questions have
been raised about construct validity (Seaberg and Gillespie, 1977).
Despite these objections, the literature seems to support the general

Table 5. Example of a Goal Attainment Scale.

Predicted outcome level	Score	Individual treatment goal (improving communication with wife)
Much less than predicted	-2	Does not talk to wife except to make commands during the week
Moderately less than predicted	-1	Occasionally talks to wife, without sarcasm, asking how she feels, how her day went, or whether she needs help, but less than four times a week
Predicted	0	Talks to wife as described above, at least four times a week
Moderately more than predicted	1	Talks to wife as described above at least once, but less than twice, a day
Much more than predicted	2	Talks to wife as described above at least twice a day

usefulness of goal attainment scaling. (See Cytrynbaum, Ginath, Birdwell, and Brandt, 1979, for an extensive critical review of goal attainment scaling.) Thus far, goal attainment scaling has been used only occasionally in clinical practice.

Group Goals

Some goals for individuals are shared by some or all of the members of the group. For example, in a victims of incest group, a shared or common goal was to be able to deal with relatives and others who were aware of their victimization as a child but who did nothing about it. Such shared or common individual goals usually increase the cohesion of the group. Moreover, as pointed out earlier, common goals are beneficial because practice of the goal by one member serves as a model to other group members.

Group goals are interactive patterns which the group aims to achieve or maintain or are products of group interactions. To clarify the concept we note some examples. If the attraction of members to the group is low, the group goal should be to increase that attraction. If the norm in the group was that members blame their spouses or parents for their patterns of violence, the group goal should be to establish the norm that each person take responsibility for his or her own violent behavior. If the homework completion rate was generally low, the group goal might be to increase the homework assignment rate. If group interaction was directed primarily from member to leader and not from member to member, the group goal might be to shift to more interaction between members.

It should be noted that group goals tend to be, in part, a function of the phase of development. In the early phase, attention needs to be paid to increasing group cohesion and establishing protherapeutic norms. Also, the new, more effective interaction patterns become important. Later, homework assignment completion rates and the selection of more relevant assignments become the focus. Finally, decreasing group cohesion becomes a goal.

Group goals may be suggested by the leader or by the members on their postsession questionnaires. Members may be annoyed by a given norm and the majority may wish to change it. How a group leader involves the group in bringing about such changes is discussed in Chapter Ten. One possible first step may be the formulation of group goal attainment scales.

Table 6. Example of a Group Goal Attainment Scale.

Predicted outcome level	Group Score	Group goal
Much less than expected	-2	Members talk amost exclusively to leader (91% or more)*
Moderately less than expected	-1	Members talk primarily to leader (65%-90%)†
Expected	0	Members talk about equally to other members and to the leader (35%-64%)
Moderately more than expected	1	Members talk primarily to each other (10%-34%)
Much more than expected	2	Members talk almost exclusively to each other (9% or less)

*The direction of interactions every ten seconds is recorded. The number is the percentage of all interactions directed toward the group leader.
†This was the level of the group at the time the goal was determined.

Just as individual goal attainment scaling is used to determine the degree to which individual treatment goals have been achieved, group goal attainment scaling is used to evaluate achievement of group goals. Table 6 is an example of a group goal attainment scale. Note that an observation system must be used in which the direction of the interactions is recorded. It is not necessary to differentiate among the members but only between members and the leader.

Group goal attainment scales cannot be developed until a problem is identified, usually by means of postsession questionnaires or observations. These same tests are used to formulate goals and establish criteria for successful outcomes. Although it is almost as difficult as individual goal attainment scaling, group goal attainment scaling appears easier for group leaders. Group goal attainment scaling is as much a group measurement procedure as it is a goal-setting and treatment procedure.

Summary

After the problems have been assessed, it is common practice to help clients determine specific goals in terms of the behaviors, cognitions, and affect they wish to modify in specific circumstances. The purposes of and the major criteria for goal formulation are outlined. How clients can be trained in effective goal setting is also explored. Individual and group goal attainment scales are described. The identification of group goals and their relationship to the treatment process are also discussed.

SEVEN

Planning for Group Interventions

The multimethod approach is basically a "planful" approach. A plan is required to determine the methods appropriate to treat the members of the group. In Chapter Three, we discussed the planning process involved in preparation for a group. Intervention planning is the process in which the general strategies, the specific actions or cognitions needed to achieve a treatment goal, and the concrete procedures required to teach those actions or cognitions are evaluated and selected for implementation. The purpose of planning is to find the best possible strategies for achieving the goals. The products of planning are group and individual intervention plans, session agendas, and plans for maintenance and generalization of change.

Planning for intervention is a continuous process that draws on information gathered before and throughout therapy. Planning is interspersed with data collection, action, reevaluation, and plan modification. In the process of planning, group leaders draw on their own and the members' training, knowledge, and experience to determine those intervention strategies most appropriate to implementing the behaviors and cognitions required for coping with problem situations. Effective intervention planning maximally involves the members through such procedures as group discussion, brainstorming, and evaluation. Brainstorming is used specifically to generate ideas from the group members as to appropriate actions they can take in a given situation and the most effective training procedures to be used.

The first step in intervention planning is to review the goals set for and with the individual client and with the group. Short-term goals are defined in terms of the actions and/or cognitions to be performed under certain conditions. Interventions are selected on the basis of these goals. Priority is given to those procedures for which the empirical literature has demonstrated a relationship to the expected outcome. The effectiveness of the intervention plan is evaluated by determining to what degree the goals have been achieved.

Types of Intervention Plans

Many types of intervention plans are generated by the planning process. The major types are individual, group, session, and generalized plans; these are interrelated. Differences and similarities among these plans, as well as examples, are presented here. All four types are developed as new information is gathered. For the most part the different planning activities overlap with each other.

Individual Intervention Plans. Individual intervention plans are plans drawn up, often in writing, for the individual members of a given group. The following plan was developed for Rob, a member of a group of men learning to control their anger. Since no plan is understandable without associated goals and monitoring procedures, these are included in the example.

Behavioral Goals: Rob's long-term goal was to develop and maintain those behaviors that would help him control his violent behavior, which appeared to surface most frequently when he felt frustrated and angry. A major stimulus to his anger was others' criticism, actual or implied. One short-term goal was to use cognitive coping statements when he began to feel angry and/or frustrated, for example, "Take a deep breath—relax, Rob. Walk away, tell her you'll talk to her later." Another short-term goal, to increase his recreational activities, would be achieved by his joining a softball league and playing three evenings a week. A long-term goal was to reduce the frequency and amount of drinking after work, which seemed to exacerbate the violent responses.

Monitoring Procedures: Rob would self-monitor by noting on a small card those situations that made him angry or frustrated and how he handled the situations. He carried the card at all times. He would confer with his friend Gary and wife Margaret to check the accuracy of his self-perception.

Intervention: The intervention strategy was to use group discussion to discover what he said to himself that exacerbated the violence. The next step would be to get help from the group as to what he might say instead. After a cognitive-modeling sequence in which someone demonstrated how he might speak to himself differently, he would practice before the others. Each week he would report back to the group how he handled the various anger-provoking situations, both successes and failures.

A similar plan was drawn up for Rob's second goal—increasing his recreational activities. He decided to break it down into steps. First, he would obtain information about the activities. Second, he would visit a game and talk to the other team members. Third, if he felt sufficiently comfortable, he would join the league. The only intervention was to report his progress to the other group members.

All group members drew up similar intervention plans, which they could modify in group discussion as they gained experience in carrying out the plan. Where the problems are very similar and in short-term groups, it is often more efficient to use a shared group plan that each member adapts to his or her own unique situation.

Group Intervention Plans. A group intervention plan is the overall therapy strategy to be used in the group and the justification for that strategy. A general plan is determined prior to the recruitment of clients and is modified as the characteristics and problems of the clients become apparent. Initial group intervention plans are part of the preliminary treatment contract and are developed as a point of departure for discussion with the group and with others concerned with the group's focus. The major components of the plan are the presenting problems, the monitoring procedures, the common goals, group composition, and group intervention strategies. The group plan may be the only intervention plan; however, in most cases, especially in groups meeting more than six sessions, individual plans are highly desirable. The following example illustrates a group intervention plan for a parent training group.

Presenting Problems: The parents complained primarily of their inability to set firm limits on their children. They also noted that their relationships with their children were largely negative and characterized by a great deal of mutual yelling.

Common Long-Term Goal: By the end of therapy, all parents would improve their relationships with their children and would demonstrate an ability to set firm limits when required. Parents would also increase the frequency with which they reinforced their children.

Common Short-Term Goals: By the end of the first four weeks, the common treatment goal formulated was that each parent bring to the group at least two situations in which they set firm limits on the behavior of their children and followed up with appropriate consequences if the children did not comply. Each parent would increase the frequency of reinforcement each week for the first four weeks. Also, at the end of two weeks, the parents would rate their relationships with their children on a 5-point scale ranging from highly negative to highly positive, as would the children.

Monitoring: The parents indicated that they would be willing to count incidents calling for firm limits and to describe their responses. They would rate the success of their efforts on a scale of 1 to 5. They would identify situations for which reinforcement was appropriate and indicate whether or not they reinforced. They would also rate the relationship on a weekly basis and ask children to do the same.

Preliminary Group Activities: The group leader would meet weekly with the group for two hours. In the early session the members would be trained in positive reinforcement strategies, as well as in time-out from reinforcement and other procedures for setting firm limits. The parents would also be taught how to contract with their children for more effective behaviors. During the second through eighth sessions, the parents would work on specific situations they found difficult using modeling, roleplaying, and group feedback. Specific exercises on the use of praise, criticism, time-out, rule setting, and limit setting would also be used.

The group plan is used as a point of departure and is to be renegotiated, if necessary, as the original procedures prove to be inadequate, new problems are introduced, or new procedures are required. The group plan can be included in the treatment contract. Plans for sessions are derived from the group plan.

Plans for Meetings: Session Agendas. Most group leaders use the session agenda to plan their weekly meetings. The agenda is a list of activities that the leader expects the group to follow during a given meeting. The agenda is either written on the blackboard or typed, duplicated, and distributed to the members. The clients are involved as early as possible in the planning of the agenda. Toward the end of a meeting, the leader may describe a tentative plan for the next meeting and ask the group for their comments. At the end of the first and all subsequent meetings, clients evaluate the session extensively and propose changes in format and content that would best meet their needs. As long as these suggestions are compatible with the mutually agreed-on purpose, the ideas are brought before the group for serious consideration. Some group leaders may arrange special meetings between sessions with representatives of the group. Thus, agenda planning is an opportunity for client involvement as well as a tool for orientation.

The agenda has several other uses. It provides a structure for the session, though not a rigid structure. Furthermore, the agenda makes it possible to set limits on consistent off-task behavior in a nonpersonal way: "That doesn't seem to be on the agenda for this week, Pete, but it is an important point. Why don't we try to include that in the agenda for next week." In this example, the group leader used the agenda to limit Pete, but at the same time found a place for Pete's contribution.

The following agenda is taken from the sixth session of a group of recovering alcoholics.

1. Briefly review homework from the previous week.
2. Review evaluations from the previous week and homework completion rate data.
3. Discuss problem of irregular attendance in group; then problem solve it.
4. Plan for next week's meeting with guests from Alcoholics Anonymous.
5. Discuss stressful situations that occurred during the week and how they were handled.
6. Select those situations that clients would like to have handled differently and suggest alternative ways of handling them.
7. Have members model, and then have person with problem rehearse agreed-on alternatives. Provide roleplayers with feedback.
8. Design next week's homework for pairs and report to the group when finished.
9. Evaluate the session in writing.

The reader should note that several items occur at almost all sessions: review of homework, review of evaluations, design of homework for the following week, and evaluation of the session. In this particular agenda, the group deals with a group problem of concern to them and the leader. If a serious group problem arises, it may be necessary to scrap at least part of the formal agenda, because discussion of the problem may consume more time than planned. The meat of the program comprises those agenda items that focus on identifying and dealing with problem situations that have occurred in the course of the week. Usually, a particular subject, such as a new skill or new information about the problem, is presented and an exercise that facilitates learning of the new material is included on the agenda.

Plans for Maintenance and Generalization of Change. The focus of a multimethod approach is not merely on change but on the maintenance and generalization of change. Since transfer of learning does not usually occur if steps have not been taken to ensure it (Stokes and Baer, 1977), a plan is established early in therapy for the maintenance and generalization of change beyond the immediate group. In the first phase of intervention, emphasis is placed on strategies for attaining change, but as the group progresses, increasing emphasis is put on the generalization plan. The following might be a typical generalization plan for a group of agoraphobics.

The group program will rely heavily on homework assignments given at the end of each session and monitored at the beginning of the subsequent session. Although, in the early phase of intervention, the members will accompany each other on increasingly more difficult ventures into the real world, gradually the members will stand further and further away from one client trying out the new behavior. Ultimately, the client will perform the behavior without the support of the group. Clients will be given increasing responsibility for their own intervention as the group progresses. The initial exercises will be provided by the leader. Later, exercises will be designed by the group with respect to their specific fears.

Procedures for generalization, and the underlying principles, are discussed in chapters Twelve and Thirteen.

Principles of Planning for Interventions

Once the client decides what she or he wants to do, say, or think to cope with a given problem situation, an intervention strategy can be selected. Many of the overlapping principles on which the selection of intervention strategies is based are described in this section. (Many of these principles have been derived from Cormier and Cormier, 1985, p. 297, and adapted to the group situation.)

Relationship to Goals. Initially selected are those procedures that have been reported in the literature or have been shown by previous experience to be related to the achievement of the goals agreed on by the client and the leader. As the various intervention strategies are discussed in subsequent chapters, the specific goals toward which each of the strategies are oriented will be pointed out.

In a postdivorce adjustment group, where the goal of most members was to relate more effectively to members of the opposite sex, both leader and members decided that assertiveness training using primarily the modeling sequence seemed most closely linked to what they wanted to achieve. As the members discovered that certain cognitive distortions concerning members of the opposite sex interfered with their learning the assertive behaviors, they agreed that cognitive restructuring might be added to the modeling sequence because the literature shows a direct connection between it and the formulated goal.

Empirical Foundation. Those procedures which have the best empirical foundation are preferred. Most of the procedures presented in this book have some empirical foundation, and where possible, this foundation has been identified to facilitate the reader's decision on the procedures. For example, group exposure for treatment of agoraphobia has some empirical support (Hand, Lamontagne, and Marks, 1974), whereas highly confrontational verbal procedures without adequate client protection may have serious psychological side effects (see Lieberman, Yalom, and Miles, 1973).

Applicability to Group. Since one strength of the group is the opportunity it provides members to help each other, the leader must consider whether a given set of procedures actually affords the members this possibility. Effective group procedures permit the maximum involvement of all the members and gradually increase the members' responsibility. They also provide diverse roles that the member can play. Although most procedures fit this category, some more readily lend themselves to group application. For example, modeling and rehearsal procedures take advantage of the many potential actors and models within the group and provide diverse sources of feedback. Although systematic desensitization (Wolpe, 1973) could be carried out in a group, it fails to take advantage of the possibilities offered by the group. There is little opportunity for mutual aid, diverse roles, and group interaction. It is desirable that procedures selected for one individual in the group be compatible or overlap with those used for other members, if the group is to be efficiently used.

The decision to include a given strategy for one client should be based on significant overlap of strategies employed with others, not on total overlap. Modeling, for example, can be used for all members, if all members have an interactive problem; moreover, it permits diverse roles for various members, significant others, observers, and discussion leaders. If the intervention strategies appropriate to a given client are not compatible with the strategies required to deal with the majority of individual problems, referral of the client to another therapy context should be considered. For example, in a group of relatives of patients with terminal cancer, two participants were having serious marital problems; they required marital intervention strategies before they could deal with their dying mother. The group voiced this observation to the participants and the leader helped them to find the counseling they needed elsewhere. Since the group was open-ended, the couple returned to the group several weeks later, after consultation with the group members and leader and the marital therapist, who continued her contact with them.

The procedures should also be feasible within the time limits of the group. Long-term insight procedures may be ill-suited to time-limited small group therapy. Modeling, cognitive restructuring, group exposure, and many relational techniques can be applied in as a few as one session and, therefore, are appropriate to both long-term and short-term therapy.

Informed Consent. Clients as well as the referring agency are informed as to the major procedures to be used and their approval is solicited. Thus, the clients must be aware of and must approve the general thrust of the procedures. For this reason, paradoxical techniques and most punishment strategies are usually not selected for the group setting. If clients were aware of the potential side effects of such procedures, they probably would not choose them voluntarily.

It is always difficult to determine how explicit the leader must be in describing to the client what will be done. Too much information too early in therapy may be overwhelming and, in some cases, may drive clients away. On the basis of a principle commonly used in informing clients, successive structuring (Rotter, 1954), group members are made aware of the basic structure of the intervention(s) used and then gradually provided more details on unique aspects of their implementation.

Emphasis on Positive Procedures. The procedures selected should basically be positive. Reinforcement procedures are preferred to punishment strategies. Group support, too, is highly valued by members in their attempts to deal with daily hassles. There is evidence that groups tend to be more cohesive if the interventions are predominantly positive (Goldstein and others, 1966). In our own research (Whitney and Rose, 1989), we found a correlation, in stress management groups, between the degree to which the group was evaluated as positive and dropouts. Even in encounter groups, Lieberman, Yalom, and Miles (1973) found that those groups in which the leader had the highest level of confrontation had the highest rate of psychological breakdown.

Of course, some form of confrontation or criticism must occasionally be used. To reduce the negative valence, clients are adequately prepared for the experience by exercises on giving and accepting criticism and are provided an opportunity to talk about negative feedback. Moreover, negative feedback is often sandwiched within positive feedback. Highly disruptive behaviors in the group are often handled by such procedures as disapproval and setting of firm limits. Group exposure, which can produce high levels of anxiety, can create panic if clients are not adequately prepared and given the choice to back out. Usually, when these anxiety-producing procedures are used, they are incorporated into a predominantly positive program of high levels of reinforcement and support.

Group Leader Competency. The group leader, or one of the co-leaders, should be trained in all procedures selected for use in the group. If the procedure is essential and the group leader is not trained in its use, training should be obtained first or a "specialist" should be called in to guide the process. All too often, group leaders and other professionals try out techniques with which they are minimally acquainted, and there are unacceptable results. If the group leader has minimal training in a given procedure and is experimenting with it for the first time, the clients should, at the very least, be made aware of the experimental nature of the procedure and of potential negative side effects.

Delegation of Responsibility to Clients. In the initial phases of therapy, the major responsibility for and activity in planning are lodged primarily with the group leader. At the beginning, it is the group leader who is best informed about the range of potential strategies, although the group members may serve as a rich source of the behaviors and cognitions that might best be used in a given situation and the coping skills that might lie within their range of competence. Furthermore, the members often have had other therapeutic experiences that the group leader could use. Wherever possible, it is advisable to empower members by involving them in planning, even in the initial phase. As therapy progresses and the members accrue greater experience and new therapeutic skills, the leader is in an even better position to get ideas from the members and to share the responsibility for the selection of strategies with the group. Thus, involvement of the clients moves from low to high as therapy progresses but is always an issue of concern.

One dramatic example of the importance of client control was reported by Langer and Rodin (1976; Rodin and Langer, 1977), who observed that when residents in a home for the aged were given a greater choice in their daily routines, they showed significant improvement in alertness, active participation, and self-rated well-being.

Flexible Structure. Plans developed early in therapy, either for strategies or for specific actions, are only tentative. As information accrues and plans are employed and found to be inadequte, the plans are usually revised and sometimes eliminated. A plan may be regarded as a point of departure to guide future planning. In a support group with elderly participants whose goals were to increase their social activity, the original plan was to discuss the various activities available to them. The members noted that this awareness was not leading to greater participation in community activities, and at the suggestion of the group leader, they decided to add field trips to the program so that they could actually try such activities as folk dancing and bowling. Later, when they discovered how shy they were with new people, they decided to add assertiveness training to help them interact more comfortably with others.

Appropriate Timing. When strategies should be employed must also be taken into consideration. Although most intervention strategies are introduced and the clients oriented to their use early in therapy, in general, the group must be sufficiently cohesive before highly demanding or intrusive intervention strategies can be proposed. Sufficiently high cohesion is indicated when members state in group discussion or on postsession questionnaires that the group is useful and/or enjoyable. Appropriate timing would be to postpone confronting clients with their patterns of response to stress-inducing situations until the clients have interacted sufficiently and disclosed something relevant about themselves.

Shaping Complex from Simple Procedures. Some procedures build on other procedures that need to be taught prior to the more complex approach. For example, most group procedures require appropriate and skilled feedback. Therefore, feedback training precedes more complicated strategies. Relaxation training is often a prerequisite for the use of cognitive-behavioral procedures and group exposure. Modeling and rehearsal strategies are components of both interactive skill training and cognitive skill training and are also taught soon after feedback. Reinforcement strategies are employed throughout therapy, and the timing dilemma in this case is when to decrease reinforcement. The timing problems faced with each intervention strategy are discussed along with the strategy in subsequent chapters.

Multiple Intervention Strategies

Finally, in reviewing the preceding principles, it is clear that one strategy is rarely, if ever, sufficient to deal with the complex problems of clients. Problems are rarely unidimensional (Mahoney, 1974). Usually, clients require assistance on a range of issues.

Multiple intervention strategies permit clients to serve as teacher of those strategies in which they are competent as well as student for those procedures they must learn. Though the intervention strategies are discussed separately in the subsequent chapters, they often are applied in combination in a well-integrated program. This combination is what led to the name *multimethod approach.*

To combine intervention strategies one must refer to original or new goals. Most goals require more than one kind of change. In identifying the nature of that change, the group leader becomes aware of the various interventions that might be required. For example, in a pain management group, most of the clients wanted to leave the house more frequently but were afraid to do so. To help them achieve their goal, it was necessary not only to reinforce the clients for devoting increasing time to other activities, but also to deal with the methods they would use to handle extreme pain while away from the house. The use of models from previous groups revealed how they managed in such situations. Group discussion members discussed their own successful coping methods. Two members who were neighbors decided to carry out the task together. The group also decided to bring in the members' spouses so that they could join in planning activities outside the home, as most spouses were intimately involved in the change of location of the clients.

Problem Solving and Planning

The initial steps in the problem-solving process have been illustrated: problem formulation in Chapter Four, generation of alternatives in Chapter Five, selection of alternatives in Chapter Six, and planning for implementation in this chapter. In subsequent chapters the process of preparation for implementation is elaborated on.

Planning as presented here may appear to occur in a linear fashion, from data collection to development of intervention and generalization strategies. Unfortunately, the paradigm is not always followed exactly. Sometimes, for example, intervention plans may precede careful goal setting. Often, in groups that have formed to learn to deal with a narrow range of problems, such as self-control groups or stress management groups, the strategies are selected in advance. Only those clients whose problems are adaptable to the common intervention package are selected. This does not mean that the intervention package is inflexible. As new common problems are discovered, the plan is often altered and new interventions are added.

Summary

Planning is the major way to attain a reasonable degree of structure in the group. Structure can protect individuals and the group as a whole against frivolous shifts in interest or manipulation by powerful group members. This is especially true if the agenda allows for a wide variety of individual input, self-disclosure, and open discussion. But the structure must be sufficiently flexible to maintain the interest of and the relevance to members and to incorporate dealing with group problems as they arise. The perfect balance is not readily attained. Goal setting and intervention planning contribute to achievement of balance.

EIGHT

Changing Behavior Through Modeling, Rehearsing, Coaching, and Feedback

The modeling sequence is the central intervention strategy in the multimethod approach. It comprises four procedures that are usually performed in sequence: modeling (demonstration), rehearsal (practice by the client), coaching (giving hints or prompts to the client), and group feedback. These procedures are also used independently or with other procedures not part of the modeling sequence. The modeling sequence is most often used in its entirety to teach the overt verbal and motor components of highly specific social skills, such as refusing a request when imposed on, approaching new people, accepting or giving criticism, asking for help, telling friends about difficult problems, and expressing emotions. These same procedures may be used in more elaborate social interactions such as a job interview, a major family decision and plan, and dating interaction over an extended period. We call modeling, rehearsal, coaching, and feedback the modeling sequence, because these procedures draw their significance from modeling theory and occur more or less in this order. Sometimes, these steps are referred to as assertiveness training, but as assertiveness is taught in many different ways and because this sequence is used to teach almost any interactive behavior, the label *assertiveness* does not seem appropriate. In this chapter, we discuss the modeling sequence primarily as it is used in the group setting. First, we present some of the major assumptions of modeling theory, most of which are drawn from the work of Bandura (1977b).

Theory

The fundamental assumption of modeling theory is that by observation, new behavior can be learned, already learned but inhibited behavior can be disinhibited, and infrequent behavior can be increased in frequency. For learning or disinhibition to occur, certain conditions must exist. The client must at the very least attend to the observational cues and must possess certain prerequisite skills. (Although speech can be modeled to an infant, the infant will not learn to speak until certain physical and intellectual development takes place.)

A number of factors enhance behavior acquisition. These factors are often influenced by the group leader in the treatment setting and include the client's skill in observing and imitating others, special attributes of the model, similarity of the model to the client along various personal characteristics, the way in which the model is presented, and the incentives under which modeling and subsequent imitation take place. Each of these factors, which can be adjusted to enhance the probability of learning and imitation, is now discussed in greater detail.

Skill in Observation and Imitation

One necessary condition for imitation is careful attention by the client to the model's behavior. If clients are restless, if the cues are too vague, if the perceptive ability of the client is limited, attention to the model may be drastically reduced. One way to increase the attention paid to a model is to give the client a structured observational role. For example, in a group of men who were substance abusers, the leader modeled how to ask for help. Prior to the modeling, the leader handed out written instructions as to the behaviors the members should look for. These included nonverbal behavior, such as eye contact, voice volume, and body posture, and verbal behavior. A second strategy for keeping the attention of the observers is to stop the modeling interaction intermittently and ask members questions on what they have seen. Third, to increase attention, make the modeling session interesting.

To increase interest, the modeling must be as realistic as

possible. Goldstein, Heller, and Sechrest (1966) point out that the more nearly the modeling exercise simulates the real world, the greater probability that the practiced behavior will be duplicated in the real world. When instructed to enter, the job candidate enters the room by opening a door. She and the interviewer proceed through the normal greeting ritual before they get down to the questions. When the interview is completed, they say their good-byes. The group leader can provide such props as a typewriter and desk for a secretary or a set of papers for the boss to look through.

If clients are involved in the process of determining suitable criteria for observation they are also more likely to attend to the observational cues. In the previously mentioned group of substance abusers, the men were asked what they thought they should be looking for in a modeled demonstration of refusing a "hit" offered to them. They suggested the criteria of firmness, brief answers, repeated simple refusal without explanation, and a calm facial expression. The group leaders recommended that they look for these characteristics in the modeling demonstration that was to follow.

Frequently, however, training may be required to teach clients how to attend to models, before they are given observational roles. One method is group exercises—relatively neutral, brief situations with clear-cut cues presented on videotape or in roleplays by co-leaders. The members are given a checklist of phenomena and asked to indicate those that occur in the demonstration. In the discussion that follows, the members compare results and give evidence to support their positions.

Prior to modeling (and rehearsal) roleplays, clients who have attention deficits are often provided a cue card with instructions to observe a narrow range of behaviors. As is usually the case with cue cards, their use is faded as soon as the members indicate they can operate without them.

Incentives for Observing and Imitating

Although clients tend to imitate certain models more readily than others, as Bandura (1977b) has pointed out, "incentive control of observational behaviors in most instances overrides the effects of variation in observer characteristics and model attributes." For this reason, modeling sessions are frequently combined with reinforcement procedures. Reinforcement of the model increases the probability that the client will imitate the model's behavior, especially if the model is rewarded in the presence of the observer. It also appears that an observer will reduce the frequency of behavior imitation in response to a model's punishment. It is important that the observer receive rewards for imitation of desired model behavior. In adult groups, the usual forms of reinforcement are leader praise, member approval (sometimes shown by applause), and success in achieving the goal established in the roleplay. Long-term reinforcement follows if the given client performs the target behavior effectively in the real world.

To make use of the principle of reinforcement of modeled behavior, one group leader invited a recently employed person to a group session of job seekers. The model was from the same general socioeconomic and educational background as the group members. Prior to the meeting, the group leader asked the model to tell the members how he prepared, what went on in the interviews, how long it took, and so forth. The members were encouraged to interview him further. The model in this case had been recently rewarded by getting a desirable job and further reinforced in the group meeting by the attention and praise of his peers. In the first step of modeling in this example, only general behaviors were modeled. In a subsequent meeting, the group leader modeled in a roleplay the specific job interview behaviors the members were likely to require. At the end of the interview, he had the "prospective employer" (a businessman invited for the purpose of the roleplay) state aloud that that was the best interview he had heard in a long time and he would have hired the group leader if he were looking for a job. In general, it is the role of the group leader to see that models are reinforced.

Characteristics of Effective Models

Although not as powerful as incentives, the characteristics of the model in part determine the extent to which a client imitates behavior (Bandura, 1977b). Some attributes of models may increase the probability that their behaviors will be imitated. These attributes include the high rewarding potential of the model, demonstration by the model of competence in areas highly regarded by the observer, and general prominence or relatively high social power with respect to the observer. To some clients, if a good relationship is established, the group leader may be regarded as having high rewarding potential. By virtue of their social role, some members may have a prominence not found in the group leader.

The similarity of models to the clients also increases the likelihood of imitation. The group leader may or may not be similar to the members in terms of socioeconomic status, race, ethnicity, and educational background. But something can be done about it. As discussed next in detail, group leaders can bring in former members, colleagues, volunteers, and others who are similar and who may also have those characteristics that increase the likelihood of imitation.

Sources of Models. Bandura (1977b) concludes on the basis of an extensive research program that the greater the number and variety of models available to the client, the greater the likelihood that the client will find adequate models to observe and imitate. The group setting offers the possibility of both number and variety. We therefore discuss a number of categories of potential models, including the group members, the group leader, invited guests, the individual client (self-modeling), and admired persons outside of the group. No one type of model possesses all of the desired characteristics. To compensate for deficiencies in one category of model, different people are selected to model a set of behaviors.

Members as Models. As pointed out earlier, the more effective models are those who show some of the observer's population characteristics (race, similar general problem area, age, sex) in addition to other attributes. For this reason, a major source of models is the group members. Two other important advantages of using members as models are that the model obtains additional practice while demonstrating to others and the group members report feeling that they are more involved.

The major drawback to this source is that many members have many socially maladaptive behaviors and only limited adaptive or coping skills. This is especially true in groups of members characterized by extremely similar problems, such as depression or common phobias. Yet, even in these groups, dramatic differences in coping skills and coping styles exist among members. Some are excessively self-critical. Some can cope with some types of situations but not others. Some have only one coping style, which is clearly not adequate for all situations. So almost all members have a skill they can model, but no one person in the group can serve as a universal model.

Another drawback to using members as models is that in roleplayed modeling, the group members who are most competent in dealing with a given situation most often serve in roleplays as models for the others. As a result, the more competent members may get much more practice time and reinforcement than the others. To offset this tendency, the group leader keeps track of the practice and modeling time and makes sure that it is equally distributed among members.

Group Leaders as Models. Although group members may be desirable models, certain behaviors may not be part of the repertoires of the clients. In these circumstances, the group leader may serve as model. Though they sometimes differ quite radically in age, education, socioeconomic status, race, and other characteristics from their clients, group leaders usually demonstrate a wider range of new coping behaviors than can clients. In addition, the group leader often (but not always) has greater reinforcement power than any one member of the group. The leader as model is able to provide a great deal more focus than the clients, with less risk that an undesirable behavior will be repeatedly modeled.

Of course, the group leader serves as a model in all of her or his actions, whether or not intended. The members select, from the total range of behaviors, often unpredictable elements. It is in roleplayed modeling that the greatest control can be brought to bear on the process. Both to focus on, and to obtain a wide range of, desirable (that is, imitation-inducing) characteristics in models, guests with such characteristics can be invited to the group and instructed in the behaviors expected.

Guests as Models. Although it is difficult to alter the membership of a group in the middle of its course, it is desirable to invite, as guests, persons who have behavioral and cognitive characteristics that are lacking in the group but are necessary to achieve treatment goals. For example, most of the members of a stress management group were successful businessmen. The level of self-disclosure was noticeably low. The group leader invited a former client to attend several sessions. (This person was even more successful in business than the group members and was willing and able to talk openly about the effects of stress on him personally.) As a result of his presence and participation, the group members became rapidly more self-disclosing. In another example, a group of black parents were unwilling to use roleplaying despite modeling by the white leader. An invited black colleague, also a parent, roleplayed with the group leader a particular common problem situation—a teenage son ignoring the requests of his parents. After several roleplays, members gradually became more willing to roleplay. The use of guests is particularly desirable when there are dramatic sex, racial, or socioeducational gaps between members and the leader.

Videotape Modeling. When videotape resources are available, it is feasible to tape modeling sessions for the clients and make VCR equipment available to review these tapes as extragroup tasks. The videotapes provide variety in the program and an opportunity for observation of multiple models. This extends treatment time beyond the boundaries of the group session. Videotaped modeling does not, however, offer the flexibility of the tailormade live demonstration. By combining live modeling with videotape presentations, both flexibility and repeated trials are achieved. A unique use of videotaping is for self-modeling.

Self-Modeling. Clients can also be encouraged to observe their own effective behavior. Even though a client complains about social deficiencies in a given set of circumstances, there are usually some situations in which a client has functioned in a highly adaptive manner.

The most powerful means of self-modeling is to have the

client repeatedly observe her or his own adaptive or effective behavior in a given situation on videotape. Before the taping, the client is well trained through observation of other models, extensive rehearsals, coaching, and feedback so that the taped performance is highly suitable for the problem situation. The tape is reviewed by the group, and, if appropriate, the client is assigned to view the tape several times a day. If the modeling is well executed, the tape may serve as a model for other clients before their tapings. This process provides a unique opportunity for mutual aid and, as a result, engenders a great deal of enthusiasm among the members. Because of the investment of the other members, the given client is more likely to make use of the tape than if it had been produced commercially or by the group leader.

Modeling Through Scripts. Sarason and Ganzer (1969) have utilized written scripts in both modeling and rehearsal with groups of institutionalized delinquents. With the understanding that most delinquents' models are antisocial adults and older clients, the scripts were used to demonstrate the effectiveness of establishing new, socially acceptable, and, hopefully, exciting models for the delinquents. In working with juvenile offenders, my colleagues and I (Brierton, Rose, and Flanagan, 1975) asked that the group members rewrite the Sarason and Ganzer scripts. The very process of script revision involved the group in formulating a realistic appraisal and definition of their situations and in developing effective interactions to resolve the difficulties they confronted. The predetermined script has been used less frequently with adults; however, it seems particularly efficacious with groups who are not very creative or have limited roleplaying skills.

Assignments to write an "ideal behavior" script can facilitate both observation of others and generation of alternative behaviors. Although scripts are mentioned here as a source of models for the group leader, we discuss them at greater length later in this chapter under Behavior Rehearsal.

Real-World Modeling. Systematic observations by the client of persons outside of the group meetings (in the "real world") provide useful and accessible models. The group leader can help the

clients to identify persons in their natural environment who can
serve as models. By assigning clients to observe these models in
particular situations, the group leader can draw on a rich and varied
source of demonstrated behaviors.

Each member of a group of parents was requested to find one
person he or she really admired and to observe that person in a
parenting role several times during the week. At the end of the week,
they were to describe the specific parenting behaviors and general
parenting characteristics of the model. Almost all of the members
discovered some characteristics they did not admire. Then each
person chose, as a target, a particular subset of behaviors the group
leader and the members roleplayed.

General Versus Specific Modeling Strategies

Most of the examples we have utilized deal with a highly
concrete set of observable behaviors. As Bandura (1969) has pointed
out, "Modeled characteristics that are highly discernible can be
more readily acquired than subtle attributes which must be
abstracted from heterogeneous responses differing on numerous
stimulus dimensions" (p. 136). The particular behaviors selected are
often crucial subsets of a complex situation. In learning these
subsets, the client may eventually be able to handle the entire
complex situation. Complex sets of interactions can, however, be
modeled in their entirety. Usually, these more general roleplays
follow, in hierarchical fashion, a series of subsets containing
required behaviors of more limited scope. In some groups, it is
possible to move directly to the more general situation. Because of
previous learning or innate capacity, some clients are able to learn
the general approach to dealing with problem situations without
learning all the detailed intermediate steps. What this means
practically is that complex behavior patterns should, as in the
previous examples, be modeled globally first and then broken down
only into those smaller units that the client has difficulty duplicat-
ing. The smaller units are more readily modeled, rehearsed, and
reinforced. Then the global situation can be modeled once again.
An advantage of doing both is that some concrete behaviors related
to the general approach may already be in the repertoire of the client

and, therefore, not all the requisite skills may need to be modeled. Moreover, the capacity of a given client to generalize from previous experiences is not ignored. Since roleplayed modeling and rehearsal are the most commonly used modeling techniques, they are discussed separately in the following sections.

Roleplayed Modeling

In this section, roleplayed modeling is discussed as a technique in the modeling sequence. Let us begin with an example and discussion of the modeling technique (or the demonstration of target behaviors), because this is the first step after assessment and goal setting. Many of the previously mentioned principles are illustrated by this sample.

Group Leader: Now that we have discussed ways of approaching Ellen's employer, I wonder if we couldn't roleplay for Ellen exactly what she might say or do in that situation. Does that sound good to you, Ellen?

Ellen: I'd really like that.

Group Leader: Marianne, you seem to have ideas that came closest to what Ellen wants to say. Would it be OK if you play the role of Ellen? And Brian, since you are an employer, would you mind playing the role of her boss?

Marianne: OK with me.

Brian: Me, too.

Group Leader: Great. Let me just review what we agreed on. [Group leader reviews the results of the brainstorming and the statements Ellen decided she wanted to make.] Brian, don't be too hard on her the first time through. But don't forget to be excessively patronizing. Ellen and the rest of you are observers. Especially keep track of what they do well. OK, let's start. Ellen, why don't you remind them of the situation?

Ellen: OK, I was in the office, and there were a bunch of people around. The boss had called me in to explain the new computer changes. Since I am supposed to be the expert, he asked me where they should be located. When I told him, he said that it amazed him how "girls" like me could do this kind of scientific work. He added that I'd probably be much happier staying at home and having babies. I get mad all over again, just thinking about it.

Group Leader: Here's your chance to put your anger into action. We've set up the room pretty much like your boss's office. Don't forget: knock at the door, enter the room, make it as real as possible. Let's begin.

Marianne (as Ellen)   [knocks at simulated door]

Brian (as boss):   Come in, Ellen. Sit down, make yourself comfortable. [Waits while Ellen sits down.] You know, Ellen, you really do good work; that's why I called you in [then, as an aside, with a little laugh], but I imagine you'd be much happier being at home raising babies like my wife.

Marianne (as Ellen):   I appreciate your approval of my work, but I'm not sure I really understand what you mean by that last remark. I'm also a little surprised that you can read my mind to tell what turns me on.

Group Leader (seeing Brian at a loss for a response, whispers): It was meant as a compliment. Not so touchy.

Brian: Oh, I only meant it as a compliment. You don't have to be so touchy.

Marianne (looking him right in the eye and speaking slowly and emphatically):   Well, I didn't take it as a compliment. I experienced it as a put-down and a sexist remark. In most ways you've been a helpful boss; I certainly appreciate your cooperation and your praise, but I really become annoyed when you make remarks like that. I'd really appreciate it if you didn't do it anymore.

Group Members (laughter, applause)

Group Leader: OK, let's stop there. That strikes me as being a great way of handling it. How about you, Ellen?

Let us review some of the principles of modeling demonstrated in this example. First, the group leader reviewed for the model what the situation was and what she might say. The leader selected as a model a person who felt comfortable playing the role and who made the best suggestion in "brainstorming" as to how to handle the situation. Furthermore, the leader attempted to make the situation as similar as possible to the real-world situation.

In choosing the "boss," the leader tried to find someone similar to the real boss. At the same time, because this was the first of many modeling trials, the leader urged the "boss" to take it easy. Roleplayers can make the model or the rehearser fail if they make the situation particularly complex and difficult.

The leader kept control of the roleplaying. He prompted the significant other (boss) when he was at a loss for words. As a first modeling session, the leader kept the demonstration brief. When the model successfully responded to the sexist boss, the leader stopped the modeling session. In this way, the model was reinforced for her success. The leader encouraged the group to reinforce her further.

One additional principle of learning theory, stated by Bandura (1977b), is that practice in the modeled behavior increases the probability that a modeled behavior will be duplicated in the real world.

Behavioral Rehearsal

After observation of one or more modeled interactions under most of the conditions described earlier, the probability that a client will duplicate the modeled behaviors in the real world increases. Practicing these behaviors in the supportive environment of a group meeting further increases the likelihood of performance of those behaviors in the real world. The client is better prepared to recognize cues and deal with a problem situation. The client is also less anxious. Such practice in a group meeting usually involves the leader or members playing the roles of significant others in the situation while the client plays his or her own role. This procedure is commonly referred to as behavioral rehearsal (Lazarus, 1966). The rehearsal is usually carried out first at the group meeting; however, assignments are often given to rehearse or roleplay a given behavior with a partner, a friend, or a family member in a setting outside the group, to increase the number of practice trials. The importance of independent and frequent trials offsets the possible damage incurred by practicing the wrong behavior, which can be corrected at a subsequent meeting.

Rehearsal techniques (often combined with modeling and other procedures) have also been used widely to teach the unemployed job-finding and interviewing skills (Azrin, Flores, and Kaplan, 1975; Kelly, Wildman, and Berler, 1980). In such programs, clients are taught to locate job openings and to present themselves more effectively in the job interview. Sometimes, clients extensively rehearse the job interview to increase their ability to convey information on past job-related experience, to direct questions to the interviewer, and to express enthusiasm in the job.

In our groups, we have used these procedures along with modeling to develop a wide range of skills such as being assertive in setting rules for children, negotiating with a spouse, dealing with daily interactions at work, asking in-laws not to interfere in the disciplining of children, requesting help from grown children, and asking a former spouse for the money owed. Before examining the principles involved in behavior rehearsal, let us review the rehearsal that followed the modeling session previously illustrated.

Group Leader: Now that you have seen one way of doing this, Ellen, would you like to try it yourself?

Ellen: It's a little scary, but I think I can do it. Could Brian be my boss, too? He was perfect. He sounded just like my boss at work.

Group Leader: Is that all right, Brian?

Brian: Yeah, I don't mind. In fact, it's sort of fun.

Group Leader: Great! Why don't you review what you are going to do again, Ellen.

Ellen [reviews aloud what she is going to say]

Group Leader: That sounds right on target. [Dramatically] Let the action begin, Brian.

Brian (jovially):   Come in, Ellen. [Seriously] Ellen, I want you to know that you really do pretty good work; I'm really surprised, since computers are really men's domain. I can't help believing that women would be much happier being at home raising babies and taking care of their husbands and home, like my wife.

Ellen: I appreciate the compliment. But that last statement! Do you really think you can read my mind and tell what is or isn't important to me?

Brian: Oh, Ellen, don't you know a compliment when you hear one? You sure are touchy.

Ellen (looking around the room and speaking rapidly):   You have a strange idea of what is a compliment. I felt that what you said was a put-down and a sexist remark. And you make them quite often. Up to now, I've just ignored them. But enough is enough. I would like you to stop it. I don't think it helps our relationship.

Group Leader: I think that's a good stopping point.

Group Members: Great, Ellen! That's telling him! [Light applause]

Principles of Effective Roleplayed Modeling and Behavior Rehearsal

A number of principles of effective roleplayed modeling and behavior rehearsal are demonstrated in the preceding example. The same principles apply to both modeling and rehearsal and are discussed here one at a time.

Eliciting Maximum Involvement. In preparing Ellen to roleplay, the group leader had Ellen review what she was going to say. In later sessions, such reviews are not necessary. Ellen also chose her own significant other on the basis of his realistic performance in the modeling session. Ellen's involvement was maximized because she was encouraged to depart from the model's verbal behavior and try out what she liked best.

The group leader could have involved the other members in Ellen's roleplay by utilizing their recommendations prior to and feedback after the roleplay. The leader could have asked the group to determine the characteristics of the significant other in the roleplay. The group could develop its own feedback system. Involving the client and the group whenever possible is a theme running throughout this book. It is often costly in terms of time, but effective in terms of the client's owning the procedure.

Reinforcing for Success. The group leader stopped the roleplay when Ellen successfully dealt with the problem situation. Often, roleplays are allowed to go on too long, which ultimately might result in failure. If roleplaying is to be reinforced it should always be stopped on a positive note. The group leader not only ended the roleplay when Ellen was successful, but in earlier sessions he had encouraged the members to respond with applause and praise at the end of the roleplay in which the given client was successful. According to Bandura (1977b), reinforcement of the imitator increases the likelihood that she or he will duplicate the behavior in the real world. Reinforcement cannot be offered unless the client is actually successful. For this reason, the group leader must structure the situation so that success in the modeling or rehearsal is highly probable.

Structuring for Success. In the early rehearsals, the group leaders or members may model only one or two responses, which the client attempts to duplicate in the rehearsal. As the client becomes competent in these few responses, the significant other in the roleplay makes an increasing number of counterstatements. The object is, first, to provide the roleplayer with early success and, then, to work toward the more complicated and extended conditions of the real world.

The client playing the significant other must be instructed to keep the situation relatively easy in the beginning. The group leader acts as a director, making sure that the difficulty created by significant others is only gradually increased. All too often in their flair for the dramatic or in a need to compete, the roleplayers enacting the significant others (often an antagonist) create situations that are impossible to solve. In such cases, the group leader stops the roleplay immediately and reinstructs the antagonist to "take it easy" on the client. To ensure early success, initial roleplays should be brief and relatively easy for the client to perform.

Increasing the Level of Difficulty. In addition to increasing the length and complexity of rehearsals as treatment progresses, new situations can be added.

Entire curricula of canned situations for different problems (developed in advance of the sessions by the therapist or others not in the group), that range from less difficult to more difficult, have been developed. An example is that of Goldstein, Carr, Davidson, and Wehr (1981), who advise that the content of the vignettes should be varied and relevant to the lives of the trainees. It is helpful to let the members revise the vignettes in the group meetings to fit their interests and circumstances.

Eventually, in long-term groups, situations are rehearsed for which no preparation is carried out and no modeling is presented. It is assumed that at this point in the treatment process, the member has learned enough basic skills to generalize to similar situations or even a novel situation. Before this phase is reached, extensive training is required.

Repeating Rehearsals. Obviously, one rehearsal is not sufficient to teach a client a given set of behaviors. Replication by others with similar problems, replication in homework assignments, and replication in pairs in the group are all ways of maximizing the advantages of rehearsal. In a group of four to seven clients, providing every client a chance to roleplay repeatedly requires a great deal of creativity and effort. (See Chapter Fourteen for additional suggestions.)

Multiple rehearsals take a lot of time. To use the group efficiently to carry out multiple trials, the group leader can provide the stimulus situation for each client one at a time in rapid succession. The group leader fits the stimulus to the individual client's situation. This is often done as a review at the end of a meeting. Obviously, this exercise works best if only one type of response is being taught; however, it is possible even if different responses are required. It should be noted that in a period of five minutes there can be as many as five rehearsals and model demonstrations since each rehearsal by one client is a model for all the others. This repeated practice exercise also requires extensive experience in roleplaying.

Setting the Stage. Actors knock at doors, enter rooms, use props, separate themselves from the audience, and rehearse under the most realistic conditions. To make the roleplay realistic, the group leader or the person rehearsing sets the stage by reviewing briefly the events leading to the situation, the situation itself, and the scene in which the event takes place. The client may take a few seconds to remember what she or he felt and thought at the critical moment.

Preparing Members to Roleplay. In early group sessions, some clients may be very anxious about roleplaying. They may even refuse to participate. In such cases, roleplaying behaviors can be introduced incrementally. First, roleplaying is modeled by members who are more comfortable. Even then, only relatively nonthreatening situations are enacted at first. Board games that instruct the participants to roleplay a simple situation have been helpful. It seems to be easier for some clients to accept and follow through on instructions for a game than on the requests of a group leader. Games can be used only if the clients feel comfortable with one another and the group leader. Otherwise, they may experience the games as patronizing.

After some preparatory rehearsals, the group leader might ask reluctant group members to simply state what they would say aloud without movement or affect. Clients may be more comfortable if they privately rehearse the lines before roleplaying with appropriate movement, affect, and voice volume. Members of the group may be instructed to rehearse in pairs without an audience to ease them into roleplaying before the whole group. The more hesitant clients might also be requested first to roleplay a significant person in another client's situation, for example, a parent or a friend. The first roleplays usually consist of one-sentence replies, as in the earlier example. Gradually, responses increase in length, again easing the client into roleplaying.

Offering assistance to those who find roleplaying difficult provides an early therapeutic opportunity and enhances relationships.

Coaching

In coaching, the leader or another member assists the client by whispering prompts or instructions during the rehearsal. Coaching is used primarily with clients who are anxious or unsure of themselves. These clients find it extremely helpful in their first roleplay. After one or a few coached rehearsals, the coaching is usually phased out.

The coach usually sits immediately behind the roleplayer and instructs her or him to speak a little louder, "to be firmer," and to ask for help. A variation of coaching is the use of cue cards or hand signals to remind clients of what they must attend to. For example, to instruct a client who speaks extremely softly to speak loudly, the coach will place his finger on his mouth. Or, the coach will remind a client to give eye contact by pointing to her own eye.

To control the level of difficulty of the roleplay, occasionally the group leader coaches the significant other. The significant other has the power to make the roleplay so easy that the client learns nothing or so difficult that the client fails. Although instructions to the significant other may help, coaching seems more effective.

Feedback

Feedback is the process of providing a given individual with information, observations, and impressions of that individual's performance or general attitudes in real life or in a roleplay. The feedback may be given by fellow group members, the group leader, and/or significant others of the client. Under optimal conditions, feedback is a highly effective teaching strategy; however, if delivered vaguely or in a hostile manner, feedback may damage the person receiving it. Constructive or therapeutic feedback from multiple sources is a major advantage of group therapy, provided that the therapeutic criteria for delivery of the feedback are met. Clients not only gain information they can use to improve their behavior, they also learn to give and accept positive and critical feedback in real-life situations.

Behavioral rehearsal accompanied by feedback has been found superior to rehearsal alone (McFall and Marston, 1970) in increasing effective assertive behaviors of adults. The importance of feedback in the learning process led Bandura (1977a) to conclude that everyday learning is usually achieved through modeling, performance, and self-corrective adjustments made on the basis of feedback.

In this section, we review the general guidelines used in providing feedback, the specific criteria used to evaluate the performance of peers, the techniques of giving feedback after a rehearsal or reviewing a tape, and training in feedback. To illustrate these procedures, we revisit the group described earlier in this chapter. The following group process described below begins just after Ellen's behavioral rehearsal.

Group Leader: Would everyone now write down as many things as you can think of that Ellen did well in the roleplay. Ellen, you can write, too. [After a brief pause] Now would you write down one thing that you might have done differently. [After a moment] You all seem to be filled with ideas, the way you've been writing. OK, first, what did you think she did well? What did you write?

Brian: I really liked the way she wouldn't let me wiggle out of it by calling it a compliment. She really let me know how she felt. Frankly, I was impressed.

Group Leader: Good, I see others nodding in agreement. That's one thing Ellen did very well. What else? Anyone else have any ideas.

Marianne: I didn't like. . . .

Group Leader (interrupting): Let's wait until we get all the ideas that you did like on the table. Then we can talk about the things you might have done differently.

Marianne: I forgot myself. Actually I thought that what she said was right on the mark. Especially, when she said that it had happened lots of times. She confronted him with the whole pattern.

Glenda: I'd like to learn how she just stood right up to him, with him being the boss and all that.

Group Leader: There's quite a bit that Ellen seems to have done well. Anything you might have done differently?

Marianne: Now's my chance! [Laughing] I guess what I might have done differently was to look Brian in the eye. I thought you were looking at the floor too much.

Glenda: What you did wrong was. . . .

Group Leader: There I go again, interrupting, but perhaps it's better to formulate it as your own opinion or what you might have done differently.

Glenda: Yeah [laughs nervously], that's something I need to work on. What I thought you might do differently was to speak a bit more slowly and with greater emphasis on some of the key words, the way Marianne did when she demonstrated it. But I agree that the words themselves were great.

Mike: I want to get back to the content. I thought it was well done for the same reasons everyone else liked it. Only I think you ought to add something positive, like "In all other areas we seem to get along really well" or "You've been helpful to me in other matters." We talked about that when we were setting goals.

Ellen: I agree with all that. I especially need to work on eye contact and speaking more slowly. I think I'd like to put something positive into it too, because he is a good boss in other ways.

Group Leader: Okay, in general, we all seem to be saying thus far that the content was good but some positive statement could be added, and that eye contact and a slower rate of speech need to be worked on in the next rehearsal. I have one last concern. There is some risk involved in taking the assertive role in this case. Ellen, you're the one that has to face that risk.

Ellen: It's a lot riskier for me to do nothing. He just seems to be
escalating the remarks. I've got to say something for my self-respect.

After this feedback session, Ellen was asked to summarize
what she had learned from the others and to consider what she
thought she might like to do differently. As often occurs, an
additional roleplay was performed so that Ellen could try to
incorporate the new ideas she liked. She was also given the
homework assignment to roleplay the situation with her "buddy"
before she tried it out in the real world.

Guidelines

Before being asked to offer feedback on a fellow member's
rehearsal, members are given guidelines, many of which are
illustrated in the preceding example.

Writing Down the Feedback. In the early sessions, all clients
are asked to put their feedback in writing. This stimulates far
greater involvement. Otherwise, the more assertive clients would
dominate the feedback presentation. This requirement is eliminated
as all members gain experience.

Giving Positive Feedback First. Positive feedback should be
offered first so that the client is reinforced as soon as possible after
the rehearsal of new skills. Also, the positive feedback increases the
probability that criticism will be accepted. The leader can moderate
by asking the critic to hold off on the criticism until the positive
feedback is stated.

Formulating Criticism as Suggested Alternatives. Criticism
should be stated as the actions or statements the observer would
carry out or make differently. "What I would do differently would
be to speak a little louder and have a little more eye contact," is a
desirable form of critical feedback. In the earlier example, when
Glenda said, "What you did wrong was," the group leader said
"you mean, what you might do differently?" In doing so, the leader

lessened the harshness of the criticism dramatically. Although criticism is an essential part of feedback, it is possible to take some of its sting away and thus reduce negative side effects.

Specifying Behavior. Whether positive or critical, feedback should be specific. To the criticism "You should be more careful in dealing with your friend," the group leader may respond "how would she be 'more careful' in that situation?" or "to be more careful, what exactly would you do or say if you were in that situation?"

Summarizing Feedback. After the first session the group leader summarizes the feedback, sandwiching the critical feedback in with specific achievements and positive comments. For example, "In summary, Ellen noted that she appreciated the compliment, expressed her feeling about the sexist statement, and asked for a change in behavior. Some of you think she might show a little more eye contact and speak just a little more loudly. All in all, she is becoming quite accomplished in handling sexist statements on her job." In subsequent sessions, the leader asks clients to keep notes on the feedback received and to summarize it aloud for the group. If necessary, in a rehearsal the member incorporates the feedback that she or he found helpful in the situation. The client is the final judge on the usefulness of the feedback.

Training in Giving Feedback. As pointed out earlier, feedback is a powerful but also a dangerous tool. Some clients are reluctant to be the recipients of it. Others do not know how to accept it appropriately. Still others use it far too critically. In teaching group members to give and accept both positive and critical feedback, we first provide them with criteria, which are developed prior to the modeling. Criteria for the earlier example might include the following questions.

Did the client ask for a change of behavior?
Did the client use good voice volume, eye contact, and posture?

Did the client express her feelings about the action of the significant other?
Did the client find something useful in what the significant other said?

A particularly useful training exercise is a roleplay in which the group leader makes a number of mistakes in giving feedback. The group then discusses the leader's performance. In requesting feedback, the leader encourages the members to adhere to the criteria. After the discussion, the leader or one of the members can model how feedback should be accepted. Finally, the leader evaluates with the group how well they adhered to the criteria and what still needs work.

Group members are taught both to give and to accept positive and critical feedback for two reasons. First, it is a skill needed to facilitate effective rehearsals and effective correction of errors in these rehearsals. Second, it provides the client with essential interpersonal skills that facilitate effective and satisfying interaction outside of the group. For these reasons, a significant amount of time, especially in the early sessions, is devoted to the training and use of these skills.

Variations on the Modeling Sequence

A number of variations are possible in the use of rehearsal. Variations add to the general interest of the members in the program and increase group cohesion. Also, clients tend to learn more when taught in different ways. Just as scripts are used for modeling, they can be used in rehearsal; however, they should gradually be dropped, as should all other structures, to increase the likelihood that the client can operate in the real world without a crutch (script).

Role Instruction

A variation of scripts commonly used with adults is role instruction. Role instruction requires that the client take a "model role" and act as if she or he were really that person. This procedure can be utilized during ongoing group interaction; that is, a new role may be played while the group discusses other tasks. For example, one member who tended to elaborate excessively on all issues assigned herself the role of a person who made only succinct comments. She permitted herself no more than three sentences per comment. She asked her neighbor to let her know if she "ran over."

Another example of role instruction is seen in the case of Doran, who rarely participated in group discussions or other social events even though he was quite intelligent and, when pushed, had demonstrated that he had many interesting ideas. The group members designed an extremely assertive role for him. He was required (and occasionally prompted) to interrupt and introduce his ideas. With an observer, it was possible to count the frequency of certain behaviors. The leader also asked Doran to double the amount of his participation in the group. A few particularly difficult situations were rehearsed in the normal manner. Doran reviewed the instructions at the beginning of the session. The group leader sat next to him and encouraged him when he seemed to slow down. After the fifteen-minute roleplay, the group evaluated Doran's performance, showed enthusiastic approval, and suggested how he might have interrupted more effectively. Subsequent roleplays were gradually increased in length to the point where Doran spent an entire session in the role.

To add greater structure to a role instruction exercise the group leader can prepare individual, written role descriptions specific to the difficulties each member is experiencing. In pairs, the members further develop instructions for each other and, during the session, play their new roles as accurately as possible. At the end of the session, members guess the roles played by each other and evaluate the effectiveness of their performances.

Fixed-Role Therapy

Fixed-role therapy, developed by Kelly (1955), is similar to rehearsal and role instruction. In this treatment modality, the initial assessment of a client is used to construct a fixed-role sketch for the individual. This sketch is carefully planned to include desirable behaviors but the details are left to the "player." The selected behaviors are usually adaptive ones that are not being performed at the beginning of therapy and are frequently markedly different from the presenting behaviors.

After the initial practice sessions, the client is urged to try the behavior in the real world and to observe the reactions of others in his or her life. At first the client is encouraged to play the role as if it were just a role. The assumption is that playing "as if" reduces the threat incurred by performing new behaviors in the real world. The role can be explored without commitment, and because of the intentional lack of detail, the client is free to modify the new role so that it is comfortable.

Group Exposure

In a unique form of modeling, group members model target behaviors for each other in the real world. The members thus provide each other mutual support in the achievement of complex and often feared tasks. As mentioned earlier, Bandura (1977a) points out that not only can modeling be used to teach new behaviors or increase the frequency of already learned behaviors, it can also be used to disinhibit behaviors that have been inhibited. Agoraphobics are exposed as a group to feared, real-world events, to disinhibit their approach responses. This method is called group exposure. This special case combines modeling and in vivo flooding. It is an in vivo (as opposed to roleplayed) modeling procedure in which agoraphobic and sociophobic clients in small groups discuss visiting public places, such as streets, markets, and crowded buses, draw up a plan, and carry it out. In carrying it out together, they observe and support each other; modeling occurs in the real world. Preparation may involve roleplayed modeling in the treatment setting. The tasks to be performed in the real world are usually graded from less to more difficult. Because group exposure is a well-developed and complete treatment package, we will look beyond the modeling component and describe the entire package and its specific support.

Clients are first presented with a theoretical justification and a description of what they can expect (for an excellent example, see Emmelkamp, 1982). Generally, clients are assured that they will not be forced to do anything they do not want to do or that they feel will bring about panic. This assurance is essential not only for ethical reasons, but also to prevent the clients from immediately dropping out. The reasons for the group are also explained (for example, the modeling effect, mutual support, sharing experiences, seeing that one is not alone with this very serious problem). Considerable time is spent explaining phobic behavior, the irrational element attached to it, and how the group will help its members face the day-to-day events that shape their world.

Most group sessions comprise three parts. In the first part, the group discusses the extragroup task completed during the preceding week, the exposure exercise they will perform as a group after the in-agency session, and any spontaneous accomplishments.

In the second part, the group members leave the meeting room and go out in the real world together to face the anxiety-producing situations. Each in a sense becomes a model for the other. Different methods are used to effect the actual exposure of the clients to public places. One method commonly used is described by Emmelkamp and Kuipers (1985). The group goes out together, the members supporting each other along the way. They are encouraged not to hold on to each other but, initially, to walk near each other. After a given period, the members are encouraged to walk at some distance from each other. The first members to complete the task serve as models for the others. In later sessions, clients go off a little way on their own. The group then returns together to the group setting.

In the third part, the members discuss their experience and design a similar extragroup task to be completed between sessions. In general, the extragroup task should not be more difficult than the task practiced in the session. Some form of monitoring of the extragroup task is advised. Extragroup tasks are always reviewed at the beginning of the next session, and success or failure, feelings, thoughts, and the degree of group support needed for the next group task are discussed.

Generally, activities are graduated, from those that produce mild anxiety to those that produce high anxiety, to avoid provoking an anxiety attack. Examples of situations that produce high anxiety are shopping in a crowded supermarket, riding in a crowded elevator, and taking a crowded bus.

The speed with which individuals are able to carry out the graduated exercises varies from person to person. The clients who learn more rapidly seem to serve as models for the others; however, it is important that clients function at their own pace, to avoid a panic attack.

The following example illustrates group exposure.

In response to a description of the program in the agency's newsletter, seven women indicated interest in a group for people who found it difficult, if not impossible, to leave their homes alone. In initial telephone contacts, the group leader assured the women that they would never be forced to do anything they did not want to do. Six women attended the first meeting. After the assumptions on which the approach is based and the nature of agoraphobia were discussed, the women decided that they would like to try out the exposure method. The leader invited a guest to talk about her experience with the procedure. The group agreed that they must be actively involved in solving their problem. With the help of the leader, they designed activities that they would carry out together in subgroups: shopping at a mall, going to a movie, visiting a number of church singles' groups, attending other functions where there would be single people, making a second visit and talking to three people whom they did not know, taking a two-day bus tour, going to a crowded dance, in subgroups. Finally, they would go to any social activity alone. As a group they ranked these activities in terms of difficulty. When they disagreed on ranking, the average was used. The members agreed to monitor weekly the activities in which they participated and the length of time spent in each activity. The leader helped the members to select procedures they could use to handle panic or intense anxiety, such as deep breathing and concentration. Also, the leader emphasized that members should look only at their own levels of achievement, not those of others, because of the differences in pace and problem severity among members. After completion of the first subgroup exercise, going to the mall, the members returned to their meeting place; they reported their experience, analyzed cognitive distortions such as "people would see that I'm crazy with fear," and discussed the difficulties encountered and how these were handled. The importance of relaxation was stressed by several women. The women showed much mutual support and shared a sense of accomplishment. They modified the next step somewhat by deciding to go to the mall just after it opened. They also agreed to spend some time alone, to ask for help from the clerk, and to ask someone for the time. These actions were modeled by those members who felt comfortable doing so and were rehearsed by the other members in extended roleplays. They assigned themselves the task of visiting a closed mall in twos or threes prior to the next session. A similar pattern characterized the next nine sessions (five-week period), with the tasks gradually increasing in difficulty.

Group Versus Individual Exposure. Compared with individual exposure, group approaches seem at least as effective and thus far more efficient (because one can deal with many clients at the same time) in achieving the same goals. A consistent trend noted by some authors is that patients treated individually show slightly less improvement than those treated in the group (see, for example, Hafner and Marks, 1976). Moreover, in some studies, there appear to be more dropouts from individual treatment. Emmelkamp and Van der Hout (1983) reported that some agoraphobics will not join a group, claiming that it is unsuitable for their problem. On the other hand, clients in groups are more easily persuaded than clients in individual treatment to try exposure exercises, probably because of mutual modeling and group reinforcement.

Long-Term Effects. In their study, Emmelkamp and Kuipers (1979) followed seventy agoraphobics, most of whom had originally been treated in groups, and found that after four years, on the average, almost all patients either maintained or continued to improve not only on agoraphobia but on other phobias and even depression. It should be pointed out that some were symptom free, some showed moderate improvement, and a few showed no improvement over baseline. Most of these clients had required some additional treatment after the original group therapy. The average number of sessions of treatment was eighteen. The content of the additional sessions is not known, but may have been necessary to achieve the success the authors describe.

Side Effects. In general, there has been no documentation of side effects of exposure on clients. Hand, Lamontagne, and Marks (1974) described a few cases in which nonagoraphobic spouses of agoraphobic clients developed various anxiety-related problems as the patient got better. At the end of treatment, several clients requested extra sessions so that they could achieve the level of performance they had seen others achieve.

Other researchers (Mathews, Jannoun, and Gelder, 1979) have reported success in involving spouses in the planning of exposure trials. Emmelkamp (1982) warns that such practices may inadvertently reinforce the dependence already existing between the client and the spouse in cases of agoraphobia. This issue must be dealt with on an individual basis. The advantages, then, of working with clients and their spouses at the same time would outweigh the disadvantages.

Summary

The modeling sequence—modeling, rehearsal, coaching, and feedback—is derived from modeling theory and is commonly used in the multimethod approach. The sequence is usually selected after the group has defined their problem situations and selected alternative interactive responses. Each component of the modeling sequence may be used alone or in combination with other procedures. After receiving feedback, clients usually rerehearse the situation, incorporating those suggestions they found most useful. Ultimately, the final rehearsal is followed by an extragroup task in which the clients employ what was learned in the group to the real world. Two variations of modeling are fixed-role therapy and group exposure. Group exposure is used primarily in the treatment of agoraphobia, and mutual modeling in the real world represents only one of the many intervention strategies employed.

NINE

Using Cognitive Strategies to Cope with Stress and Promote Change

In recent years, highly concrete strategies have been developed to help people change the way they perceive themselves or the situations they face. (See Ellis, 1974, 1977; Beck, 1976; Mahoney, 1974; Meichenbaum, 1986; D'Zurilla and Nezu, 1982; D'Zurilla, 1986). Often, the techniques employed consist of observing how clients describe and evaluate the actual situations and their thoughts in these situations. Also, the client is assisted in making a more realistic appraisal of a situation by talking him- or herself through it. To learn how self-talk and situation evaluation are related to anxiety, one must examine some assumptions about the nature of anxiety and stress.

Some Assumptions About Anxiety and Stress

Most clients who come to group therapy, regardless of the nature of the initial complaint, manifest some anxiety or stress. (We have not made a distinction between stress and anxiety, because both appear to be emotional responses with similar explanations.) These emotional reactions often occur in, prior to, and/or during the performance of certain tasks or in crucial situations. This anxiety often impinges on the client's ability to perform those tasks

Note: Many of the considerations discussed here are drawn from the ideas of R. S. Lazarus (1980).

appropriately or to act effectively in the given situations. Some people feel anxiety in so many situations that the anxiety is said to be generalized.

Anxiety or stress can be manifested in a number of ways, for example, heart palpitations, difficulty in breathing, tension, dizziness, tightness, shaking, and other physical complaints, such as headaches and stomach aches. (It is not always clear what is an anxiety/stress response and what is a purely physiological response; the two appear to be linked.) The intensity of anxiety seems to vary from person to person and situation to situation; the actual manifestations overlap but each person's experience is unique. Although the anxiety is usually related to a particular situation, it is not caused by the situation. It is mediated by the person's thoughts about or evaluation of the situation or his or her ability to deal with the situation. Sometimes, the anxiety itself is evaluated so that its intensity increases. It may eventually become an automatic sequence that occurs repeatedly under various conditions.

Anxiety warns people that they are in danger, that their physical well being is threatened. It is an emotional response that tells a person to change his or her present course of action. Some situations—a car suddenly cutting across one's path, for example—demand a rapid change in behavior. Sometimes, the danger is the client's own creation, the result of faulty evaluation of the situation. On being called into her boss's office, Lou Anna was certain she was to be fired because of a small mistake she made on an account the previous week. She was overwhelmed with anxiety until the boss merely asked her for some help on another important project. In most cases, the situation is evaluated as inherently threatening (primary appraisal) and an estimate is made of the availability of internal and external resources to deal with the threat effectively (secondary appraisal).

The threat may be perceived as physical harm or as rejection by others. The perceived threat seems to induce behavioral arousal (perhaps as a means of mobilization of the body in the face of threat). The arousal might take the form of fighting with persons in the situation, flight from the situation, freezing or inability to act in the situation, and/or total collapse of the person experiencing the anxiety. The intensity of the anxiety appears to be proportional to the estimate of danger in the situation.

Another example illustrates how anxiety is a function not of the situation but of the perception of the situation as a threat and the ability to cope with the threat. On seeing a red splotch on his forehead, Rodney immediately interpreted it as skin cancer and felt there was nothing he could do. He scarcely thought of anything but his impending death until he saw his physician. When the doctor informed him it was a simple skin allergy, the intense anxiety he was experiencing disappeared. Walter, on seeing a similar red splotch on his forehead, interpreted it as a cue to see the doctor. He said to himself, "it could be anything, so there is no sense in worrying yet." Thus, two persons confronted with the same situation experienced completely different reactions. Because they have different learning histories and different genetic makeups, they evaluated the same situation differently.

It is assumed that cognition occurs in response to external and internal stimuli. These cognitive responses are usually conscious or inferred thoughts, evaluations, expectancies, unstructured mind "noise," and images and their accompanying affect. Zajonc (1980) makes a distinction between "hot" or emotionally laden cognitions and "cold" cognitions to which little affect is attached. It is to the emotionally laden cognitions that much of the intervention is addressed. Cognitive responses may be logical or illogical, rational or irrational, self-defeating or self-enhancing, effective or ineffective.

Therapy is focused on determining clients' perceptions of anxiety-inducing situations and helping them to evaluate and respond to the given situations more effectively. Group members are often quite perceptive in identifying each other's ideational distortions of each other and in suggesting functional alternatives.

Several cognitive procedures are commonly used in groups and have some empirical support in the treatment of anxiety- and stress-related problems: provision of corrective information, cognitive restructuring, and self-instructional training. These approaches overlap each other as well as other noncognitive procedures. As each of these strategies is examined, the overlap is noted.

Provision of Corrective Information

Some clients are anxious or fearful simply because they do not have enough information about a situation they commonly encounter. More often, the client does not have adequate information and also holds onto distorted or inefficient beliefs or lacks the necessary coping skills. In the first case, providing the information is sufficient. In the second case, the corrective information is merely the first step in cognitive restructuring.

For example, in a group of persons with sexual disorders, a good part of the program was devoted simply to identifying commonly held beliefs and providing the members with information and research debunking the myths. In the earlier example, in which Rodney feared that he had skin cancer, the doctor corrected the cognitions of the client and as a result immediately reduced his anxiety. The role of the group was to help him to identify the limited basis he had for his assumption and to get him to his physician.

The group is an efficient context for the dissemination of information, if effective teaching procedures are used. Outlines, handouts, exercises, and overhead projectors elicit interest in the presentation and promote more effective learning in groups. Group discussion often clarifies issues. Moreover, the facts are more palatable when confirmed by several peers than the group leader alone. Of course, the risk of distortion of facts by ill-informed but totally convinced members is ever-present in groups. In such cases, the leader should note that he or she disagrees on the particular matter, but will check sources to make sure that the members get the best information available.

Orientation to the various techniques, as they are introduced, is a specific method of providing corrective information, which is integrated into other cognitive procedures such as self-reinforcement training.

Self-Reinforcement Training

Self-reinforcement is an important skill that only a few clients are able to master early in treatment. It is also a component of other cognitive intervention strategies. For example, throughout the self-instructional paradigm (see Figure 3) but especially in the last phase, clients are expected to covertly reinforce themselves. Also, in cognitive restructuring, employment of self-enhancing statements (to be discussed later) requires skill in self-reinforcement. We have found that simply instructing members to reinforce themselves more frequently is not sufficient because of the strongly accepted cultural norm that people should not brag, even to themselves. To this end, self-reinforcement training is utilized. Self-reinforcement training includes a brief orientation in which the importance of being able to describe oneself positively is stressed and its use in subsequent training strategies is explained. This exercise follows the orientation:

> Describe, in writing, at least two positive characteristics for each person in the group.
> In a loud, assertive tone, describe each person in the group in terms of the positive characteristics you have just written.
> As you are being described, write down what is said and, in a summary, list those characteristics you agree with (even a little).
> State your positive characteristics as convincingly as possible to the other group members.
> Provide feedback to each other on the presentations.

After the exercise, the group leader assesses the need for additional training. Usually, however, members are asked to consider self-monitoring their positive self-statements and to read them to the group at the next session. In long-term groups, the exercise is repeated at least once at a later session.

To a group of women who met because of what some described as a lack of self-esteem and others as depression, the group leader explained the importance of self-reinforcement and how it would be used in subsequent exercises. She then used the preceding reinforcement exercise. The leader had listed, in writing, the positive characteristics of each member prior to the meeting to make sure that each person received her share of praise during the exercise. She would have used the list only if there were insufficient comments from the members. The members and the leader came up with such statements as "she makes good suggestions to others in the group," "she listens carefully to others and is concerned about them," "she keeps us on task when we get off task," "she asks for help when she needs it," and "she pays attention to what others are saying." Some members were not sure of what they should include in their summary lists; the leader reminded them that if at least two other members of the group had described it as a characteristic, it should be included. Members checked with each other to verify the statements. When all members had completed their lists, they insisted that the leader also compose a list, and each member, amid much laughter, delineated the leader's positive attributes. The leader asked the group members to save their lists and to add positive self-statements as they observed them. She also noted that "because she was a quick learner, she would do the same." Several members committed themselves to keeping track of positive self-statements during the week and reporting to the members. On the postsession questionnaire, most members stated that they found the exercise somewhat difficult in the beginning, but noted that it was interesting or fun to do.

Cognitive Restructuring

Cognitive restructuring is the process of "identifying and altering the client's irrational beliefs and negative self-statements or thoughts" (Cormier and Cormier, 1985, p. 405). There are many approaches to cognitive restructuring. The approach discussed here is one that we have found particularly amenable to the group context and for which, as part of a larger package, we have found some empirical support (Tallant, Rose, and Tolman, 1989; Tolman and Rose, 1989; Subramanian and Rose, 1988). In general, this form of cognitive restructuring involves training in determining distorted cognitions through group exercises, ascertaining each client's own distortions, and identifying more functional cognitions to replace them. The client is then taught to replace the distortions through such techniques as cognitive correction, cognitive modeling, and cognitive rehearsal.

One of the earliest approaches to cognitive restructuring is rational emotive therapy (RET), developed by Ellis (1974). Because we sought a more behavioral approach that permitted a wider variety of potential interventions, we adapted the approach developed primarily by Meichenbaum (1977) and Goldfried, Decenteceo, and Weinberg (1974) to group treatment. Because Meichenbaum borrowed heavily from Ellis (1974), RET is briefly described first.

RET assumes that all anxiety-related problems are the result of magical thinking or irrational ideation. Some of these ideas lead to self-condemnation, others to anger, and still others to a low tolerance for frustration. The RET leader helps the client to identify those irrational ideas they hold as evidenced by their self-statements in stressful situations, their emotional reactions, and their behavior. Thus, the major intervention strategies in RET are verbal persuasion and teaching. The RET group leader uses the members as the major source of feedback, persuasion, and disputation of the irrational ideas. Ultimately, the client is taught to dispute his or her own irrational beliefs for which there is no supporting evidence and to recognize the effects of holding such ideas. Listed here are some of the more frequently occurring of Ellis's (1974) irrational ideas that we have encountered:

1. It is an absolute necessity that I be approved of or loved by every significant person with whom I come into contact.

2. I should be thoroughly competent and successful in every area, if I am to be considered worthwhile.

3. It is terrible when things are not the way I would like them to be.

4. All my troubles are due to external circumstances and there is nothing I can do about them.

5. If something is extremely difficult, troublesome, or fear inducing, I should think about it all the time.

6. It is better to avoid problems and difficult situations than to face them.

7. There is a perfect solution to every problem and my failure to find it is catastropic.

The multimethod approach draws on these irrational ideas to help identify and later to dispute distorted ideation. This list also serves as a basis for justifying why some thoughts appear to be self-defeating or self-enhancing, for definition of these concepts (to be discussed later). Ellis assumes that these irrational ideas are universal, whereas the authors cited earlier tend to individualize their approach by determining the irrational components unique to each person in each situation. Although in recent years Ellis has proposed additional techniques to supplement his major strategy of self-disputation of irrational ideas, the Meichenbaum (1977) approach to cognitive restructuring lends itself to a much wider variety of group and behavioral interventions. Finally, Meichenbaum places less emphasis on identifying negative statements and more emphasis on teaching coping alternatives. In fact, if a client is unable to identify the specific self-defeating ideation, the group leader can move immediately to training in coping behavior and cognitions.

It should be pointed out that people do not form well-developed, clear thoughts all the time. Many clients even fail to identify their thinking in stressful situations or images. They may first have to be trained in perceiving and identifying their thinking.

After they are oriented to the assumptions underlying the approach and demonstrate some skill in identifying their cognitions, members must logically analyze these cognitions. In this analysis, the client's appraisals of cognitions relative to problematic or stressful situations are examined. As faulty logic or dependence on nonfunctional cognitive events is identified, disputational procedures are applied to the evaluations. The group analyzes a given member's thinking in a specific situation and disputes the logic or the usefulness of certain cognitions. Once identified as self-defeating, the cognitions become the immediate target of change. Later, as a new list of self-enhancing cognitions is generated within the group, the self-defeating cognitions are replaced by the self-enhancing ones through cognitive modeling and practice, just as in self-instructional training (described later in this chapter). To clarify cognitive restructuring, the steps (Figure 2) as used within the context of the small group, are discussed here in detail.

Providing a Rationale

As Cormier and Cormier (1985) point out, the importance of providing an adequate rationale and overview cannot be overemphasized. It is a gradual process. The following rationale, adapted from Meichenbaum (1977), is one way to begin.

> One thing you will learn in this group is that how we think about and talk to ourselves influences how we feel and act. We can frighten ourselves by telling ourselves we are frightened. We can make ourselves feel bad about ourselves by calling ourselves names or putting ourselves down in other ways. We can also get rid of painful feelings by thinking about ourselves differently. Sometimes we tend to exaggerate, to make a terrible tragedy out of one small failure. And then we allow ourselves to put ourselves down because of the tragedy that we created in our head. We can often make ourselves feel better if we reexamine stressful situations with the help of our friends here in the group and find new, more accurate ways of thinking about problem situations and our responses to them.

At this point the group leader asks the members to provide examples of situations in which their thinking made them feel angry or unhappy or kept them from acting. If the clients have no examples, the group leader should have some case studies available to distribute to the group. It is also a good idea to bring up examples that arose in earlier discussions and to remind members of these examples. After a discussion, the group leader provides an overview.

> In this group, one of the things we will be doing together is looking at situations that make you unhappy or anxious and studying how you think about these situations. If what you are doing or thinking is not working for you, we

Figure 2. Steps in Cognitive Restructuring.

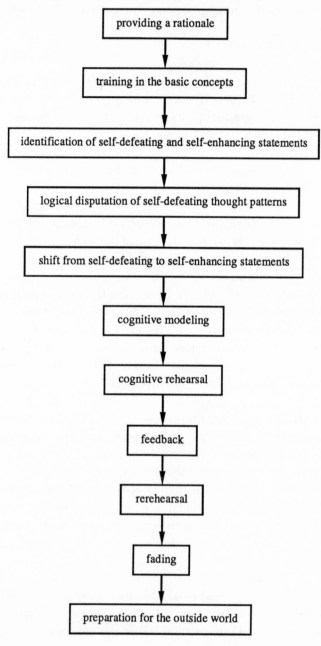

will try to help you find better ways of thinking and behaving in the situations.

In open groups or in groups in which there are members with previous group experience, we generally encourage the experienced members to provide the orientation. It may not be as polished as the leader's orientation, but members report that it is more acceptable. The group leader often helps prepare the client-orienter.

Training in the Basic Concepts

Clients should be made aware of at least two concepts of how people describe their cognitive responses to (or appraisals of) troublesome situations: self-defeating statements and self-enhancing statements. The statements are often silent but may be verbalized. These concepts, derived for the most part from the work of Meichenbaum (1977), and supporting examples are presented to the group members in the terminology given here. (The following material may be given as a handout to the group members and discussed rather than presented as a lecture.)

Self-Defeating Statements. Expressions of ineffective responses to difficult, stressful, or anxiety-producing situations are self-defeating statements. They are ineffective insofar as they prevent the person from acting in his or her own best interest. The statement itself makes the person more unhappy or anxious than did the actual response. For example, Harry would like to talk to the new employee. He says to himself, "Oh, she'll think I'm awfully forward coming up to her that way." Harry walks away, as he always does with people he would like to get to know. The statement leads to inaction, self-doubt, and increased anxiety. It interferes with Harry's goal to make friends. As such, it is self-defeating. Although there are many kinds of self-defeating statements, they all produce similar results. Sometimes they are quite obvious; at other times, they are inferred from actions or other statements.

To facilitate the identification of self-defeating statements, other, somewhat overlapping concepts may be used to describe what an individual is doing when making a self-defeating statement. These concepts, derived partially from Meichenbaum (1977) and Ellis (1974), but mostly from Beck (1976), are exaggeration, catastrophization, absolutizing, prophesying, self-put-downs, selective perception, excessive self-demand, and "centering." Depending on the intellectual skills of the clients, these concepts may or may not be shared with the group, but the leader will find them helpful in analyzing the unique aspects of a given self-statement.

Exaggeration, making a relatively insignificant situation important, is a common characteristic of self-defeating statements. For example, Jerry was not made a supervisor at work, although co-workers had said that he did better on the line than anyone else. He thought, "I'm not considered very highly at this place." His evaluation exaggerates the supervisor position and will probably be followed by an increase in the level of his anxiety.

Catastrophization is a gross exaggeration that makes a tragedy of some trivial event. In the preceding example, "I didn't get that job, my life is ruined," would be the catastrophization. Beck (1976) has found that this phenomenon is fairly common among sufferers of anxiety.

Absolutizing is making statements that suggest a given situation will remain unchanged regardless of changing conditions and nothing can be done to alter the situation. Such statements often contain absolute words such as *never, always, can't,* and *impossible.* When Harry states that no one will ever like him or Jerry says that he'll never get the job he wants, they are absolutizing. These statements generate a feeling of hopelessness that is clearly unrealistic and, hence, self-defeating.

Prophesying is predicting future unfortunate and unknowable outcomes. Jerry might prophesy, "Even if a new supervisory job opens up, it's my luck, I won't get that either." Many absolute and catastrophic statements also fall into this category. The danger of prophesying negative outcomes is that such statements may serve as self-fulfilling prophesies. The statements "I'm going to fail, I know I will" and "I'm sure I won't be able to sleep tonight" may contribute to or result in the failure and sleepless night.

Mind reading statements imply that one person knows what another person is thinking: "I can just feel he won't like me." "They think that what I do is stupid." "If I do that everyone will think I'm foolish or helpless." Anxious people often make such statements with no external evidence.

Self-put-downs are essentially negative and critical self-descriptions made without adequate evidence. Such statements lack any positive component unless this is sarcastically expressed. Usually, such statements are quite general. When Henry spilled the milk, he thought, "What a dumb, clumsy idiot I am. I can't do anything right." (Also note the exaggeration and absolutizing in this example.)

Selective perception is focusing on one small negative event and discounting the rest of the situation. Arona, who is an excellent cook, made a mistake in the amount of salt she used in a certain dish. No one noticed, yet she said to herself, "See, I made a mistake. I hardly know anything about cooking." (This example also contains exaggeration.)

Excessive self-demand is reflected in the setting of unrealistic goals. Often the word *should* or *must* is in the statement: "I must get that job." "I must never make a slip of the tongue when I talk to others, or I will be a social failure." "I should always be pleasant and good natured, no matter what I really feel."

In *centering,* the client sees her- or himself as the object of others' statements. An assumption is usually made: "The boss really picks on me" (when in reality the boss picks on everyone).

Self-Enhancing Statements. Statements that are accurate, realistic self-appraisals or evaluations of a problem situation are self-enhancing. They may suggest appropriate action and facilitate an individual's movement toward set goals. These statements may be self-encouraging, for example, "that's something I've done well before and I can do it now if I try," or self-instructional, for example, "just take one step at a time." Usually, self-enhancing (or coping) statements do not stimulate strong negative emotions. They may even stimulate positive emotions, such as satisfaction or pride in achievement. Here are some additional examples of self-enhancing statements:

When his employer criticized him in a way he thought both general and unfair, Alan thought, "Wait a minute, that doesn't seem fair to me; I'd better ask her exactly what I did." Although, clearly, he was emotionally aroused by the criticism, he responded with a problem-solving statement.

In response to a feared encounter with a prospective employer, "Even though there are a hundred applicants, I'll get the job" would not be self-enhancing because it is unrealistic. A self-enhancing statement would be: "Although there are over a hundred applicants, by being prepared and clearly presenting my qualifications, I will give myself the best possible chance of getting the job." As for self-defeating statements, some clients may need help in identifying the self-enhancing statement appropriate to a given situation.

Identification of Self-Defeating and Self-Enhancing Thoughts

After defining and providing examples of self-defeating and self-enhancing statements, the group leader asks the members for examples.

As further practice, the leader distributes the following exercise and asks members to identify the self-defeating and self-enhancing statements. The group leader also asks members to explain why the cognition is self-defeating (that is, what type of self-defeating statement it is).

Read the following statements carefully. On the basis of our discussion thus far, indicate which statements are self-defeating and which are self-enhancing. Give reasons for your answers (for example, the person is *catastrophizing* or *absolutizing* the situation).

1. (before taking a driving test) No matter what I do, I'll never be able to pass my driving test.
2. (Theodore explains why he goes to pieces in interactions with his wife.) When she "pushes my button," I just can't control myself.
3. (Sylvia has just received news about the loss of a small

amount of money.) See that's just my luck. What can you do when you have luck like mine?

4. (Henry sees a young woman at a dance with whom he would like to dance.) If I ask her to dance, I know she'll refuse me. Women like her don't like men like me. So what's the use?

5. (Manuel was typing a letter and forgot a word.) Oh my God, I made a mistake! That's disastrous. I'll have to fix it. What a waste of time.

6. (during a job interview) I may not get the job, but I certainly won't get it if I don't try.

7. (before a job interview) No sense in trying to get the job, with all those applicants I won't get it anyway.

8. (after being assigned a new complicated task at work) Sure it's difficult, but if I take one step at a time, I'll probably get it done.

9. (on opening a test booklet) I can see that this test is too hard for me. I can't answer the first question.

10. (just before a physical examination) It's going to be an awful experience. Those doctors seem to want to embarrass me and scare me half to death with their questions. I won't even be able to talk.

After individually responding to these statements, the members discuss their responses in the group. If the group is large (eight or more), division into two subgroups may provide a greater opportunity for participation. The purpose of the exercise is to give members the opportunity to identify both self-defeating and self-enhancing statements and to help them understand how these might influence social functioning. On the postsession questionnaire, members rated this exercise as very valuable.

The next exercise makes it possible for clients to disclose cognitive statements they have been known to make. To encourage self-disclosure, the leader relates his or her own experience first. We have found that when the instructions for self-disclosure are written, as in an exercise, compliance is more likely.

1. In this exercise, write two statements, one self-defeating and one self-enhancing, that you have used in the face of

stressful or problematic situations. Your statement can be
similar to one in the preceding exercise but should fit
your situation.

2.   Divide into subgroups, present your statements, and let
other members explain why the statements are self-
defeating and self-enhancing.

Once again, the members discuss in subgroups the self-
defeating and self-enhancing statements they have identified. We
have combined the two in order to avoid a completely negative
focus. If a person cannot think of one or both statements, he or she
is encouraged to use statements a friend or family member makes.
(In early sessions, some clients are not prepared to reveal self-
defeating statements; however, group pressure and modeling by
others eventually encourage most members to disclose relevant
material. No one, however, should be forced to self-disclose.)

Once each group member has identified several situations,
response patterns may become apparent. For example, in one
situation, Millie responded, "I can't meet new people. I'm sure I'll
blow it so I don't even try." In another situation, she said, "I'm
always too tired in the evening to go anywhere." After the second
comment, Ryan suggested that maybe Millie tends to absolutize her
responses to most situations, as evidenced by the frequency of
"never," "always," and "can't" in her responses. He suggested that
maybe she could focus in the group on reducing such absolutizing.
Ryan described the pattern in the form of a hypothesis: He
suggested a reason, provided evidence, and told Millie what action
she might take. As the same types of self-defeating statements
appear in response to most stressful events, patterns can be
identified.

It is useful to help the client to identify these patterns and to
focus on finding alternative cognitive strategies as early as possible
in treatment. By dealing with cognitions that are frequent, the
leader can more readily generalize from one situation to another and
prepare the client for situations that have not yet occurred: "I
wonder if Peter's tendency to see himself as the center of almost all
events at work, which he has identified, is apparent in his life
outside work?" "Isn't this situation similar to the time Peter became

upset with an overly demanding delivery man?" Such questions help the leader to elicit group comments.

Logical Disputation of Self-Defeating Thought Patterns

After a member identifies a problematic situation and the self-defeating statement used to respond to that situation, the group leader models the situation and self-defeating response first and asks the group members to do the same. After everyone has presented a situation, the group leader reviews his statement and asks the members to dispute it using the following criteria (most of which have been adapted from Beck, 1976):

Is the logic faulty?

Are any of the logical errors mentioned earlier present (for example, exaggeration or mind reading)?

What evidence is there that the statement is accurate?

What is the probability that the feared outcome will occur?

What is the client's perception of the "degree of awfulness" of the predicted outcome?

What is the client's evaluation of his or her ability to prevent the feared outcome from occurring and to deal with the worst possible outcome should it occur?

What past success has the client had in predicting dire outcomes?

As the members discuss the example, the leader coaches them in the use of these criteria.

One at a time, the members present their statements for disputation. Even if the clients have already recognized their statements as self-defeating, they are encouraged to present the statements, because group disputation brings out the specific self-defeating characteristics of the statement. All of the disputational techniques are applicable to group therapy provided that the members are trained in disputational argument. It is often easier for the members to dispute the arguments of others with the aid of their peers than to dispute their own statements. Through peer pressure and self-modeling, the clients learn to dispute their statements.

In the following example, the group disputes a statement made by one of the members in response to the earlier exercise.

Shearon: Well, when I'm a little depressed or feeling bad about something, I tell myself that I can't do any simple task, like writing a letter. Maybe, I really can, but at the moment it seems impossible. Yesterday, for example, I wanted to read that material you asked us to read for the meeting. It had been a bad day and I said to myself, "I just can't read it. I'm just too down." It was only two pages, too.

Group Leader: If I understand you, sometimes when you're a little down, you might tell yourself you can't do something, when in fact you have the ability to do so? [To group members] Why would that be an example of a self-defeating statement?

Millie: Well, the way she describes the situation to herself keeps her from doing anything. It certainly doesn't help her to get out of her depression.

Ann: Besides, because she doesn't do anything, she feels bad about herself. Maybe it makes her even more anxious. I'm an expert on that since I do the same thing.

Jean: Isn't that what we called absolutizing? She says she can't and that's final. I suppose if you tell yourself you can't, you're finished.

Several Others [laugh, then nod agreement]

Group Leader: Shearon, I wonder whether you can't summarize, with feeling, the reasons that your statement is self-defeating?

Shearon: Well, I'll try. Let's see. When I say I can't do something when I'm depressed, it keeps me from doing anything. It's kind of an excuse, I guess. It's . . . what do you call it . . . ah, absolutizing, too. Nothing is that absolute. Let's see now. Oh yeah, it makes me feel worse about myself. My self-esteem drops to nothing. That's all I remember. In any case, it doesn't do me much good.

Group Leader: That's fantastic. You sounded compelling. Are you and the rest of the group convinced it is a self-defeating statement? [Everyone, including Shearon, nods agreement.]

To develop more effective responses, the group leader in the preceding example continued:

Group Leader: Since you seem to agree, Shearon, then it seems to me it would be helpful in such situations to be able to tell yourself something different, like: "At times like this, it sure is difficult to do anything, but I should at least try." Why don't we all write down any ideas we have as to what Shearon might say that would be self-enhancing, under the same conditions.

As is always the case in brainstorming, no one, not even the leader, should be permitted to evaluate a given suggestion until all the suggestions have been presented. Often, this process is sufficient to generate a large number of potential self-enhancing statements. Sometimes, in the initial phase of treatment, clients may have very few ideas. Presenting theory in advance, with examples thrown in, enriches the brainstorming process.

In cases of centering ("I'm the only one his criticism is meant for"), Beck (1976) suggests a procedure called decentering, in which the client is asked to respond as if she or he is *not* the focal point of all events, for example, "She's aloof from everyone, not just me."

Watzlawick, Weakland, and Fisch (1974) use a procedure called reframing for clients who label their behavior in such a way that anxiety increases. Reframing attempts to change the point of reference against which the clients judge their behaviors and cognitions. For example, when a parent says, "I'm a bad parent because I'm so anxious when my kid does anything wrong," another group member or the group leader might reply, "You are a concerned parent. You need only a more effective way of showing that concern." Another procedure, reattribution, is utilized when the client assumes an excessive amount of control over negative outcomes. There was a general cutback in the workforce at the plant where Arthur works, to which he responded, "It's my fault I've been laid off. I'm a failure as a husband and a father. If only I had worked harder." A reattributed statement might be "It's really rough being out of work, but I can't put the blame on myself. There are two hundred other men, some senior to me, who are also out of work.

I've always been a hard worker and good provider. Now, I've got to pull myself together and see what my alternatives are."

Whatever the method used, after potential cognitive or verbal alternatives are developed, they are evaluated by the client, who selects those statements she or he finds most accurate and most useful. Although the other group members and the leader may help in the process of evaluation, the ultimate decision as to the kinds of self-enhancing statement to be utilized is the client's.

Shift from Self-Defeating to Self-Enhancing Statements

After identifying their self-defeating statements, clients must replace them with self-enhancing statements. They are taught to make transitional statements such as: "Stop!" "Shift!" and "That's no way to look at it!" after they make a self-defeating statement. They should voice these loudly and assertively. (Later they may whisper them.)

The client describes the sequence: situation, self-defeating thought, emphatic transitional statement, self-enhancing statement. On the basis of this initial summary, the client may choose to try out the new responses in the real world. Disputation, discovery of self-enhancing alternatives, and summarization may be sufficient preparation. Two very powerful tools that help clients become more comfortable in the application of new cognitions are cognitive modeling and cognitive rehearsal. Cognitive modeling and cognitive rehearsal can be used to train clients in positive self-talk alone, without disputation or transitional statements.

Cognitive Modeling

In the next example, the group leader and the group members have helped Vern to identify his self-defeating statements in a specific situation, a possible transitional statement, and self-enhancing alternatives. Vern has just summarized what he wants to do.

Group Leader: OK, I think I understand what you want to do.

Let's see if I can't demonstrate it to you. Correct me if you want to do it differently. First, I'll describe the situation.

[As Vern] I'm feeling really down because of all the arguments at work. I get home and the first thing my wife says is, "Hon', would you mind taking out the garbage, and I need some help with the table." I think to myself, "Why does she always dump on me. She knows I'm tired." I really feel angry. [Emphatically] "Cut it out Vern [firmly], just take a deep breath and relax; she can't mind read and besides, she doesn't always pick on you—that's just not true. You can calmly ask her if she doesn't mind waiting until you get your stuff together."

Did I get the situation pretty much as it was?

Vern (nods approval):   Yeah, that's the way it is.

Group Leader: Is that pretty much what you wanted to say?

Vern: Yeah, but I doubt if I can do it that well. That's what I'd like to do.

Group Leader: Would you like me or someone else to demonstrate this again for you. Just to get another picture of it?

Vern: I don't think so. I guess I'm ready to try it myself.

Group Leader: Just use your own words. It doesn't have to be perfect; my words certainly weren't. I'll set the situation for you.

The interaction between the group leader and Vern is cognitive modeling. The purpose is to demonstrate how Vern can shift from a self-defeating statement to a self-enhancing statement. The model describes the background to the situation, the self-defeating statement, and the transitional statement ("Cut it out," "Stop!") and then models the agreed-on alternative response. Although, early in treatment, the group leader does most of the modeling, as the members grow in experience, models are drawn from the group.

Cognitive Rehearsal

The same example is used to illustrate cognitive rehearsal. Note that the first time, the group leader sets the scene.

Group Leader (flatly):   It's a familiar scene. Get yourself into how it feels. OK? You've had a tough day at work. Everyone seemed to be on your case. You no sooner get through the door than your wife shouts, from the other room [dramatically], "That you, hon'? Would you mind getting the garbage? And see what you can do about the table." [Whispers] OK, respond!

Vern: I think [angrily], "Who does she think she is, bossing me around like that? Doesn't she know what a hard day I've had? Why does she always pick on me like that?" [Pauses to think, then loudly] "Cut it out, Vern! Stop it! Take a deep breath—that's it; let it out slowly. You know damn well she can't read your mind. She's not picking on you—she's just asking for help."

[In the session from which this extract was taken, Vern later behaviorally rehearsed what he wanted to say aloud to his wife.]

A number of variations of cognitive rehearsal are available. In one, the leader or another member can initially make the transitional statement if that is easier for the client. Eventually, however, the client assumes responsibility for the entire sequence— description of the situation, original response, transitional statement, and new self-enhancing statement.

Feedback

After covert rehearsal, as after overt rehearsal, the group members provide feedback. The feedback is usually focused on whether there was a response to each critical moment in the given situation and the quality of those responses. In addition, in most groups, feedback is also focused on the fluency, completeness, logical consistency, realism, and tone of the self-statements.

Group Leader: That's quite good, Vern. I hope you convinced yourself. What did the rest of you write down that you liked about what Vern said?

Howard: He changed it a bit from what you demonstrated, but I liked what he said better. It was more realistic. It was more "him." He said it as if he really meant it.

Warren: Vern, I think you were complete in what you said. You told yourself to breathe slowly and then you corrected yourself. I even like the loudness of your transitional statement. I'm sure it made you take notice.

Michael: You pretty well kept to the things you said you wanted to be able to do when you made your plan. I guess that's the most important for me.

Group Leader (after a brief pause):   Is there anything that any of you might think or communicate differently?

Vern: I was still angry when I shifted the responsibility to myself, but I transferred my anger to myself. But I never did stop being angry. I don't know whether that was good or bad.

Warren: My feeling is that that was good. In the way you did it originally, you were threatening the relationship. In the way you did it in the roleplay, you were likely to come up with something that enhanced the relationship.

Michael: I felt that you said it to yourself a little fast. You didn't let it sink in.

Group Leader (after a brief pause):   I think these comments should be helpful, Vern. Why don't we try it just one more time? Is there anything you want to change? OK, only this time you might try setting the scene yourself.

Rerehearsal

Once the feedback is given, the cognitive rehearsal is usually repeated. The second time, the roleplayer takes into consideration the nature of the corrections. After the second cognitive rehearsal, the group leader goes on to the next person in the group. When all the members have practiced their own situations aloud, the next step is *fading*.

Fading

In fading, each client simply repeats the covert rehearsal, first whispering it, then saying it to herself. In the group, we have found it useful to whisper responses in pairs, so that the number of trials is increased and the partners can monitor each other. Moreover, after several trials, the members no longer need the leader to monitor them. Since the rehearsal cannot be heard and thus is not disruptive to the others, all the members in the group can rehearse their covert responses at the same time. The group leader, as shown here, guides the final rehearsal, after requesting the members to review the stress-producing situation and their typical responses.

Group Leader: OK, imagine you are in your situation. If you forget the details, look at your card. Think of others involved—what are they saying or doing? Now think how you would normally respond to the situation. Imagine how you would feel. Now [emphatically] stop yourself and go on to a self-enhancing statement. OK, let's stop and discuss how it went.

Variations. Simply practicing aloud for too long a period may gradually satiate the client, making him less attentive to the rest of the learning process. Interest can be increased by variations in the procedure. The process can be videotaped and shown to the group for more careful perusal and feedback. Clients can be assigned home exercises in which they argue with themselves in front of a mirror. Group members can be instructed to reinforce each other for each appropriate counterargument. Round-robin group argumentation is used, in which group members, one at a time, argue with the client who must practice the self-enhancing statements very quickly. This last technique is similar to the "point-counterpoint procedure" suggested by Beck (1976) and readily lends itself to the group context.

Imagery Training. To prevent clients from losing interest in the roleplaying, imagery can be used in cognitive modeling and rehearsal. Imagery is the process of calling up visual, auditory, and olfactory images to the client (Anderson, 1980) as realistically as possible. Its purpose in treatment is to elicit cognitive and physiological components of emotional arousal to situations that are impractical to reconstruct in the real world. Imagery also permits the identification of emotional themes and patterns of importance to the client. Clients may also use imagery to help them relax, as discussed in Chapter Ten. Two other common uses of imagery are in systematic desensitization (Wolpe, 1973) and in preparation for group exposure (Hand, Lamontagne, and Marks, 1974).

Some clients find it difficult to generate scenes with a sufficient sense of reality (Wolpe, 1973). For these clients, such cues as sounds or smells associated with the situation may facilitate the visual cues. Some members must be trained to improve their imagining skills. The group leader asks the members to imagine a neutral scene visually, and then gradually adds other sensory characteristics. The leader monitors the process by having the members indicate if the imagery is being realized. If not, she asks them to clear their minds and start over again with a simpler image.

In one group of clients with general anxiety and depression, the leader asked all the members to imagine they were sitting in bumper-to-bumper traffic. She provided them with as many cues as possible, and then asked: "Now tell us what you hear, feel, see, and smell." The members responded, "I can smell the car fumes and it's making me sick." "I hear the honking and people swearing at one another." "I'm getting mad waiting in line." "I'm so hot I can't stand it." "Everywhere I look I see cars: red ones, green ones, sports cars, station wagons." The members then discussed how vivid the images were. They compared the intensity of their images. Then the leader repeated the exercise with a combination of the most prominent images, and once again the group discussed the intensity of the images. The same exercise was repeated in pairs, with each person in the pair being the leader for the other, to provide additional practice in imagery and to let each member serve as the leader.

Imagery plays an important role in preparing clients for performance in the real world. We have postponed the discussion of this phase of cognitive restructuring until the end of the next section, since self-instructional training and cognitive restructuring employ the same procedures for such preparation. Self-instructional training is similar to cognitive restructuring in its reliance on cognitions, cognitive rehearsal, cognitive modeling, and preparation for the real world, but is different in purpose and in some of the steps.

Self-Instructional Training

The purpose of self-instructional training is to help the client get through a difficult and usually ongoing situation through the use of subvocal instructional self-statements. To clarify self-instructional training, the steps are examined in detail relative to the small group (Figure 3).

Providing a Rationale

As in cognitive restructuring and most other procedures discussed in this book, the first step in self-instructional training is to provide the clients with the rationale for its use. The following explanation has been used both with adults and with adolescents.

Today, we are going to learn a technique for helping ourselves get through difficult situations. As you know, almost everyone talks to themselves. I certainly do. We can employ that tendency to help us face a series of changing situations one step at a time. For example, last week I was supposed to give a speech to the staff at the agency. I was really nervous about it. So as I went into the meeting room I told myself to be calm and to remember that I knew more about my subject than anyone else in the room. I kept reminding myself to look at them and not at my notes, because I knew what I was going to say. When I made a slight mistake, I reminded myself that everyone can make a mistake, and just kept going. It really helped.

What we are going to do is to learn special ways of talking to ourselves that might help us to get through difficult situations. First, we are going to take a look at the steps that

Figure 3. Steps in Self-Instructional Training.

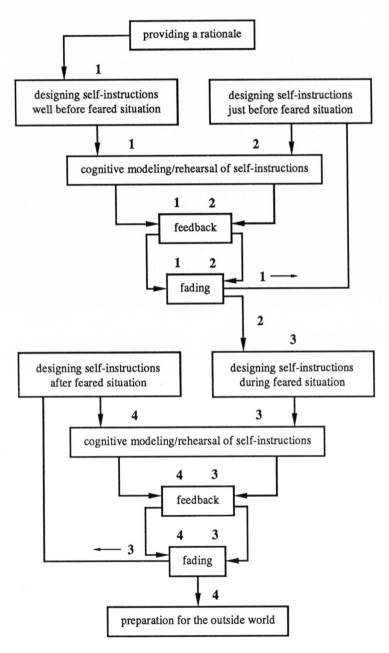

need to be performed in each situation. Then we are going to demonstrate to each other what each of us could be saying to ourselves to get through these steps. We will practice these self-statements, first aloud and then to ourselves. Are there any questions? [Group leader answers questions.] Does anyone else have any experience with this? [Encourages others to tell of their own experiences.]

There are many different tasks that we can talk ourselves through, for example, when Naomi has to make a speech in class, or when Eugene has to go through the sequence of events involved in being interviewed by a prospective employer, or when Phillipe has to put together the swing set for his son Luke without exploding at everyone in the house.

In the preceding example, not only did the group leader explain the procedure, she demonstrated how it might be used in a problematic situation (her own). Finally, she drew on situations that she knew were problematic to group members, to link the procedure to their experience. After presentation of the rationale, the leader helps the members to analyze the problematic task (situation) by breaking it down into its component parts. It should be noted that tasks can be interactive (as in going through the steps of telling one's spouse how one might feel) or noninteractive (as in balancing one's checkbook).

Self-instructional training is similar to cognitive restructuring insofar as self-instructional statements are often self-enhancing or coping statements that the client is learning. (A self-enhancing statement is a form of coping statement. In self-instructional training I prefer to use *coping statement*, since the statement is used to help the client cope with the situation.) It differs from cognitive restructuring in that less emphasis is placed on disputational techniques and self-defeating statements and more emphasis is placed on the client's development and use of a unique set of instructions and self-supportive statements for each of four different phases: before the event (several hours or even days before the event, usually when the client starts worrying), immediately before the event, during the event, and immediately after the event.

Designing Self-Instructions

In each phase, coping statements appropriate to that phase are developed. Initially, coping statements are suggested by the group leader. As the group gains experience, the other members may propose ideas to the client. Clients select those self-instructional statements with which they are most comfortable. Note these examples of phase-specific, self-instructional statements (adapted from Meichenbaum, 1986):

Well Before the Event

No sense worrying about it until it's in front of me.
Just relax, you've done it before, you can do it again.
Focus on what you have to do now, not on then.

Just Before the Event

You've done it before, you can do it again.
Concentrate on those first few words.
Take one step at a time. The first step is take a deep breath and let it out slowly.
Pretend this is just another rehearsal.

During the Event

Take one step at a time.
Take a deep breath, let it out slowly. Now concentrate on the job to be done.
Keep it up, you can do it.
Focus on the task.
Slow down. Remember to problem solve. What are some other alternatives?

Immediately After the Event

Hey, you did it, and you didn't fall apart.
If you talk it through you can do it.
OK, now relax, walk off with the confidence you deserve.
I've done it again. It'll still be better next time.
It wasn't perfect, but I keep improving.

Cognitive Modeling, Cognitive Rehearsal, Feedback, and Fading

After generation of self-statements for the four phases, just as in cognitive restructuring, the group leader models, the members rehearse and receive feedback, and the overt behaviors are faded. It may not be necessary to go through all the phases. The client need only go through those phases with which he is having difficulty. Self-instructional training is a time-consuming process. If one person gets too much attention, the rest of the group may lose interest. For this reason, when self-instructional training is used in the group, the leader either focuses on common situations from which all members will profit or provides each member with an active role regardless of whose situation is being handled. Also, by plan, those who do not deal with their situation one day should be assured that they will have an opportunity in the next session.

Variations in Cognitive Rehearsal Procedures. As in overt rehearsal, it is sometimes useful to coach the client, especially when the client is anxious. The leader may coach or may designate a member to be the coach. Coaching should eventually be eliminated.

Beck (1976) suggests that clients be instructed to roleplay a situation with a feared outcome as if they had no fear. The one persistent self-instruction the client uses throughout is "act as if I have no fear." The client may also be continuously coached with the same expression. The group members can discuss how disabling the anxiety appeared to be. If this procedure is used, modeling may not be required. Although most clients seem to find this generalized instruction extremely difficult, a few clients rapidly learn the desired behaviors and associated cognitions.

Combination of Behavioral and Cognitive Rehearsals. As Coyne (1982) notes, shifting from self-defeating to self-enhancing cognitions or being able to talk oneself through a difficult situation is useless if the fundamental behaviors are not in one's repertoire. If a person does not have the substance (content) for a speech, no matter how much cognitive restructuring takes place, the individual will not be able to make the speech. It behooves the leader to investigate whether the requisite overt behaviors are available to a client before initiating the cognitive procedure.

It is not always possible to ascertain the presence of a behavior in the repertoire of an individual, but a simple description or a roleplay of what a client perceives she or he would do in a given situation might provide some evidence. Often, clients describe or perform in great detail what they would do, but comment afterward that they never could do it in real life because of one or another faulty assumption about themselves or their situations. In these instances, some form of cognitive intervention is appropriate.

On the other hand, failure to perform or even describe adequately indicates that some training in overt target behaviors through problem solving, the modeling sequence, or other strategies is first required. Often, even though there are cognitive barriers to performance, the modeling sequence alone may be sufficient to train the client in the desired performance.

The combination of the modeling sequence and cognitive restructuring is effective in bringing about change. These strategies can be supplemented by operant, recreational, small group procedures to further enhance the learning climate.

For the reasons mentioned earlier, a final rehearsal, in which all phases are integrated into one long combined cognitive rehearsal/overt rehearsal, is often added. The cognitive elements are emitted in a stage whisper and the overt elements are spoken aloud. In this example taken from a parent group, Edna rehearses meeting her child's first-grade teacher.

Edna: Let's see now. The situation is this. In an hour I have to see the teacher. I begin to feel anxiety mounting. I think to myself, "Edna [she talks in a loud stage whisper], it's all right to be a little nervous—you haven't done this before. You know what you have to say. It's perfectly all right to tell the teacher that Jay is not getting enough time reading. If she doesn't like it that's her problem."

Group Leader: OK, it's an hour later now. There's the teacher, Mrs. Simna. You begin to feel the tension.

Edna (in stage whisper): "OK, Edna, just relax. That's it. Remember, you have every right to ask her. Walk over to her with confidence. Good. Get her attention." [In a loud voice] Hello . . . hello, Mrs. Simna.

Group Leader (as Mrs. Simna):   I only have a few minutes. The kids will soon be back from lunch.

Edna (in stage whisper):   I feel tense. I think to myself, "I can do it. I've done things like this before. It's important for my child. Just relax, concentrate on breathing normally, regularly. OK, focus on what you have to do. Now begin." [In a loud voice] Mrs. Simna, I would like to speak to you about Jay's reading. He really likes what you have been teaching him. [In stage whisper] "You are doing fine. Keep it up—just breathe naturally." [Aloud] I was wondering if there is any way that you and I could make a plan to increase the help he is getting? [In a stage whisper] "Now you've done it, Edna. It wasn't as bad as you expected—good for you!"

Group Leader (as Mrs. Simna):   Well, if you think it is necessary.

Edna: Yes, I do think it is necessary, but of course I need your help, since you're the expert. [In stage whisper] "Well done, Edna. That's the way to do it."

Group Leader (stopping the rehearsal):   Good for you, Edna, you did a great job. I hope it wasn't too confusing going through all those phases and back and forth between your thoughts and your words. It didn't seem like it.

Edna: Actually, it wasn't bad at all.

Edna utilized the self-statements to tell herself to breathe regularly, to focus on the task, to remind herself that she had sone similar things before, and to experience her initial anxiety as being all right. She could have also urged herself to use positive imagery as she focused on the task.

Preparation for the Outside World

Preparation for the outside world is the same for cognitive restructuring and self-instructional training. Modeling repeatedly, rehearsing repeatedly, fading verbalized self-talk, teaching the general principles of effective self-talk, and providing clients with an opportunity to teach others are all strategies for increasing the likelihood of transfer of the new cognitions to the real world. Group members are also instructed to record in their diaries more complex situations, which they present to the group at the next session. The group leader may, at the same time, design hypothetical situations with gradually increasing levels of difficulty, in the event that a client does not have an inappropriate situation. Of course, the final means of effecting generalization is for members to assign themselves the task of carrying out the newly learned self-instructions in the real world. Although such assignments are not readily monitored, the clients do describe their experiences to the group at the beginning of the next session. In Chapter Thirteen, specific strategies and homework assignments are discussed more fully. Here, we introduce some of these principles as they apply to assignments with cognitive components.

The ultimate goal of self-instruction is performance in the real world of the tasks the clients set as goals. At the end of each session, clients design a plan for trying out what was dealt with in the group during that or earlier sessions. A number of principles (most of which have been suggested by Beck, 1976) should be considered in development of the plan. Clients should be advised that they do not have to do anything they cannot or do not want to do. Clients should be encouraged to choose an activity that interests them. It is usually preferable, if there is a choice, that the clients do the easy assignment first. If there is no choice, then the clients should proceed only with the first part of the task (subtask). Even when clients attempt to do the entire task, they should be encouraged to focus on one subtask at a time and not to dwell on the final product. As the client achieves one step, he should check how it feels and, if it is an acceptable level, try something a little more difficult. Clients should continue to monitor their anxiety level as well as their thinking while performing the assignments. Beck (1976) also advises that the assignments be neither too specific nor too general and that flexibility be permitted. Not every situation the client will face will be the same as those that have been practiced. The purpose in assigning homework is to engage the client in dealing with feared situations and not to do them perfectly.

The criteria should be reviewed with the group prior to the development of assignments. Although the group leader encourages certain types of extragroup tasks and there is mutual encouragement among the members, each client is the arbiter of his or her own assignments.

Assignments are usually designed in pairs, and after partners provide feedback to each other, they read the assignments aloud to the group as a form of public commitment. These and other principles of homework construction are elaborated on in Chapter Thirteen. At the beginning of the next session, the group leader should ask each member to summarize her or his achievements. What was tried out in the real world is reinforced by all the members when the achievement is described in the session.

Summary

Assumptions concerning anxiety and stress are outlined to explain why various cognitive procedures are used in treatment. Cognitive change procedures, including cognitive correction, self-reinforcement training, cognitive restructuring, and self-instructional training, are discussed and their application in the group is emphasized. Some problems inherent in these overlapping procedures are considered. The possibility of combining modeling and cognitive procedures with each other or with other procedures, or both, is briefly considered.

TEN

Involving Group Members in Relaxation, Breathing, Meditation, and Sociorecreational Activities

Relaxation procedures refer to self-inducement of a relaxed state by means of neuromuscular relaxation, breathing exercises, and meditation. In group treatment, these procedures have several purposes. First, they are used as the major form of intervention in the treatment of problems such as stress disorders. Second, and more often, relaxation procedures are used in conjunction with other intervention strategies in dealing with anxiety- and stress-related disturbances. Third, relaxation is taught as a skill that enhances the quality of life. Finally, relaxation procedures serve as a group contingency and as a stimulator of increased group cohesion. Let us examine each purpose briefly.

In a number of studies, the major structured intervention strategy in at least one of the research conditions was relaxation. For example, Reynolds and Coats (1986) found that short-term relaxation training in groups significantly decreased depression in adolescents. Cragan and Deffenbacher (1984) and Turner (1979) found that relaxation groups were either as effective as or more effective than other combined procedures in reducing anxiety and maintaining that reduction. In the treatment of test anxiety, Deffenbacher and Hahnloser (1981) discovered that relaxation was as effective as coping skill training. In summary, there is reasonable support for the use of relaxation training in groups as the only specific intervention to improve the ability of members to cope with stressful and anxiety-producing situations.

Although the context of treatment was the small group, none of the previously cited authors reported using group strategies or other interventions concomitantly with relaxation training. Even when relaxation training is the major intervention strategy, other nonspecified strategies are used as well. For example, in almost all cases, homework is encouraged and reinforced when carried out. In addition, the cognitive self-instruction to relax, to control one's respiration, or to meditate in the face of a difficult or feared situation is often incorporated into relaxation training and practiced in the group. Members often talk about stressful situations in the relaxation group. They problem solve informally with each other. Members applaud each other on success and offer sympathy about failure.

In other studies relaxation has been reported to be used as a part of a more complex package including cognitive restructuring or cognitive coping skill training, social skill training, and relational and group intervention strategies (for example, Cragan and Deffenbacher, 1984; Lyles, Burish, Korzely, and Oldham, 1982). In most of our groups, this combination has been the most common set of interventions. Use of this package is supported by a number of studies of quite diverse populations. Applications of relaxation and other cognitive behavioral and group strategies include teaching cancer patients coping skills, treating bulimia, coping with recent divorce, reducing the severity of depression, and reducing anxiety and stress.

In some groups, these relaxation activities become so highly valued that they can be used as group contingencies for the work done in the early part of sessions. Because most members seem to find the activity so enjoyable and restful, the relaxation training also seems to increase members' attraction to the group. Through the example and encouragement of other members, home practice is often established as a group norm. Since home practice is central to the achievement of stress reduction, it is not an insignificant reason for training clients in relaxation procedures in groups. Group norms may be established that pressure clients to carry out the home practice.

There are many excellent texts on neuromuscular relaxation (for example, Bernstein and Borkovec, 1973), respiratory control (Hewitt, 1977), and meditation (for example, Shapiro, 1980). Therefore, this chapter focuses on the unique application of these procedures in groups. The reader is advised to refer to the cited texts for more details on the procedures and further applications.

The role of the group in encouraging participation in another form of relaxation, sociorecreational activities, is also discussed in this chapter.

Neuromuscular Relaxation

Although the relaxation training referred to in most of the studies cited earlier was progressive relaxation, the variability across procedures is extensive. In this section, we focus on the specific group application of progressive relaxation training. Several basic approaches are presented because of the different intellectual and physical capacities of our clients. Variations on these approaches, specific uses of the group, and strategies for attaining generalization to the real world are also discussed.

Teaching Relaxation. Prior to training in relaxation as in all other intervention strategies, clients are provided with a rationale. The following points might be included:

Many authors have noted that relaxation comprises activities that are incompatible with anxiety and stress. For example, Everly and Rosenfeld (1981, p. 90) have stated that with persistent practice, you can build an "antistress" disposition. For some, with sufficient practice, relaxation can even become a life-style activity that may replace more stress-inducing activities. When a person is deeply relaxed, troubling situations often lose their importance. They can be placed in their true perspective. Many people find that they feel better about themselves after relaxation.

If it is learned through pregroup interviews that some members have had successful relaxation experiences, these members can be asked to discuss their experiences as part of the orientation. They are also asked to warn the other members about potential pitfalls. If they do not, the leader advises the group about the extremely rare but possible dangers of relaxation.

Although extremely unusual, some danger is associated with relaxation. If you are on medication, please ask your doctor whether the combination of relaxation and medication might produce uncomfortable side effects. If you have suffered whiplash or muscle cramping, avoid the tension part of the exercises. Occasionally, people have strange, frightening thoughts or experience dizziness along with the relaxation. In any case, do not get up quickly. Gradually end the relaxation and return slowly to activity. These side effects are extremely rare but, should any occur, feel free to stop what you are doing and talk to us or the group about it.

A brief group discussion of these potential problems follows. Training usually begins at a subsequent session to allow members time to check with physicians if necessary. For most clients, relaxation is taught primarily through demonstration, instruction, and practice in groups. As training progresses, members gradually teach and monitor each other, and the exercise becomes self-instructional; that is, the members instruct themselves silently through the various steps of the process.

The leader verifies that the clients are tensing a muscle group correctly before giving the instruction to relax. As soon as all members can correctly tense and relax one muscle group, the leader moves on to the next muscle group. The literature abounds with patterns of instruction, although alternate tension and relaxation prevail. The order in which muscle groups are tensed and relaxed and their size are the major factors. We describe here the procedure that we most commonly use with clients without major physical or intellectual disabilities. Before beginning, a relaxing atmosphere is created by dimming the lights, playing soft music, and hanging a "do not disturb" sign on the door. The leader orients the clients to the technique and possible reactions.

Last week we talked about the different ways of using relaxation. This week, as we agreed, I will demonstrate how you can use relaxation to deal with those situations that you feel make you tense, nervous, and angry. The first few times we do this, you may find it difficult to follow the instructions; you may itch or may feel the urge to laugh or move. [Note that the group leader gives the members permission to do what they are highly likely to do anyway.] Don't worry about it. You may feel at certain times or in certain parts of the body slight or extreme relaxation. When the relaxation is extensive, it may even scare you a bit. But you will learn to enjoy it. Now listen to me carefully and try to follow the instructions as best as you can. OK, loosen tight belts or other tight clothing. Take off your glasses and remove your contact lenses. Lie on your back [where there is sufficient room] or sit comfortably in your chair with your feet slightly separated. Place your arms alongside your body [on your lap if sitting] with your palms up and your hands open. [The group leader looks around and praises correct posture.]

I am going to ask you first to tense a certain part of your body, for example your fist, and then to relax it. Then I am going to ask you to notice the difference. Do not tense too hard; stop tensing if you feel the muscle group tighten up. In fact, feel free to stop any time you want.

Let's try it first with your right hand and right arm, and see how that goes. Focus on your right hand. Slowly make a tight fist, but don't squeeze too tightly. Concentrate on the tension in your fingers and your hand. Hold it for a few seconds. One, two, three, now give your attention to your right arm. Try to feel the muscles and then concentrate on tensing the muscles in that arm. Increase the tension throughout the arm from the hand to the top of the shoulder. Stretch the arm, but don't lift it, or you will tense other muscles. Keep your attention on the tension in your arm. Remain this way for five seconds. Slowly release the tension in your fist and then your arm. Your hand should be slightly opened once again with your palm up. Try to think about what is happening in the arm. Each of you will feel different things happening. Some may feel that the arm is becoming quite heavy and is sinking into the mat. If that worked all right, we'll go through the rest of the body that way. Now focus on your left hand and left arm. [The group leader goes through the same steps with the left fist and then left arm.] Now concentrate on the right foot and leg. Push the heel away and draw the toes toward you to avoid a foot cramp. [The group leader looks at each member to make sure the exercise is being done correctly.] Slowly increase tension until it reaches maximum, from the foot to the thigh. Stretch the leg but do not lift it. Wait five seconds in this tensed condition, focusing as much as possible on the leg. Now slowly release the tension in the leg. Some people feel the leg becoming heavy. Some feel it sinking into the floor. Some feel relaxation. Some note no difference. [The leader proceeds through the same steps with the left leg and then reviews the extremities.] Relax the right arm as much as possible, then the left arm, the right leg, and once again the left leg.

Turn your attention to the pelvic girdle. That's the area around your waist. To tense this area, tighten or contract the stomach (abdominal) muscles and draw them slightly upward. Then draw the buttocks toward one another. [Because with some clients, the word *buttocks* will stimulate laughter, this area can be avoided the first few times.] Forget the rest of the body and concentrate on this one tensed area. Slowly release the stomach muscles and the buttocks and let them sink heavily into the floor.

Direct your attention to the muscles of the chest. Gradually tense these muscles. Move your shoulders toward each other from behind. Tense the back and rib muscles. Gradually relax the chest box, the shoulders, the back, and the rib cage. Let your lower and upper body sink into the floor. Relax your arms and legs once again.

Focus on the neck. To tense it, pull back the neck toward the nape; hold it a few seconds and slowly release. You may note a difference between the tensed neck and the resting neck. Focus on the face. Clench your jaws; tense the cheeks, mouth, and eyelids; wrinkle the forehead. One by one, release the tension in the jaws, the cheeks, the mouth, the eyelids, and finally the forehead. Let these muscles feel the pull of gravity. Let your mouth fall open slightly. Go slowly once more through the entire body relaxing, without tensing, the feet, the legs, the pelvic area, the chest, the back, the arms, the shoulders, the neck, and the face. If possible let your body sink even further into the mat or chair. Hold it for a minute [later two to five minutes].

Don't jump up and run off. Move your fingers slowly, now your toes, now your arms and leg just a little, then a little more. Move your shoulders. Move your head back and forth. If you feel like stretching, stretch, increase the depth of your breathing, sit up, stretch some more, hold it momentarily. Now, if you feel ready, stand up. [Great care is taken to exit from the relaxed state slowly.]

Generalization of Learning. To achieve generalization of relaxation skills, relaxation is taught (following the suggestions of Cautela and Groden, 1978, pp. 7-78) in different positions: sitting, standing, walking, and lying down. Relaxation is practiced in different settings such as the workplace, the car, sports events, restaurants, every room of the home, and wherever the client experiences tension. It can be carried out in these different settings only when the client has learned a shortened form of relaxation.

To make relaxation a skill that can be used as the need arises, clients must first become competent in the procedure through practice at every session and daily between sessions. Home practice is encouraged through the use of tapes, which are eventually eliminated, and through family and friends who serve as monitors. The most important generalization procedure is elimination of the tension phase (not always effective), followed by gradual reduction of the number of muscle groups relaxed in a given session. In line with Bernstein and Borkovec (1973), we gradually decrease the number of muscle groups into which we divide the body, from seventeen to seven to four, in the course of treatment. Finally, the members practice relaxation on command. Although the relaxation experienced may not be as deep as that elicited by the detailed instruction to relax, many clients note that the word *relax* does stimulate a drop in the level of tension. Relaxing on self-command can be carried out only after the client has learned a shortened form of relaxation.

In Chapter Four, we discussed how clients are taught to identify stressful situations. In relaxation training, these stressful situations are reviewed. The clients are asked to imagine the situation and proceed through the steps of relaxation at the critical moment in the stressful situation. Thus, in line with a strategy proposed by Paul (1966), the initial onset of stress or anxiety becomes the cue to relax.

Homework, of course, is an essential part of any generalization package. In 60 percent of the research projects reviewed by Hillenberg and Collins (1982) homework was required, and most of the authors who used homework claimed it was essential to training. Unfortunately, there are no studies that examine the difference between training with homework and training without homework. In work with adults, compliance with homework is difficult to obtain, even when the clients are committed. Special strategies must be employed to increase compliance. Audiotapes and daily practice with buddies seem to enhance compliance. Some group leaders arrange special daily or semiweekly relaxation sessions at times convenient for the clients. These extra sessions are gradually faded until the homework is carried out without such a structure.

Variations in Teaching Procedures. As noted earlier, many variations of the relaxation procedures exist. Longer versions that consider, for example, the voice box and very small muscle groups have been described by Jacobson (1929) and Bernstein and Borkovec (1973). We have found these versions especially useful for clients who are unable to relax a particular muscle group or for whom a very small muscle group is the focus of the tension. In most cases, however, the paradigm described earlier is sufficient.

Many older clients and/or physically handicapped clients may find the paradigm described excessively demanding. Also, the procedure may be too complex for the intellectually or emotionally impaired. Therefore, the group leader must be able to modify the commonly used paradigm to fit these special populations.

Using the Group. Almost all of the procedures described so far can be taught efficiently in a group, provided that the leader is able to observe the clients separately to detect individual problems. A good time for the leader to do this is when the group members are working in pairs. Wherever possible, and as soon as possible, better functioning clients should be allowed and encouraged to teach and monitor each other, usually in pairs. Thus, each client proceeds through the relaxation procedure twice in a session: once as the instructor and once as student. Before clients reach this phase, the group leader will have demonstrated the necessary steps repeatedly. Furthermore, the client must be "certified" as a coach before being permitted to instruct another client. The group leader remains nearby, circulating around the room and carefully observing and prompting.

Often, in groups, there is too little time to give relaxation training the attention it deserves. Clients may find it useful to seek additional relaxation training outside the group. If the group uses relaxation only occasionally, the use of in-group time for training may not be warranted. Of course, relaxation training is usually only one of many intervention strategies used to achieve group and individual goals. The appropriateness of the relaxation strategy and the extent of its use depend on the nature of the target behaviors. Certainly, for clients who complain of chronic or acute anxiety or stress, relaxation training should be a central feature of the program.

Breathing Exercises

Hundreds of diverse patterns of respiratory control have been described in the literature. It has a long history as a part of oriental martial arts, yoga and pranayama practices, and Zen. It is one of the most flexible means of stress control (Everly and Rosenfeld, 1981) and, for many, the most effective. It is less disruptive in social situations to alter one's breathing pattern than to initiate meditation or tension–relaxation responses. Unfortunately, in addition to the side effects mentioned in reference to relaxation training, breathing exercises are associated with the danger of hyperventilation, which results in diminished carbon dioxide levels in the blood and, within a short period, potentially numerous physical symptoms. Therefore, we focus on those procedures that are least likely to result in side effects and on the strategies for avoiding the effects. First, it is relatively easy and harmless to teach the client to pause and breathe more slowly than usual. Clients frequently report that they achieve a more relaxed state by breathing more slowly. Should the client feel lightheaded, he or she should return to normal breathing.

Diaphragmatic Breathing. In diaphragmatic breathing, the client first inhales slowly through the nose (to warm the air) for two to three seconds; during this period, the air causes first the abdomen and then the chest to expand slightly without discomfort. The client may be instructed to lift the chest slightly to permit the entry of the air. Without a pause, the client expels the air (first from the chest, then the abdomen) through either the nose or the mouth (depending on personal preference) for two to three seconds. After a one-second interval, the client may inhale again. The cycle can safely be repeated for several minutes without the danger of hyperventilation. The client should be advised to stop if lightheadedness is experienced.

In a variation of diaphragmatic breathing, the client is instructed to count the number of seconds in each phase. In the beginning, the group leader does the counting; however, this works against individualizing the capacity of each person, so after several demonstrations, the members count.

Stress Reduction Breathing. Stress reduction breathing has been shown to induce a state of relaxation in thirty to sixty seconds (Vanderhoof, 1980). Because of their common use in our group, the modified instructions of Everly and Rosenfeld (1981) are provided.

Research has shown stress reduction breathing to be effective in reducing muscle tension and subjective reports of anxiety as well as heart rate (Everly, 1979a, 1979b; Vanderhoof, 1980).

After explaining the purpose of the procedure and how it can help reduce stress, the leader instructs the group members to assume a comfortable position and to place their left hand on their abdomen and the right hand on top of the left. Then they are directed to relax and imagine an empty bottle or pouch lying directly under their hands. They are next told to begin to inhale so that the imaginary container fills with air and their hands rise gradually. The exercise, which will take about two seconds at the outset, will probably take two and a half or three seconds after further practice. (This first step can be eliminated after several weeks and replaced simply with the instruction to breathe in deeply.)

Group members are told to close their eyes and think, while holding their breath for about two seconds, "My body is calm." Then, as they slowly exhale, they should tell themselves, "My body is quiet." This last step takes about four seconds—that is, about as long as the first two steps combined.

Clients are cautioned to stop if they experience any dizziness or light-headedness and to reduce the length of inhalation in subsequent sessions. They are also advised that they may not immediately experience beneficial results but that persistent practice (ten to twelve times a day) will enable them to relax at will during stressful periods. It is important for the group leader to designate the time and place for subsequent relaxation practices before the initial group relaxation session disperses. (For further details, see Everly, 1979a; 1979b.)

In teaching this exercise, the group leader demonstrates the procedure and then monitors members one at a time while the others look on. After the criteria for effective breathing and the danger signs are well established, a system of paired supervision can be used. The observations of the partners are then examined in the larger group. Where necessary, further modeling may be carried out by the leader or accomplished group members. Because of the ease with which this procedure is both learned and practiced, it receives the highest evaluation of all relaxation procedures and most other interventions as well.

Meditation

Meditation is "a family of techniques which have in common a conscious attempt to focus attention in a nonanalytical way and an attempt not to dwell on discursive ruminating thought"

(Shapiro, 1982, p. 268). Carrington (1978a) developed a procedure called clinically standardized meditation (CSM), which is a Western version of more esoteric Eastern practices. He instructs clients to repeat a soothing sound such as the word *one*, without a conscious effort or concentration. Meditation is particularly attractive to members who consider themselves out of or on the edge of main-stream middle-class culture. Our experience with the procedure has been primarily with groups of adolescents and college students.

As no consistent difference is noted in the research literature between relaxation and meditation with regard to their effectiveness for the treatment of anxiety and stress (Everly and Rosenfeld, 1981), it is possible to offer clients the choice, provided that the group leader is skilled in both. Because the experience with application of meditation in treatment groups is limited, we recommend that the interested group leader consult the works of Carrington (1978a, 1978b) and Shapiro (1980).

CSM can, for the most part, be taught similarly to relaxation. It is more difficult to use ongoing group monitoring procedures in meditation training, and the buddy system does not appear to be useful. Meditation can be taught in the group because it is just as easy to demonstrate, explain, and teach it to many people as to one person; however, it does not take full advantage of the interactive nature of the treatment group, because interaction disrupts the meditative process. Interaction can occur after the meditative process through discussion; however, discussion immediately after a meditative session is also disruptive. In general, when given the choice, most adult clients prefer relaxation, probably because they are more familiar with it. Where the program is advertised to teach meditation among other procedures, clients who indeed are interested and willing to include meditation as a preferred part of their program refer themselves.

Of course, meditation is not suitable for all people. Shapiro (1980) warns that people with perfectionistic, self-critical, and goal-oriented approaches to problems, associated with the type A personality, might bring these attitudes to meditation. This is also true in my experience with deep muscle relaxation. These attitudes are likely to interfere with the meditative process and increase anxiety. Some clients experience adverse side effects when meditating, especially if it lasts too long. Effects noted by Shapiro (1980, p. 47) are increased anxiety, boredom, depression, restlessness, and decreased reality testing. Similar side effects have been found for neuromuscular relaxation. To reduce these potential side effects, Carrington (1978a) recommends that clients initially meditate with, and under the direct supervision of, the group leader. After demonstrating the process, the group leader can monitor the members one at a time (as with the breathing exercises), while the others look on. As they gain expertise in meditation, some members may be able to monitor others. After termination of treatment, relaxation activities are done primarily alone.

Sociorecreational Activities

Recreational activities are those activities in which an individual participates during free time for purposes of relaxation, for example, sports, theater, movies, TV, and arts and crafts. Sociorecreational activities are recreational activities that involve other people. Some are participatory, whereas others are passive (observational). Many of the clients we see in our groups have limited skills in the participatory activities and few skills in passive activities. A large percentage merely indiscriminately watch TV. Many express boredom with much of what they do in their free time and some have specifically stated as a goal the expansion of their recreational activities. Sociorecreational activities can also be used to learn other skills. For example, Quinsey and Varney (1977) used a board game to teach social skills to their group.

In assessment, we specifically ask clients how they use their free time. If we find that at least several people in the group have limited skills or participate in few activities they rate as interesting or fun, we add sociorecreational activities to the agenda.

In proposing the topic for consideration, the leader explains (provides a rationale for) why a balanced sociorecreational life is valuable in managing stress or improving the quality of life. The leader discusses with the members what each does recreationally in a typical week. Usually, the group has prepared for this discussion the previous week so that members can keep track of their activities. (It is interesting to note that many members report that they have increased their sociorecreational activities as a result of the monitoring, and find the increase quite satisfying.)

After the members discuss the week's activities, the leader suggests that they try out each other's activities during the next week. That is, the members choose buddies, and the buddies trade activities for the week. In this phase of treatment, at least several members may set a goal of greater participation in sociorecreational activities. When a majority of the members set such a goal, especially in long-term groups without a specific theme or in stress reduction groups, they may organize an extragroup recreational program, usually without the group leader—for example, bowling nights or checkers clubs to which members are required to bring nonmembers. Another group went to professional sports activities together. In yet another group, one member taught the others folk dances, and later they all went to a large folk dance.

Often, part of a session is devoted to discussing how to get involved in already existing activities. A group of recently divorced persons assigned themselves the task of listing all the activities available to people of their age and status. At the next session, after the list has been compiled, the members plan to gather detailed information on activities. At the third session, each member reports on his or her observation of at least one sociorecreational activity. In a group of agoraphobics, this same program was carried out over a longer period, with members accompanying one another to the activity of choice.

Where the necessary approach responses are not in the repertoire of the individual, modeling may be used, for example, in asking someone how to join the Y. Moreover, cognitive barriers ("People who don't know me will reject me") to expanding sociorecreational activities are often discussed and steps are taken in the group to break down these barriers through cognitive restructuring or self-instructional training.

Sociorecreational activities are readily incorporated into the multimethod approach and may become the most important intervention used by a group. Such skills are essential to a client's well being and, in the face of serious deficiencies, should be incorporated into most group programs. As a side benefit, sociorecreational skills provide program diversity, which increases the interest in, and hence the cohesion of, the group. Furthermore, sociorecreational activities provide a real-world topic around which interaction can take place.

Summary

The purposes, advantages, and limitations of relaxation training in group treatment have just been discussed. Three general relaxation procedures are described: neuromuscular relaxation, respiratory control, and meditation. Each procedure is useful for different types of clients. All three procedures are helpful to most clients in the treatment of stress and stress-related disorders. The group leader may have some difficulty in selecting the appropriate strategy. It is not advisable to use all three. A rule of thumb is that the group leader should develop skill in one procedure after becoming familiar with all three. The procedure about which the leader is most enthusiastic is usually the one the members like best. Moreover, although research supports all three procedures, the most research has been carried out on neuromuscular relaxation, which as a result has the strongest empirical support. Also, most clients are familiar with neuromuscular relaxation because of the popular literature and because it fits their expectations about treatment.

Certain clients cannot use any of the three procedures without side effects, which, though rare, can occur. The group leader should be aware—and make the clients aware—of these potential side effects.

Relaxation procedures readily lend themselves to the group setting, where pair monitoring and group discussion are possible. It is difficult to individualize training in groups, but the leader must make individual observations to ensure that the procedures are used safely. Although groups exist in which the sole focus is training in one relaxation procedure (these are called relaxation, meditational, or recreational groups), most often these procedures are taught as part of a larger multimethod approach.

Sociorecreational activities also enhance relaxation. Relaxation training and sociorecreational training are excellent group procedures that can be used to treat a wide range of complaints and to increase group cohesion. The group leader must be well prepared, and adequate time must be allotted to practice. Furthermore, the leader must take advantage of the potential of the group in teaching, setting up practice sessions, and encouraging home activity.

ELEVEN

Resolving Problems in Group Structure and Process

Every action we have suggested to group leaders, throughout this book, has been discussed in light of its implications for the group. The group is a dynamic environment whose elements must be actively considered if interventions are to be effective. All interventions in the group setting should be considered as group procedures even if the target of the intervention is an individual. A person sets individual treatment goals in response to feedback from others in the group. Each client designs an individualized treatment plan within the group context and with broad assistance from fellow members. If the mutual support system is not operative, all of the advantages of group therapy, described in Chapter One, are negated. Failure to use the unique attributes of the group weakens or eliminates the effect of the interventions.

In Chapter Two we described the group structures and processes that impinge on the treatment process. Chapter Five was devoted to the operationalization of most of these concepts. In Chapter Six, group goals were defined in terms of desired changes in these interactive patterns. Most empirical configurations of group phenomena either enhance or detract from learning. Some phenomena may have little import one way or the other. The goal of the group leader is to create and reinforce those configurations of group phenomena that enhance the treatment process and help the group members to achieve their goals and to resolve those group conditions that interfere with the treatment process. These latter conditions are referred to as group problems and fit into the problem-solving paradigm. In this chapter, group problems are scrutinized. Strategies for resolving group problems and achieving group goals are also illustrated. Through this analysis, the procedures for modifying undesirable group conditions and maintaining desirable ones are explained.

Group Problems

Definition of Group Problem. Patterns of behavior, norms, expectations, roles, and relationships can be identified in all groups. Some of these patterns enhance goal attainment; others appear to detract from it. A group problem can be defined as an intragroup interactive event (or series of events) or a product of interactive events that interferes with effective member task performance or goal attainment. The responsibility for amelioration of that problem cannot be attributed to a change in behavior of a member or the group leader but to interactive changes among all members. Such a definition is relevant primarily to goal-oriented groups, and the problems and strategies discussed in this chapter also pertain to such groups.

Group problems can best be dealt with if they are indicated by observed phenomena. They may be subjectively observed by the group leader, reported on by the members during or after a session, or systematically observed by a nonparticipating observer. Member perceptions are neither more or less valid than observations of a neutral observer or the perception of the leader. They merely provide a different perspective.

Advantages of Identifying and Dealing with Group Problems. Group problems can arise at any time throughout the history of the group. If ignored, they become a "hidden agenda" that interferes with the work of the group. For example, if relationships among pairs and triads of members are vitally important to the group, the group interaction may focus on maintaining those subgroups, until the issue of "pairing off" (Bion, 1959) arises. Under these conditions, no matter how persuasive the leader's arguments for a given cognitive-behavioral intervention or exercise might be, full support would be slow in coming. Similarly, if one member dominates the interaction and the others resent it, unless the leader deals with the issue, it is unlikely that members will disclose their problems to each other, because mutual trust cannot exist in such a disparate communication pattern.

In the identification of a problem, in discovering each individual's contribution to that problem, in planning for and carrying out interventions to resolve a problem, and in evaluating the outcome of the entire process, the group leader both models and offers members multiple opportunities to practice a systematic problem-solving approach around a significant common issue. Members have the opportunity to view their own pattern of behavioral, cognitive, and affective response to interactive events of the group, to evaluate with the help of the group which are ineffective, to attempt remediation strategies, and to observe the consequences of success or failure in the change process.

Finally, in ascertaining a group problem, no one member is forced to assume sole blame for it. On the other hand, no one in the group can escape at least partial responsibility for the existence of the problematic situation and its eventual remediation. Since blame is not ascribed to any one person and responsibility is attributed to all persons, members are more readily able to participate openly and actively in the process. In the outside world, responsibility for most communication problems must also be shared with others, if a particular situation is to be improved. Learning to deal with mutual problems is an important task in its own right.

Let us examine some structures and processes that are often perceived as group problems. In Table 7 we have outlined major group problems that we have encountered, how they were ascertained, and what strategies, in addition to systematic group problem solving, were employed.

Table 7 oversimplifies the process of group problem identification and resolution. We now describe in far greater detail many of these problems and the strategies employed by the group leader in concrete situations. Problems are rarely only of one category or type, such as low cohesion or unequal distribution of participation, but rather include many diverse phenomena. One problem usually stands out, and the following illustrations assume that this is the case.

Table 7. Group Problems.

Group Problems	Observable Evidence	Possible Strategy
Low cohesion	Drop in satisfaction.* Attendance/promptness rate is low. Ratio of critical statements to positive statements is high. Assignment completion rate is low.	Present data to group and discuss with group. Brainstorm about possible strategies.** Introduce variation into program. Serve coffee and food.
One or two members dominate interaction	One or two members speak more than twice as much as other members.	Prepare low-frequency members prior to meeting; prompt them in meeting. Reinforce low participants. Cue high participants when talking too much. Set limits for all members.
Members withdraw from interaction	Several members speak less than half of their share of the available time.	Usually occurs in conjunction with preceding problem. Handle in same way.
Too much off-task behavior	Off-task behavior more than 10 percent of total interaction.	Help group to define "off-task," than have group monitor set limits on each other's "off-task" behavior.
Too little self-disclosure	Participants talk about others but not selves. They blame others or circumstances for their problems.	Discuss similarities of cases to self, to own problems. Gradually increase demand for self-disclosure.
Excessive subgrouping	Twenty percent or greater interaction in the group occurs in pairs or triads during general group discussion.	Use subgrouping exercises with new subgroup formation. Use fewer subgrouping exercises in general. Develop "buddy system" that changes every week.
Dependence on leader	Members ask leader for ideas, suggestions, or help throughout meeting. Leader answers most of the questions. Interaction occurs primarily between leaders and members.	Use frequent brainstorming. Ask group for answer; advise before giving it. Reinforce all member initiatives. Bring in models who are more independent. Examine pattern with group.

Table 7. Group Problems, Cont'd.

Group Problems	Observable Evidence	Possible Strategy
High fight state	More than 10 percent of statements reflect anger, "put-downs" of others, or passive aggressive behavior. Attendance is usually irregular. Some members do not participate at all.	Describe observations to group. Use critical feedback training exercises. Reflect on same pattern in real world. Train in positive feedback alternatives through roleplaying and exercises.

*Almost all group problems are indicated by a drop in satisfaction.
**In dealing with almost all group problems, presentation and group discussion of the data and/or impressions are used first. Brainstorming and evaluation of possible strategies, including some of those mentioned here, are also useful.

Problems in Group Cohesion

As pointed out earlier, attention to group cohesiveness is essential to maintain attendance and concentration on the work to be accomplished. The relationship to work is complex. Highly cohesive groups tend to achieve their goals better than do less cohesive groups. Of course, when the relationship to the leader is poor or the leader is excluded from the definition of the group, members tend to choose a non-treatment-oriented goal toward which they zealously strive. Basically, two states seem to impinge on the successful achievement of group goals: excessively high cohesion and excessively low cohesion.

Too Little Cohesion. When a group begins, the cohesion is usually too low for effective learning to take place. One exception is a previously established group, such as a family or friendship circle, although major communication problems exist even in these groups. To start out and remain as attractive as possible, groups are usually composed of persons with similar problems. The treatment program planned is one in which members are likely to be interested and in which roleplaying is used extensively. The group leader uses both observations and responses to a questionnaire to determine the level of cohesion. Under these prophylactic conditions, it is rare to find a group with low cohesion. Unfortunately, groups may not be as similar as a leader might desire. Interests may initially overlap but then change in unpredictable ways; individuals may arise who, because of their behavior, detract from the cohesiveness of the group; and the leader may fail to involve the members adequately in the treatment process. One such experience is described here to demonstrate what additional measures can be taken to increase the cohesiveness of a group that data suggest has a relatively low level of cohesiveness.

Group Leader: Last week, I noticed on the postsession questionnaires that the satisfaction level and your response to the question about the helpfulness of other members had dropped quite a bit and that a number of you had commented that the meetings were getting somewhat repetitive. I wonder if you still feel that way. I think it's important that we discuss this before we go any further.

Patrick: It was kind of a boring meeting last week. Several of us were talking about it as we left the meeting. Frankly, Al, you did quite a bit of talking about stuff a lot of us didn't understand, that cognitive restructuring stuff. Some of us aren't sure how it affects us.

Group Leader: Anything else of concern?

Charles: Well, I didn't think it was so boring maybe as the others did. But I found it confusing, too. And I guess I didn't feel very involved.

Group Leader: Well, I see you are all here this week, so the content didn't seem to drive you away. Were you tempted?

Patrick: I thought of it, but I've learned a lot in the group and you can't expect it to be great every week.

Group Leader: I think there is good reason for concern. Let me try to summarize the problem. If I've got it straight, there was too much lecture last week, without sufficient clarification or examples. Some people feel that they were not adequately involved. Are these general concerns? Do most of you share them?

Others (nod agreement)

Group Leader: I wonder what we can do about it. As we had discussed earlier, in such a problem, everyone plays a role—the group leader, each of you, the group. It might be helpful if we all wrote down anything we can think of to make the meetings more useful. Make at least one comment on me and at least one comment on the group or yourself. I'll do it too.

Group Leader (after a few minutes): You seem to be finished, most of you. What did you write that I might do differently? I'll put it on the board. [Quite a few suggestions were made: give better examples, don't use so much jargon, give a few exercises to make sure we understand, don't rush so much, take at least two sessions to explain difficult ideas, don't wait for the people who are late, and lay off the bad jokes!] That's quite a list of suggestions, all of which I should seriously consider. We'll come back to them later. Now, what did you write that you or the group should do differently? [The answers may include: ask for clarification when I don't understand something; try to take examples from my own experience; come on time—then maybe I won't be so confused; talk more; read the handouts (I have to admit I didn't).] That's also a thoughtful list. Why doesn't each of us, including me, decide to try at least one of these suggestions at this and the next meeting to see if we can improve the level of satisfaction? Let's do it in pairs. Each person in the pair will serve as consultant to the other. When we're finished, each of us can read the plan to the group.

The major strategy was first to reflect on the results of the postsession questionnaire and then to identify the problem in this group. The intervention was to proceed through the first phase of problem solving. The effectiveness of the intervention would be indicated by the increase in satisfaction from this meeting to the next. The lack of cohesion seemed to be related to the group leader's failure to involve the members in discussion and to the group leader's tendency to overload them conceptually. Without losing the treatment focus of the group, the group leader helped to increase group cohesion by encouraging the members to talk about their complaints and to design, within specified limits, their own plans for improvement. It should be noted that the leader did not become defensive in response to the criticism, but in fact incorporated their ideas into his approach. An underlying relationship problem may have existed that the leader did not recognize. If the plan had failed, it would still have been possible to examine the leader's relationship to the group and the members' relationships to each other. Sometimes the problem is what it appears to be!

Other strategies have been used to increase cohesion. In a single parents' group, the leader scheduled an extended coffee break; the first week, she provided refreshments, and in subsequent weeks, the members arranged to take turns providing refreshments. During this break, the parents had the opportunity to talk informally about their own children. As most of these parents were quite lonely, the opportunity to socialize was a powerful tool for enhancing cohesion. Because high levels of reinforcement appear to lead to high cohesion, groups commonly use a reinforcement exercise where members, one at a time, reinforce the person to their left for concrete, effective in-group behavior; then the circle is reversed, with each person reinforcing the one to the right. Satisfaction and cohesion indicators usually increase after this exercise.

As pointed out earlier, using these tools, the vast majority of groups we have worked with are able to achieve a high level of cohesion quickly without problem solving. This may be possible because the program itself elicits the maximum involvement of the participants, delegates leadership responsibilities, builds in "enjoyable" activities such as roleplaying, and is basically a positive approach with lots of positive reinforcement and a minimum of critique. As Goldstein, Heller, and Sechrest (1966, pp. 392–430) concluded in a review of the literature, creation of a positive climate with a high frequency of reinforcement is an extremely important precondition of high cohesion.

We note that some groups attain a high level of cohesion more quickly than other groups, even if they are following the same program. Most often, the leaders in these highly cohesive groups are judged as being less serious and "more fun" than their low-cohesion-group counterparts. These findings are related to personality differences, which we are unable to teach. Unless the characteristics are extreme, the outcomes do not seem to differ (see Antonuccio, Lewinsohn, and Steinmetz, 1982). A person does not have to be a professional stand-up comic to be an effective group leader. A little humor will go a long way. Of course, humor may not be compatible with the style of the group leader. In the earlier example, one of the comments to Alan was to "lay off the bad jokes."

In summary, to increase or maintain cohesiveness, the program should be moderately structured; group problems should be dealt with as they arise; all members should be maximally involved in the interaction; the group should remain focused on what the clients find important; food should be provided, at least in the early sessions; the program should be varied and sufficiently attractive to maintain interest and to provide, initially, various reinforcements for the group and individual members.

High cohesion results in mutual trust and support, increased self-disclosure, increased sense of intimacy among members, and the perception of the group environment as a protected opportunity to test reality. These have been identified by Yalom (1985) as some of the major curative factors we discussed earlier (Chapter Two).

Too Much Cohesion. Three situations illustrate the effects of too much cohesion. In the first, the group invests so much effort in maintaining high cohesion that it is kept from working toward individual treatment goals. In such cases, the leader must remind the members of the group purpose and discuss how their present behavior is interfering with that purpose. If the group indicates a strong preference for a social club over a therapeutic experience, the appropriate arrangements could be made, but under other auspices. In our experience, this rarely occurs.

The second situation arises as the group moves toward termination. If the group is too cohesive, the members will have major problems in separating. Plans should be made to reduce the cohesion. If equally attractive alternatives do not exist, it is not uncommon for maladaptive behaviors to return when an extremely cohesive group terminates. Clients should be helped in the search for other groups and individuals to replace the therapy group. Members are encouraged to bring guests to the last few group meetings (preferably newly made friends) and to join new nonthera-peutic interest or friendship groups (see Chapter Thirteen for more details). (The leader must be aware of the problem of possible abuses of confidentiality in the use of guests. Prior to their intro-duction this issue must be discussed and the types of situations and content dealt with should be at a level that the members would speak to nongroup members about. If this cannot be done, visitors should not be employed.) The leader reinforces less and trains members, and their families, in self-reinforcement.

The third example of excessive cohesion is the group in which the leader is excluded from the members' psychological definition of the group. The members feel close to one another but not to the leader. They see the leader as an imposition on the group experience. Perhaps they expected a different sort of therapy program, or maybe a member emerged and successfully competed with the leader for control of the group. This state may result in the group's working solely toward nontherapeutic goals, such as maintenance of the group, recreation such as horseplay and private jokes, sabotage of the leader's recommendations, and exclusion of the leader from significant interactions. Though not a common feature of short-term structured groups, this phenomenon occurs occasionally. It can be avoided by careful preliminary clarification of the group goal and the importance of focusing on activities that contribute to that goal. This is especially important for people who have been in encounter groups or other nondirected groups.

The ongoing monitoring may also reveal a problem before it becomes full blown. If the cohesion is high and the criticism of the leader excessive, the inconsistency should be presented to the group for their consideration. If the members agree, several of the strategies can be used to resolve the problem: involving the members in planning for the subsequent session, increasing (slightly) opportunities for discussion of general issues, and having group members monitor themselves for off-task behavior.

Problems in Communication

The communication structure of a group is the pattern of communication in the group. Who communicates with whom?

How is participation distributed in the group? What are the prevailing communication themes in the group?

A common problem in discussion groups is dominance by one or two people of, and withdrawal by others from, the group interaction pattern. Attainment of individual treatment goals usually requires that there be broad participation in discussion and other activities. If some people describe their problems, give help and support to others, and generate ideas frequently while others do so rarely, the former will profit more from the group than the latter. Often, the high participators are concerned about how the low participators are judging their disclosures. Furthermore, where the discrepancies are large, group cohesion and reported satisfaction tend to be low. If the members are to perceive each other as mutually supportive and the group as a protected setting for self-disclosure, communication must be even.

One way to modify the proportion of participation is to lay out the problem to the group. If they perceive it as a problem as well, the group problem-solving process can be invoked. In groups with little experience, the leader serves as the major source of suggestions for solutions:

Group Leader: As we look over last week's participation data, which I have written on the board, it's clear that John, Everett, and I did most of the talking while the rest of you had little opportunity to talk. I guess we have a group problem, since some of us leap in before others get a chance, and some of us leave long gaps for the rest of us to spring into.

John: I know I do a lot of talking, but I have a lot of concerns.

Emily: That's true, John, and this may sound a little hard, but you might consider the fact that the rest of us do, too.

Group Leader: I'm the leader, and I'm supposed to give you all an equal chance to talk about your concerns; and as we look at the participation data, I'm forced to admit that I am encroaching on your time.

Gordon: Of course, but you've got a lot to say that's really important.

Group Leader: That may be so, but you didn't come for a lecture. This is supposed to be participatory learning. What about those of you who haven't been speaking up much?

Anthony: Well, I don't like to speak up in groups, so I'm glad when others do it. But I guess that's one of the reasons I'm in this group. I suppose if I leave it the way it is now, I won't learn anything.

Donna: I have to agree with that for me too. But what can we do? We all seem to have to do something different about it.

Group Leader: That's what I think, too. We have to do something together and something on our own. One way to approach it might be for each of us to make a plan for ourselves and then together a plan for the group as a whole.

Group Members: (nods of agreement)

John: I guess I should just shut up. Is that what you are saying?

Anthony: I'm certainly not saying that. You say some pretty good things. I just need to find a way to hold up my end. I could use a little encouragement.

Group Leader: I agree that's the direction we need to go in to find ways to increase or decrease, but not eliminate, the participation of all members so that it's a little more equal.

Group Members: (nods of agreement)

John: Well, we could sort of brainstorm about how each of us could move toward the middle better. Each would sort of suggest things he can do for himself?

Group Leader: Judging by the nods of approval, that seems like a good idea. That being the case, at this very moment let's write down whatever ideas we have so that we all get a chance to say what we think we should do.

Among other ideas, the group requested the observer to report more often on the frequency of their interactions. The observer would report to them after the break as well as at the beginning of the subsequent meeting. Each person would set a goal for himself or herself and then see whether the data registered movement toward that goal. The "talkers" would remind each other by saying, "Is this statement really necessary?" Using a cognitive approach, the leader would request all members first to say to themselves what they want to say to the group. Those whose negative self-talk prevented them from speaking would be assisted, through cognitive restructuring, to replace such self-statements as "I don't have anything important to say" with "My ideas are as good as the next person's." The members went on to establish individual plans for themselves and a group plan, which they monitored weekly to ensure that interactional goals were maintained.

In another group, the leader, at the suggestion of a member, provided all of the members with stopwatches and had them monitor themselves. The group was then asked to balance participation by dividing the fifteen-minute period among seven people, including the two leaders. The low participants were occasionally coached by the co-leader. They planned what they would discuss; members were encouraged to take notes. After a brief practice session, they proceeded to discuss the day's agenda for fifteen minutes. Individuals were warned when their two minutes were up. This procedure provoked a great deal of laughter. The content of the discussion was of less value than the process. A second attempt later in the meeting was less intrusive. No third trial seemed to be required, even at subsequent meetings.

Another technique occasionally used to decrease participation by excessive talkers (who do not seem to listen very well) is recapitulation. The member must summarize aloud what the preceding speaker said before being permitted to add something new to the conversation. This technique works better than more direct interventions because most individuals discover their own nonlistening behavior patterns as they attempt to recapitulate their predecessors' remarks. The group leader profits most from this procedure.

Normally, this procedure is applied only for a short period to obtain the necessary effect; however, to give members practice in listening and in monitoring their listening, repeated trials at various intervals are recommended. If continued too long (more than fifteen minutes), the conversation can become stilted, non-task oriented, and aversive. The procedure is more effective when used sporadically rather than regularly. Taping and replaying the meeting is also an excellent way to allow members to recognize their particular pattern of communication.

Many of the preceding techniques were developed by groups to respond to a specific problem. The techniques are effective to the degree that the members are involved in the planning or at least in the decision to use them. The variations are unlimited and depend on the creativity of the group.

Problems in the Subgroup Structure

In most groups, communication is not distributed equally either in direction or in amount. That is, members communicate more frequently with some than with others. They work more often with some members than with others. These mutual preferences lead to the formation of subgroups.

Subgrouping is inevitable in the group setting. Particularly at the beginning, members have difficulty interacting evenly with everyone else. Some clients are comfortable in initiating social contacts with others only within subgroups. As a result, leaders usually encourage subgroup activities to elicit at least some participation. More often than not, the subgroup activity enhances rather than detracts from the attainment of group goals. For example, in some groups we have found that the cohesion level is higher for sessions with subgroup activities than in those without. On occasion, the subgroup may be so much more valued than the group that it disrupts the ongoing group process. At this point, the leader should increase group activities and reduce or entirely eliminate subgroup activities. The leader can also change the composition of subgroups by reassigning the members; however, the leader must be careful to avoid combining people who punish others or trigger maladaptive behaviors in each other. There must be some basis for positive interaction, for example, common interest or reciprocal skills. Subgroups can comprise two or more persons; however, we have found that triads sometimes have more difficulty in making decisions. Furthermore, occasionally, two members of the triad pair off, excluding the third person.

In a stress management group comprising men with a history of cardiac arrest, the search for the cause of the drop in satisfaction led to the conclusion that some members were working primarily with one or two others and excluding the other members of the group. In the problem-solving process, the members initially evaluated four suggestions from a brainstorming exercise and decided that subgroup exercises should no longer be used in the group and that the seating arrangement should change every week. The basis for their conclusion was that the same people clustered together when subgroup programs were announced, and also, members rushed to sit with their friends at the beginning of meetings.

Problematic Group Norms

Many group norms have been found to be unproductive or, in some way, to hinder the achievement of group goals. We have already noted excessive or inappropriate criticism, or both; inadequate mutual reinforcement; excessive dependence on the leader; excessive off-task behavior; and inadequate concern for the problems of others. All of these problems have been dealt with in similar ways. To illustrate some of these strategies, we draw on our experience with a group of anxious and depressed clients who sought to manage their anxiety more effectively and to function more fully in the real world. In this group, the prevailing interactive norm was excessive criticism.

Calvin: Wayne, you're such an idiot! You make everything complicated and difficult for yourself. Why don't you just use the relaxation exercise? It's so easy!

Wayne: I can't speak for the rest of you, but I'm sick and tired of all these put-downs. I know some people think they are funny or even helpful, but I for one can't concentrate on what we are trying to do in the group. I didn't even want to come back this week. I talked to Rina [the group leader] and she said, "Bring it up in the group." I think this is as good a time as any.

Group Leader: And what do the rest of you think? Is this a common problem, or does it just affect Wayne?

Calvin: I think it's an exaggeration. We're only joking.

Anita Ann: Joking, shit! I find these so-called jokes and the people who make them offensive. Frankly, I think that Rina should say something when these put-downs are made. [The discussion continues in the same tone; most of the members are upset with the high frequency of put-downs and critical statements.]

Maynard: Look at the way we're dealing with this problem. We're practically killing each other here, too. We always seem to be blaming somebody for our own behavior or attacking somebody.

Group Leader: Perhaps this way we don't have to look at ourselves or deal with everyday hassles. That is supposed to be the focus of our discussions?

Several: Yes. Yeah. That's about it!

Group Leader: I think this is a serious problem, and I'm glad it was brought up so that we can try to do something about it. But first I want to say that to a large degree, I feel coresponsible for the emergence of this problem. I have permitted free flow of criticism before we have even discussed, much less practiced, various styles of effective feedback. Moreover, I didn't say anything earlier even though I have been a little upset with the tone of the conversation for some time.

Maynard: I, for one, am going to do what Wayne just did. I'm going to let people know when I feel put-down or unfairly criticized. [Others agree.]

Anita Ann: But even criticism of criticism has got to be handled in a new way. Otherwise, everyone will just get defensive and we'll never break the cycle.

Wayne: I agree with both of you. But, Rina, I think you ought to call it to our attention if we aren't seeing it. And could you tell us more about that feedback exercise?

The group members then proceeded to select a strategy for remedying the omnipresent put-downs; thus, the leader did not have to initiate additional problem-solving measures. From then on, however, she carefully monitored the frequency of put-downs or unfair criticism in the group to make sure the plans were working. Furthermore, she built into the next session an exercise on giving and accepting criticism.

In this group, a member complained to the leader who, rather than work with the individual alone, encouraged him to bring it up in the group at the first opportunity. This not only placed that person in a leadership position, it prevented the leader from taking over the solution process. Sometimes, the leader must offer his or her perception of the group, but the members' perceptions usually have more weight. Clearly, the problem was not solved, but a plan was made to deal with it.

Where norms of excessive mutual criticism, put-downs, and defensiveness exist among members without their recognizing it, the leader can present the group with a similar (actual or fabricated) case. In one group, a fictional client, who was being put-down in a work situation, was described. First, the group identified the thoughts and behaviors of all interacting parties in the case. Second, the members were asked to design a plan in which all the interacting parties had to change a pattern of thinking or behaving to improve the general group climate. Members then discussed how they were similar to or different from the actors in the case study. This led to discussion of their specific group situation and to formulation of a plan to modify members' behavior to remedy the group problem. The case should be sufficiently similar that members can identify elements of their own problem, but it should not be identical.

A more direct approach would be for the leader to give his or her opinion of the situation and then ask members for their perceptions. The group leader must be careful not to identify too closely with the victim or to place responsibility solely on the others, or the group may become unwilling to deal with the problem. Solving problems that involve more than one member must be viewed as a common rather than an individual responsibility.

Problems in the Leadership Structure

One particular role structure that warrants consideration in its own right is the leadership structure of the group. (See Fiedler, 1971, for an empirically based theory of small group leadership.) Although usually associated with individuals or roles in the group, leadership can be more usefully described as a set of behaviors that facilitate the attainment of group and individual goals and the maintenance of the group (Cartwright and Zander, 1968). Often, these behaviors may be attached primarily to one person, the group leader, as she or he strives to give the group a focus. Later, these behaviors may also be associated with one or two group members. As we pointed out earlier, because high status and power are often associated with the leadershp role, the major function of the group leader is to facilitate the distribution of those behaviors associated with group leadership so that at least some of the rewards and control of leadership accrue to all members. Thus, an important function of the group leader is to eliminate gradually the central leadership role. The process is gradual because the work of the group must be carried out. The group leader must maintain sufficient responsibility until the members themselves are able to provide guidance to the group. As a result, the group initially appears to be highly managed and structured by the group leader. Gradually, the group is managed and structured to an increasing degree by the members. The role of the group leader shifts from direct leader to prompter and consultant.

What is the value of members' trying out their own leadership behaviors? First, practice in the leadership functions that facilitate the attainment of treatment goals often extends the members' area of competence to other social groups, where leadership is usually highly valued. (And, as a result, leadership skills learned in the treatment group have the opportunity to be reinforced in other groups.) Second, the more the members provide their own leadership, the more likely they will choose to work on problems of central concern and try out new methods. Third, as suggested earlier, members of treatment groups are more likely to be in low-status situations in their social world. They experience powerlessness in a wide variety of social situations. The successful performance of leadership activities enhances their perceived power or self-efficacy in the group. This does not mean that all members become leaders, but they do achieve increasing control over their own programs and, it is to be hoped, their own lives. Of course, there are also dangers in the delegation of responsibility. The process becomes less efficient. Occasionally, private agendas of the clients interfere with goal achievement. Once in a while, the leader must reassert her- or himself. But, as long as the leader remains aware of the dangers, the advantages of delegation far exceed a controlling position by the group leader.

For these reasons, the group leader is constantly concerned with training all members in leadership behaviors and transferring leadership responsibilities to them. In fact, by the end of treatment, members should be helping to clarify problems, suggesting treatment plans, developing contracts for each other, choosing their own tasks, and organizing roleplays.

Leadership behaviors are taught in the same way as other behaviors. The group discusses what the leader specifically does as leader. The members are asked which of the behaviors the leader is demonstrating at a given meeting. Subsequently, members are encouraged to perform these behaviors whenever possible. Approximations of leadership behavior are reinforced in the group. In subsequent meetings, members practice being leader; the group leader acts either as coach or as co-leader. Some group leaders, on the request of a client, set up leadership seminars in the later phases of treatment to focus on the extension of leadership skills. Both discussion-leading and discussion-participation skills are taught in these seminars. After treatment ends, some members may serve as group aides; they are trained in an in-service program that further reinforces their leadership ability. Obviously, this type of program is limited to clients who are not too restricted by their problems. Stress management clients may view such a program as one more burden; the intellectually impaired may find it too demanding.

In the following example, the problem was initially viewed as belonging exclusively to the two group leaders, who then involved the group in helping them solve the problem. As the situation evolved, it became clear that in addition to the leaders' domination of discussions, there existed a more important problem: too little delegation of leadership functions to the members.

According to the observer's data, the two leaders of an adult social-skill-training group were speaking more than 45 percent of the time. Obviously, this left the members a relatively short time to discuss and practice new social skills. Most members highly valued the contribution of the leaders and did not want to alter the situation. Satisfaction in the group was relatively high. The leaders suggested that it was primarily their problem ("I talk too much? I interrupt too much?") Several members disagreed. One person stated that if the members were sufficiently involved, the leaders would not have to talk so much. The leaders decided that to involve the members, they would talk less to one another. The leaders requested the group's feedback. Based on the members' suggestions and their own ideas, the leaders elected to analyze their speaking patterns (when and what they said) and to change their behavior. The leaders were aware of their tendency to amplify unnecessarily each other's statements; therefore, they established a *rule* that the group leaders could not talk back-to-back. They asked the members to monitor their adherence to the rule. They also decided to increase the time they would wait before responding to a group member's statement, from two seconds to three. An observer kept track of both response latencies and back-to-back talking by group leaders.

But it didn't work! There was a brief drop in the leaders' activity but it shot right back up. The leaders somehow managed to get around the proscriptions. In a group discussion of the situation, it became apparent that in not viewing it as a group problem, the members assumed no responsibility for resolving the problem. Moreover, the leaders retained the major leadership functions. The group members discussed what they could be doing and saying that the leaders were currently doing and saying. They had to provide feedback more often and not depend on the leaders for it; they could even serve as discussion leaders now that they had observed what was happening; they could do the summarizations themselves. The group decided that at the end of each meeting, one member would meet with the leaders to help plan the next meeting.

In this example, the leaders took sole responsibility for changing, and it failed. The leaders modeled self-disclosure and other strategies used to modify behavior in the group. They involved the group in monitoring the changes. The leaders appeared to involve the members in the process, but it was not enough. Specific leadership functions had to be isolated and delegated. These functions were well within the behavioral repertoire of the members.

Problems with Productivity

The group leader and members can ascertain whether or not the group is moving toward achievement of individual treatment goals by measuring the amount of work performed by the members, or the group's productivity. Estimates of productivity have been shown to correlate significantly with outcome in assertiveness training groups for adults (Rose, 1981). As pointed out in Chapter Four, group productivity for a session is measured at the beginning of the next session as the number of extragroup tasks completed. Alternatively, productivity can be rated by the group. Thus, for a specific point in time, the individual's productivity records and the group record, which is usually the average for all the members, are obtained. Because extragroup activity is central to productivity and because extragroup task completion correlates highly with outcome, productivity is dealt with at every meeting. Low productivity is a common group problem. In many of the previous examples, low productivity was a side effect of other problems, such as poor communications, nontherapeutic norms, and differential status of roles. Sometimes, low productivity is the major target of change.

The following example describes how one group leader used systematic problem solving to deal with productivity as well as with several interrelated group problems. In this group, as in most groups, several problems were detected in addition to low productivity. Dominance by one person or decrease in participation is often accompanied by a drop in the task completion rate or other index of productivity. The crucial targets were program participation and low productivity.

Parents of handicapped children had been meeting for four weeks. They had developed the common goal of learning stress management skills, such as relaxation and self-talk, to deal with stressful situations. Even though they were enthusiastic about these procedures during the session, they were not practicing relaxation as they had agreed to do at the end of each session. Most of them complained that their lives were just too busy to spend time on relaxation. When the leader pointed out the pattern and suggested that perhaps they didn't want the assignments, the members disagreed strongly. They came to the conclusion that it was a matter of discipline, not unwillingness or motivation, and they needed to help each other acquire that discipline. The members brainstormed and came up with a number of suggestions. They decided to call each other three days after the meeting to see how they were doing; they would distribute practice tapes on which each individual would also record practice time and listening time. They decided to complete the self-talk assignment in the group. The rate of assignment completion increased from 42 to 90 percent in one week and leveled off at 85 percent for the rest of the sessions. Satisfaction showed a similar pattern. The success resulted not only from the use of these techniques, but from the involvement of members in suggesting, evaluating, carrying out, and monitoring certain actions. The leader provided only the framework within which the solution was obtained.

Other groups have developed other procedures by using the problem-solving process. For example, members of a group of highly stressed persons, all of whom had had an initial heart attack and were working to manage stress effectively, decided to do away with all assignments. The amount of actual work performed increased dramatically. These clients simply did not like "being assigned something." They experienced too much of that in their daily lives.

In another group of weight losers, the members chose to take smaller steps. They had made dramatic gains the first few weeks but found it increasingly difficult to accede to their self-imposed demands. The leader helped these clients to design individual programs that were less punishing and more realistic. Although the weight loss rate slowed down, the task completion rate increased. Because productivity is an important issue, much of Chapter Twelve is devoted to the assignment completion problem.

Emotional Group Problems

As described in Chapter Two, at least three predominantly emotional problems can be identified: dependence on the leader, group fight-or-flight, and pairing off. Pairing off was discussed with respect to subgroup problems. The first two problems are discussed here.

Dependence on the Leader. When leadership functions are not shared or not accepted by group members, the members become dependent on the leader for decisions. The problem with dependence on the leader is that clients lose an opportunity to make decisions about their own behavior. Moreover, they do not have to take responsibility for failure: "My group leader made the decision; it's her fault that I failed."

As shown in Table 7, members who are dependent on the leader direct most communication to the leader and not to each other. Requests for help characterize these interactions. Rarely do members take responsibility. In response, leaders can employ a variety of interventions, in addition to posing the problem to the group for clarification and problem solving.

One strategy employed is planned fading of the leader from the interaction. If the group becomes anxious or concerned, these reactions are discussed in terms of their implications for learning and application of skills taught in the group to the outside world.

Another strategy is subgroup assignments, for example, in the development of extragroup tasks. At first, the leader floats among the subgroups. Later, the leader withdraws completely from the process. As the group progresses to the middle phase of treatment, all requests for assistance are thrown back to the group; however, as shown in this example, the criteria for answering the question must first be made explicit by the group.

Al: Sheldon [the group leader], I just can't figure this out. Is this a good way of designing the homework? [He describes the homework assignment he designed for himself.]

Lon: Yeah, I can't either. Nothing goes right. [Lon describes his plan.]

Group Leader (to the group):   I wonder whether we might not first review the criteria we established last week for a good contract? That might help you to judge whether these assignments are good.

Lawrence: One thing, it should be highly concrete. You should know exactly what you are supposed to do, and when you are supposed to do it, and with whom.

Gary: Didn't we talk about the task being a small step on the way to achieving the goal?

Francis: The criterion that was most important to me was that it was something I could do between sessions.

Other Group Members (continue to elaborate on criteria)

Group Leader (when the group pauses):   In terms of those criteria to what degree, Al and Lon, are the assignments you just described useful?

The occasional request for help does not constitute dependence on the leader. Only when such requests become commonplace should they be the focus of the group. Members' insistent demands on the leader or others to solve their problems can be evaluated in terms of their interference with effective relationships and problem solving.

Group Fight-or-Flight State. Another affective group process discussed in Chapter Two that may interfere with effective group problem solving is fight-or-flight. Manifestation of this state works against mutual assistance and satisfying working relationships. The fight phenomenon is readily detected as an increase in sarcasm and generalized criticism of other members and the leader. The flight phenomenon is recognized as a decrease in participation, high absenteeism, and general indifference. These phenomena are often middle-phase group problems, appearing only when a certain level of intimacy has been achieved. They are relatively uncommon in short-term groups (ten weeks or less). The platitudes of polite conversation fall away and members deal with each other as they would with spouses, siblings, or close friends. They blame each other and the leader for the lack of rapid cures to their problems or current frustrations. Such behavior often suggests that new and more relevant goals be set.

Usually, the first move is to stop the problem-focused inter-action, describe the leader's observations, ask members first whether their observations are similar and then what they are responding to. Often they do not realize what they are doing until it is pointed out to them. The leader may wonder aloud if these behaviors are patterns of their responses to frustration in the outside world. Sometimes, it is helpful to use a cognitive exercise, in which everyone writes down and then reads aloud what they were thinking and feeling before the leader stopped the interaction. A number of cognitive distortions can be identified and dealt with in this manner. On occasion, the group leader might encourage systematic group feedback to individual affective responses. The group might brainstorm about why a group of relatively similar people would suddenly stop communicating openly and/or start communicating aggressively.

All of these strategies are applied to obtain a better picture of the problem. Usually, with this state as with other dysfunctional emotional states, it is only when the parameters of the problem are fully exposed that systematic problem-solving procedures can be initiated. This particular group problem may also be described as a group norm (mutual aggression, put-downs) or as a nonfunctional communication pattern.

Some Concerns About Group Problems. Initially in dealing
with group problems, the group leader may expect that the group,
on seeing the data, will agree with his or her assumption. Data are
often convincing, especially when there are multiple indicators
such as low attendance, low satisfaction, and uneven distribution of
participation. Occasionally, however, for various reasons, the data
are regarded as nonproblematic by the group. There may be
insufficient evidence to convince the group that a problem exists, or
the problem may lie with the group leader. In either case, it is
usually advisable for the group leader to ignore the problem until
more data become available and to examine his or her own stake in
the "problem." In short-term groups, leaders often ignore group
problems to keep to the agenda. If the problem is serious, it will
persist and limit the effectiveness of the group. Often, ignoring the
problem wastes more time than handling it. As an intermediate
step, some group leaders proceed on their own without involving
the members. For example, in a group in which interaction was
directed primarily toward the leader, the group leader, without
consulting the group, asked the members to direct their statements
to the group. He also backed away slightly from the group circle; he
responded to questions with, "I wonder what others think."
According to the data collected, this simple solution seemed to work
in this case; however, in a similar situation in a parent group, the
leader's interventions were ineffective. If the problem is not too
disruptive, it may be worth avoiding the intensity of the problem-
solving process as a first step, but only in short-term groups. The
process itself provides an important therapeutic opportunity, often
enhancing the relationship of the leader to the group and increasing
group cohesion.

Resolution of group problems, though valuable, is a time-
consuming process. When group problems abound, the group does
not accomplish the work for which the clients were originally
referred (learning unique social and cognitive skills). For these
reasons, preventative practices are necessary to preserve the possibility of treatment goal attainment. Long-term groups may not find
these practices necessary. Certainly, in psychodynamically oriented
groups, prevention may be undesirable, because dealing with group
problems is the major work of the group. Thus, prevention, though

not universally desirable, may be sound treatment in groups of short duration and have primarily an educational or skill-training focus.

Basically, prevention strategies are good interventions. If attraction to the group is maintained at a high level through a balance of effective work and interesting programming, if group leaders ensure equal participation, if leaders hold well-planned meetings with reasonable and achievable agendas, and if leaders make judicious use of humor, then it is unlikely that many group problems will arise. Fortunately, we are not perfect, and in the absence of perfection something is overlooked or someone is slighted. Group leaders, too, vary in mood, experience, and ability to handle complex group stimuli. And, unusually difficult groups and persons can create problems under the best conditions. So problems are inevitable and an approach to group problem solving is necessary.

Conclusions and Summary

Throughout this chapter we have emphasized the involvement of members in the solution of group problems. Direct leader intervention without consultation was the exception. The primary vehicle through which this involvement was achieved, in most of the examples, has been systematic problem solving and, within that approach, the techniques of brainstorming, evaluation, and monitoring. These take advantage of the real-life experiences of our clients and provide them the opportunity to help one another. As Yalom (1985) pointed out, a major curative factor in groups is "altruism," in this case defined as helping others. Another curative factor noted by Yalom (1985) is "empowerment," which occurs when clients are maximally involved in planning and carrying out their own treatment.

It should be clear from the content of this chapter that modification of group structures also involves, and has as its purpose, the modification of individual behavior. If the attempt is made to modify the behavior of an individual without regard to group cohesion, group norms, individual status, and group communication patterns, the likelihood of success is dramatically reduced. Individual behavior within a group depends largely on the behavior of others in the group.

Many of the problems described earlier can be analyzed from several perspectives. A productivity problem can be viewed as a communication problem, and a communication problem can be perceived as inappropriate norms. There is considerable overlap, but in each case it was clear that a group problem existed and that it needed to be dealt with. Intervention strategies depend more on the behavior manifested in the group than on the particular label used to describe it.

Problems in group structures and processes involve identification of patterned responses. By pointing out recurring patterns and helping members find more rational ways of responding, leaders prepare members to deal more effectively with real-life systems, such as the family or the work situation.

Only a few of the problems that can arise in a group are reviewed, including excessive cohesion, insufficient cohesion, uneven distribution of participation, off-task behavior, pairing off, dependence on the leader, and conflict. Various strategies are utilized, but common to all of these are the use of concrete evidence to present the problem and use of the group problem-solving process. The leader or a member presents a concern to the group based on the weekly data or a subjective impression. If the members concur, they explore the problem in greater detail. On the basis of this analysis, the members and the leader develop strategies to deal with the problem through brainstorming and problem solving. The resulting strategies, agreed on by the members, are implemented in the group where their effectiveness can readily be evaluated. Wherever possible, the group leader attempts to link both problem and problem-solving strategies to similar situations in the real world.

TWELVE

Extending Treatment into the Real World Through Extragroup Tasks

During the week I intend to keep track of the urges I have to get angry and to write down how I handled it. I will also relax three to four times this week for a period of ten minutes each time. I will roleplay one time the situation I roleplayed in the group in which I asked the clerk what type of programs they had. Then I will go to the Y and actually ask for information.

The diverse tasks in this example were designed by a client in an anger control group. These extragroup tasks, also called assignments, homework, home tasks, and home exercises, are characterized by their specificity; they indicate what, where, when, and with whom certain behaviors or cognitions will occur within a given period. The word *assignment,* though more commonly used, is not entirely accurate, because the activities are planned together by the group members. The word *homework* is also not quite suitable, because the tasks are intended for a number of settings, including the home. What these activities do have in common is that they occur outside the group. In most cases, the clients report to the group the results of their experiences.

Reid (1978), Stokes and Baer (1977), Goldstein and Kanfer (1979), and many other authors have noted the importance of extragroup tasks in treatment and described their use. Several books have been written (Maultsby, 1971; Shelton and Levy, 1981; Shelton and Ackerman, 1974) on the theory and principles of behavioral tasks. All of these authors found that the extragroup component of treatment is central to the therapeutic process.

Purposes of Extragroup Tasks

The extragroup task has many uses in the multimethod approach, but none is more important than the transfer of knowledge and skills acquired in the group to the real world.

Transferring Acquired Knowledge/Skills to the Real World. To a considerable extent, behavior is specific to the situation in which it is learned. One may excel at roleplaying requests for help from an employer in the protected setting of the group, but find it difficult to do the same with the real boss. It is, therefore, necessary to provide real-life opportunities to try new behaviors. Thus, tasks are the central means, though not the only means, as we shall spell out in Chapter Thirteen, through which learning is transferred from the clinical setting to a real-world setting.

Extending Treatment Beyond the Sessions. Even in long-term therapy, two to four hours a week is clearly insufficient to bring about significant changes in major behavioral and cognitive patterns developed over a lifetime. The client must profit therapeutically from the remaining 105 waking hours to achieve meaningful change. Repeating lessons learned in the group, reading material discussed in the group, practicing roleplays initially tried out in the group, and, above all, attempting to engage others in the real world in those situations practiced in the group are all ways of extending treatment.

Increasing the Client's Independence. Because in the group all training and practice occur under the supervision of the group leader and fellow clients, conditions must be set under which the members can try out new behaviors independent of the group leader. Thus, the extragroup task also helps clients to become the principal agent of their change and to decrease their dependence on the group. Success in completing the task alone enhances the client's perceived control of his or her environment and, hence, his or her sense of self-efficacy (Bandura, 1977a).

The absence of immediate supervision, however, reduces the control exerted over the client and the assurance that the behavior will actually be performed. In fact, failure to complete the task might diminish the client's sense of self-efficacy. Fortunately, there exist strategies that promote compliance, even in the absence of the leader or other monitor. These strategies are discussed later in this chapter.

Creating Opportunities for Additional Trials. For behavior to be maintained, repeated trials are necessary. Extragroup tasks provide time not available in group sessions. In any one session, only a limited number of roleplays can be carried out for each person. Extragroup tasks, especially those involving roleplays and relaxation practice, represent agreements to continue practicing.

Providing Access to Private Events. Extragroup tasks provide the opportunity to treat private behaviors, such as sleeping disorders and sexual disturbances, or private thoughts in special contexts or under unique conditions, that is not possible in the group setting. In the early sessions, clients assign themselves to monitor these private behaviors. They bring these observations to the group for consideration and, if necessary, remediation. Furthermore, they commit themselves to try out new forms of self-talk or cognitive restructuring in extragroup situations, the results of which are reported to the group.

Providing an Index of Ongoing Productivity. Extragroup tasks, as discussed in Chapter Eleven, constitute an index of productivity. Since we have found a tentative relationship between outcome and task completion rate (Rose, 1981), this index would seem valuable as a gauge of group and individual achievements.

Completing the Problem-Solving Process. Finally, the extragroup task and the subsequent monitoring in the group represent the last two steps in the problem-solving process. Once a client has been prepared to deal with the problem in the real world

through roleplaying, cognitive restructuring, and other group
procedures, she or he designs a plan to implement these newly
learned behaviors or cognitions in the real world. Reporting back
to the group or a buddy is the verification phase of the process.
Thus, after the assessment phase, almost the entire group session
is devoted to preparing for or reporting back on extragroup assignments.

Types of Tasks

The preceding purposes cannot be achieved with only one
type of task. Different types of tasks contribute in different ways to
the therapeutic process. Included are behavioral interactive,
cognitive, combined behavioral interactive-cognitive, mutual
modeling, simulated, observational, and noninteractive tasks.

Behavioral Interactive Tasks. In behavioral interactive tasks,
the client talks with or in other ways interacts with people outside
the group in highly specific ways. These tasks are observable social
phenomena limited in terms of time, place, and action.

The assignment I have given myself for next week is to
apply for the job at the gas station. During the interview, I'm
going to take a deep breath, let it out slowly, and remind
myself to speak slowly and clearly. As soon as I have the
interview, I'll call Orrin and tell him just what I said and what
I was thinking during the interview.

The task that Gary and I designed for me during the
coming week is to try out the relaxation techniques we learned
in the group this week on at least four different days, for ten
minutes each day. After each successful practice I will record
it, as well as any problems or other reactions I might have had,
in my diary. (I was going to do it longer, but this is going to be
a busy week.)

Asking for the job and relaxing four times in one week are
examples of behavioral interactive tasks. Since these are readily

observable, their completion can readily be monitored and reinforced. As a result, they are the most common type of task, and most of the generalizations we make on compliance later in this chapter are applicable to this type of task. Preparation for behavioral interactive tasks is most often done through group modeling and behavioral rehearsal procedures, described in detail in Chapter Seven.

Simulated tasks are special behavioral tasks that prepare clients for behavioral interactive tasks:

> What I intend to do during the week is to practice at least four times in a row with my buddy the same roleplay I did in the group today. That roleplay is to tell my co-worker in a matter of fact voice that I object to her smoking and, since it is illegal, I insist on her stopping. After I've practiced four times, I will talk to my co-worker at the first opportunity. Whatever the result, I shall call my buddy.

The simulated task differs from the interactive task only in that the behavior performed in the real world is a roleplayed interaction rather than an actual interaction with a significant other. Often, the group has only limited practice time. To provide more practice time, simulated tasks are assigned. These multiple trials also increase the probability of transfer to the real world.

Simulated tasks are useful only if the situations to be roleplayed are clearly spelled out. Therefore, an abbreviated script is often written by the group for the protagonist, who also directs the roleplay. Usually, this type of task is used in the middle phase of treatment and with individuals who have previously demonstrated roleplay skills. It is especially useful for clients who require much preparation before trying out a new behavior.

Cognitive Tasks. Cognitive tasks involve examination and change of the self-talk associated with problematic situations. In addition, clients explore how basic assumptions concerning the self and the world interfere with everyday functioning. These tasks may also involve a shift from negative self-talk to positive expressions of attitudes. For example, Sterling constantly points out to family and friends that he is too unlucky to do anything and that he is sure to fail if he tries. After being trained to recognize these statements and to rehearse alternative statements in the group, Sterling decides that whenever he is faced with a difficult task, he will say to himself, "I think it will be difficult, but if I am well prepared, I will certainly give it my best effort and have a good chance of succeeding." Finally, cognitive tasks may involve self-reinforcement after completion of an interactive task or another cognitive restructuring task. After Sterling describes his success, he will be taught to reinforce himself. He is not only to repeat the earlier self-statement, but also to praise himself each time he succeeds. These and other cognitive homework procedures are explained in more detail in Chapter Nine.

Often, clients are assigned a combination cognitive and behavioral interactive task. In the behavioral task example referred to earlier, the client had to ask for a job (behavioral) and, at the same time, remind himself to speak loudly and clearly (cognitive).

Mutual Member Tasks. In Chapter Seven, we discussed group exposure as a means by which agoraphobics and social phobics could confront the real world. This type of task is also used to help people apply for a job; the client can be accompanied to the office door. One group leader helped a dating group plan and organize a party; the members coached each other in asking for dates and picked up their "dates" together. As the goal is to perform the task alone, this mutual support task can be regarded as an early step in the treatment process.

Noninteractive Tasks. Noninteractive behavioral tasks comprise behaviors that do not directly involve the client in interaction with other persons—for example, keeping a budget, writing down one's treatment goals, keeping an exercise program, or reading an article or chapter in a book.

The major procedures used to prepare for this type of task are careful definition of the task, usually with the help of the group; intense monitoring of the task; and other cognitive and self-control strategies. These tasks often have concrete products, which, when shown to the group, are praised by the group members or group leader. Examples of such products are budgets and data that support how each budget item was met, a written statement of treatment goals, and a report on a book or an article.

Among literate clients, reading tasks are the most common noninteractive tasks. For example, the assignment to read the first chapter of *Your Perfect Right* (Alberti and Emmons, 1985) saves a social skill group much time because the chapter outlines the basic principles of such a group. Almost all groups are assigned readings. Parent group members are commonly requested to read excerpts from *Families* (Patterson, 1975). Members of stress management groups read from our *Leader's Guide to Stress Management Training* (Rose, Tolman, and Tallant, 1985a). In family violence groups, we recommend readings from Edleson, Miller, and Stone (1983), and in pain management groups, we have encouraged members to read excerpts from our *Leader's Guide to Pain Management* (Rose and Subramanian, 1987).

To make the most of the assignment, the leader should point out the major issues covered in the reading when making the recommendation:

Most clients find it extremely useful to read this handout on how anxiety and stress are related to how we evaluate and think about situations. In reading the material try to come up with an example from your own life, which we can then discuss next week. You might want to pay particular attention to the categories of self-defeating statements used by the author and to see if you can find examples of any of these from your own or others' activities. I've put these questions down on the handout. Do you have any questions?

At the next session, the leader should bring up the major issues for discussion in the group:

What were the most important points in the handout for you? [discussion] Can you give us some examples of the relationship? [discussion] What about examples of self-defeating statements? [discussion]

When the noninteractive task is too complicated to be dealt with in the group, for example, repairing a small engine or doing one's accounting, the client is encouraged to take a course on the subject. For the more fearful, taking a course may mean first getting information on the telephone, visiting the agency, talking to the class instructor, trying out the class for one session, and eventually actively participating. This combines the noninteractive task with behavioral interactive, cognitive, and even observational tasks.

Observational Tasks.

As for me, I'm going to continue keeping track of what I say to myself just as I begin to experience stress. I will pay special attention to situations in which I put myself down or tell myself I can't do something.

Observational tasks involve self-observation or observation of others. Self-observation may focus on either behavioral, cognitive, or affective responses to stress situations and the situations in which the responses occur. It also involves the systematic recording of these observations. In the early assessment phase of treatment, self-observation is common (see Chapter Four). The client usually continues to self-monitor to assess progress, for example, monitoring one's level of anxiety in given situations on a scale of 1 to 10, counting the number of arguments with a spouse, keeping track of the amount of time spent in chore behavior, recording one's thoughts in stressful situations, and keeping a diary.

Where insufficient models exist in the group, potential models in the community can be observed. A group of elderly outpatients were assigned to observe those people they admired who came to the Senior Center, to keep track of what these people did during the day, and to report back to the group. Care was taken to note only positive behaviors to avoid interpersonal conflict with the model. (See Chapter Eight for more details on this type of modeling.) Regardless of the type of extragroup task used, the value lies in the clients' compliance.

Use of Tasks to Increase Compliance

A very common group problem is failure to complete tasks. Therefore, strategies have been developed to maximize the probability of compliance. These strategies and their empirical foundation, as they apply to individual therapy primarily for adults, are described, among others, by Shelton and Levy (1981). Here, we elaborate on these strategies as they apply to groups.

1. *Involve clients.* Involvement of a client in the selection and planning of a task increases the likelihood that the client will complete the task. Clients are far more likely to complete an assignment that they have developed themselves and own than one imposed on them by the group leader or other group members. Initially, clients may not have the basic skills to design their own tasks. Thus, the group leader plays a major role in modeling the planning of tasks in the first few sessions of treatment, but even in this early phase she must take into consideration the client's interests, which should have been elicited in the pregroup interview.

As she presents tasks, the group leader points out the criteria that guided her in development of the tasks. After learning the principles discussed next, members are better able to assume responsibility for the design of their tasks. In addition, clients can pair off to design tasks. Each partner gives the other feedback on whether they have met the criteria.

In yet another procedure, the criteria are written on the chalk board and the leader presents the group with a task containing some clearly observable errors. The group then discusses the "case" in terms of the criteria.

2. *Be specific.* Clients should be well versed in the specific details of their tasks if they expect to complete them. That is, each group member should know when the task is to be carried out, with whom, under what conditions, what behaviors or cognitions are to be implemented, and if and how the results are to be monitored and reported back to the group. It takes considerable time to achieve this specificity in a session, but failure to do so is one of the major reasons for noncompliance. The clients simply do not know when,

where, or what they are supposed to be doing. Note this example of a highly specific and well-articulated task:

> I agree to go to the church dance for the Singles Group on Saturday evening and to ask a friend (Walter M. or Steve G.) to go with me. I will call him on Tuesday evening and as soon as he agrees, I will call my "buddy" in the group who has indicated he will be home on Tuesday. If I can't succeed on Tuesday, I will try each subsequent evening.

In this task the client knows exactly what has to be done and the time frame within which it needs to be done. Earlier, she had briefly discussed what she might do, and one of the other members had modeled a roleplay. She had roleplayed the phone conversation several times in the group. In later sessions, such specificity is not desirable. A task is assigned that covers a wider set of circumstances and allows greater independence and creativity on the part of the client.

3. *Prepare adequately.* In the preceding example, the client was prepared for the task by roleplaying the most difficult part—asking the man to go to the dance with her. If a client is unsure how to carry out an interactive task, preparation in the group through behavioral or cognitive rehearsal may be necessary. If no preparation is required, the task may not be sufficiently difficult to warrant the group's attention.

In preliminary sessions, preparation may consist merely of obtaining the information necessary to carry out the task. For example, Wilfred, who was isolated socially, decided that his task would be to join a class; however, he also assigned himself the preliminary task to obtain information about the various classes available, costs, class size, and available transportation (because he had no car). Had he simply assumed the task of joining a drama class, he would have been more likely to fail.

To ensure that each group member is well prepared, at the end of each meeting, the leader or the buddy reviews with the client exactly what will be done as a task prior to the next session and whether the client has performed all the necessary prerequisite activities. The tasks are usually written down at the end of the meeting; in doing so, the members often discover that they are lacking information or are prepared inadequately. For example, Ann wrote that she was going to list all the activities she wanted to do and had to do. Moreover, she would prioritize the items on the list. When she reported back to the group, she realized that she did not know how to prioritize and had to work on that before completing the assignment.

As the group approaches termination, less preparation is required for extragroup tasks. In the final sessions, no preparation is given, to simulate the conditions of the real world.

4. *Reinforce success.* When a task is successfully completed, the client is usually reinforced at the time he tells the group about his success. Reinforcement takes the form of praise by the members and the group leader and, after a particularly difficult task, by the applause of the entire group. Some clients reinforce themselves with such activities as reading a novel or watching a favorite TV program. In the earlier example, Ann stated that only when she had completed her task would she work on the sweater she was knitting for herself. If the client plans to reinforce himself at the successful completion of the task, he should include this information in the written task description. This statement, which defines both the task and the reinforcement, is called a contingency contract. Although commonly used with children, it is occasionally used with adults at their own initiative.

The client is also trained to reinforce herself covertly for performance of the task at the time it is carried out. A self-reinforcement exercise is incorporated into the agendas of most groups we have worked with. In this exercise, each person writes down one thing she has recently done well. If she cannot think of anything, the other group members give her ideas. The group brainstorms about a list of self-reinforcing statements that are written on the chalk board. Then each member tells the group in an assertive tone what she or he has done well and reinforces her- or himself with one of the statements on the chalk board. The exercise is usually repeated several times, with members using different self-statements and different achievements.

5. *Gradually increase the level of difficulty.* The most powerful reinforcement is success. Initial tasks should be relatively

easy to perform so that success is achieved and reinforcement received; however, the task should not be so easy that it is not a challenge. The level of difficulty of subsequent tasks should gradually be increased to approximate the difficulty of the treatment goal. We have found that as a client moves closer to the goal the level of difficulty can be increased dramatically, provided there is a history of early success. This principle is most dramatically demonstrated in Chapter Nine in the example of group exposure, in which the design of successively difficult tasks is the major treatment planning activity. Another example is found in a group of couples with sexual problems, who were assigned a sequence of tasks to do at home, under what both partners agreed were the most romantic conditions (soft lights, soft music, favorite perfume, candlelight dinner). The clients were instructed to go no further than the first task in the following sequence after the first session, and to add on the next tasks session by session: fondle partner briefly with clothes on; fondle partner for an hour with clothes on; fondle partner without clothes on; fondle partner for an hour, stimulating erogenous zones; engage in sexual intercourse.

A less dramatic example is a group of parents of children with attention deficit disorder. The parents are first asked to roleplay with their partner at home how they will reinforce their children for modest achievements. The second week, they reinforce their child at least once for an achievement using the criteria for good reinforcement. The third week, they reinforce, at least once a day, specific behaviors of their children. And in the fourth week, they attempt to reinforce every occurrence of predetermined behaviors.

6. *Cue the Client.* When a task is complex (that is, it has many diverse steps), clients may have difficulty remembering all the steps necessary to complete the task successfully. To facilitate their remembering, the group leader uses a variety of cueing strategies to remind the client when and what is to happen. For example, Herbert arranged to be called by his buddy every evening to remind him to practice relaxation, which he had forgotten to do the week before. At work, Allyson set her computer to ring on the hour, at which time she wrote down her level of anxiety and what was happening in the environment about her. On the mirror in her bathroom, Maria placed a large calendar on which she wrote her

tasks on the appropriate day. In the evening, if she had completed the tasks, she circled the day.

All of these techniques serve as cues to perform a task at a specific time. Although frequently used in the initial phase of treatment, cues, like other devices, are rapidly faded as the clients gain competence. If such cues seem insufficient, the client may be reacting to the excessive structure imposed by such techniques. This issue should be discussed in the group.

7. *Use multiple monitors.* It is our experience that the greater the number of monitors, the greater the likelihood of task completion. Cognitive tasks, however, can be monitored only by a given client; even behavioral tasks may not be monitored by anyone that the client chooses. Although we explore with the client as many external monitoring sources as possible, we have not often been successful in finding more than one, the client. For adult clients, the primary monitors are buddies from the group, relatives, or friends not in the group. Unfortunately, as many friends and family members have a history of nagging or adversely cueing the client, their involvement as monitors may produce more trouble than benefits.

Even if the client succeeds in finding additional monitors, they should gradually be phased out; only self-report should be used in the late phase of treatment, to reduce the artificiality of the treatment procedures.

8. *Select a task that is possible.* It is possible to complete a task only if the conditions for carrying out that task exist. For example, one member of a stress management group was very interested in the task of planning a vacation together with his wife, because taking a vacation and improving communication with his wife were areas of concern to him. When the other members asked him when he would do this, he realized that he would have to postpone the task, because his wife was visiting relatives and would not be back until a week later.

9. *Encourage clients to commit publicly to the task.* Members should be encouraged to make a public commitment to the group and, eventually, to the immediate social circle on which the task impinges. After the client describes the task to the group, the leader asks the client why the task is important to him or her. If

the client does not know, the leader may ask the group. In our experience, a client who believes that a task is important and states his intention to carry it out is more likely to complete it. The use of multiple monitors is also a form of public commitment. Public commitment by everyone else in the group pressures a client to make a statement as well. The research of Levy and her associates (Levy, 1977; Levy, Yamashita, and Pow, 1979; Levy and Clark, 1980) lends support to this assumption.

Kanfer and Gaelick (1986, p. 310) warn that "caution must be exercised in the use of public commitment, because the client might set the criteria for the contracted behavior higher than she or he can reasonably achieve, in order to impress others." They also warn that the clients may try to avoid those who have knowledge of the commitment. Discussion in the group of these issues reduces the likelihood of their occurrence.

10. *Encourage clients to commit privately.* Although difficult to ascertain, private commitment or motivation is an important prerequisite for completion of a task. Rough indicators are the time and effort invested to define the task, to meet the criteria for planning, and to carry it out. As noted earlier, public commitment and maximum involvement may increase private commitment to completion of the contract. Another strategy proposed by Shelton and Levy (1981) is to discuss with group members what they have already done to help themselves with problems.

As a task is designed, the group member should be encouraged to explain how the task is related to the problem for which the client was referred to the group. The group discussion that follows is an excellent opportunity to talk to members about their beliefs and fears with respect to a given task. Members should be encouraged to ask questions. This is also an opportunity to incorporate a model into the group who testifies to the value of the various tasks. If a live model is not available, audio- or videotapes can be used. Cognitive rehearsal may be used to practice statements indicating private commitment. These statements usually have evolved out of the group discussion.

11. *Correct cognitive barriers to task completion.* Sometimes, behavioral tasks are not completed because cognitive distortions interfere with the client's capacity to perform the desired be-

havior. For example, a parent in a parent training group decided to set firm limits on her son whenever he had a temper tantrum. She repeatedly failed to carry out this task. When the members looked at her parallel cognitions, they discovered the statement "He won't love me any more if I don't let him do what he wants." Correction of this distortion through disputation and cognitive rehearsal led to completion of the task. How such procedures are explicitly carried out is described in Chapter Nine.

12. *Monitor all extragroup tasks at subsequent sessions.* As mentioned earlier in this chapter, all assignments are monitored at the beginning of the subsequent session. Failure to do so almost inevitably results in failure to comply and in lack of reinforcement. The leader asks the members about their week. When a client reveals a success, the leader is careful to reinforce him and encourages the members to do likewise. If a client fails to complete a task, the leader simply goes on to the next client without asking for an explanaton. After all the members recount their experiences, the leader summarizes their achievements. This provides the leader with a second opportunity to reinforce. The leader then asks that they later examine the reasons for both success and lack of it when they plan the next week's extragroup tasks.

13. *And if members still fail to complete extragroup tasks?* Even though leaders pay a great deal of attention to the preceding principles, in some groups, the tasks remain incomplete or unimportant to a majority of the members. In two groups, after the leaders had discussed the reasons for failure with the members they concluded that the homework overstructured their activities. As a result, the leaders agreed to temporarily do away with structured tasks. The leaders of both groups merely gave the members a list of activities that some people found useful to perform between sessions. Unless the members requested clarification, they were given no further help or encouragement. In both groups, the amount of extragroup activity appeared to increase, although without formal monitoring, it was difficult to be certain.

Summary

In summary, tasks are a vital means of transferring what members have learned in the group to the real world, but only if they are completed. They increase the amount of treatment time available to the client without adding to the cost. They increase the client's independence and sense of self-efficacy. They create opportunities for multiple trials of behaviors attempted only once in the group. They provide access to private events. They provide an index of productivity.

There are many different types of tasks, of which the most important for transfer of change are behavioral interactive and cognitive tasks. Tasks are central to the problem-solving process. Performance of the task, which represents the implementation phase, and monitoring of the task, which represents the validation phase, constitute the first cycle of the process.

A number of principles were described that can be used as guidelines by both group leaders and members to enhance compliance. These guidelines can be integrated into the task planning process, where they serve to prevent low compliance and the concomitant side effects. It is important to note that most of these principles, such as "be specific" and "prepare adequately," change as the group develops over time.

THIRTEEN

Principles and Strategies for Maintaining New Behavior

Clients may learn to be good group members. They may also learn to roleplay what they have learned with accuracy and flair. They may even demonstrate the target behaviors under the comfortable conditions of the group setting. Yet they will have achieved nothing useful unless they can apply the behaviors and cognitions they have learned in the group in a variety of circumstances outside the treatment group. This chapter explicates the strategies employed in transferring the learning beyond the group.

Generalization is extension of learning beyond the boundaries of the training or therapeutic session in terms of time, behavior, setting, or any combination of these. Generalization in time refers to maintenance of acquired behaviors/cognitions after termination of the clinical experience. A client is said to maintain what she has learned in the group if, six months after the group experience, she is still able to relax in the face of daily hassles, a skill she learned in the group.

Generalization of behavior refers to the practice of behaviors similar but not identical to those learned in the treatment session. For example, the client who learns to control anger in the group may generalize what he has learned to control stress responses outside the group.

Generalization in setting refers to application of what is learned in the treatment setting to settings outside the group, for example, the client who, after learning to refuse others who impose on him in a roleplay in the group meeting, applies these roleplayed behaviors at home with his brother-in-law or in the office with a bothersome co-worker. This is also one of the major purposes of the extragroup task, discussed in Chapter Twelve. Combination of all three types of generalization is demonstrated by the client who, having learned in the group to ask for help from a roleplayed physician, applies that behavior with his real doctor in the office setting or with a friend whose help he needs, and continues to demonstrate that help-seeking behavior long after the group has terminated. For treatment to be considered effective, generalization must take place at all three levels.

The most fundamental observation about generalization is that it rarely occurs if nothing is done about it (Stokes and Baer, 1977, p. 350). Generalization must be planned. In the multimethod approach to group therapy, a gradual, systematic program for the generalization of changes from the group to the client's natural environment is planned for and carried out, separate from assessment and intervention planning. Once the changes in behavior are manifested on a regular basis in the group, the focus of planning and treatment activities shifts to maintenance of these new behaviors outside the group.

The group has a number of advantages over the therapeutic dyad in teaching generalization. Some of these were noted in Chapter One. The group provides an environment that more nearly simulates the real world than does a one-to-one relationship. Multiple models and modeling experiences are available in the group setting. The group provides frequent and varied opportunities for members to assume responsibility for helping others. The group supplies to its members a variety of experiences, situations, and demands. As the reader will note in the subsequent sections, each of these circumstances represents an opportunity to apply a unique principle to training for generalization.

As discussed in Chapter Twelve, the extragroup task is a major strategy of generalization in setting, as most tasks consist of practicing new behaviors learned in the group in the external environment. Because the extragroup task was thoroughly discussed in Chapter Twelve, here we discuss other principles of generalization of change that are commonly used to guide group intervention planning. At least three sets of principles of generalization can be identified. The first set pertains to the process of target selection.

Certain targets of intervention are more readily generalized than others, and certain targets mediate the attainment of the client's self-selected targets. The second set of principles relates to variation in the program, and the third set involves training in the extragroup environment. A firm empirical foundation does not as yet exist for all of these principles. They were, for the most part, derived by extrapolation from some modest research, often in nonclinical settings, and extensive clinical experience.

Many of the principles espoused here overlap. In addition, subprinciples can be identified.

Principles of Generalization Related to Target Selection

The first two principles in this category concern the criteria for the selection of target behaviors. The leader should focus on behaviors considered important by the client and significant others in his environment. In so doing, the leader is also likely to select behaviors that will be reinforced outside the group. The next four principles are concerned with teaching target behaviors or cognitive frameworks that mediate the client's self-selected goals. These include positive self-talk, independent behavior, conceptualization of the general principles of maintenance of change, and problem-solving skills.

1. *Focus on behaviors considered important in the real world.* If a client does not consider a behavior important, he or she is unlikely to invest much effort in acquiring it. Often, the assignment of a client to a given group is determined by the description of the group. But clients may change and/or misunderstand what the group is all about. In thematic groups, it may be better to encourage such clients to find another group that better meets their needs rather than mold the goals of the client to fit the parameters of the group. As members are encouraged to become more specific within the group theme, it is helpful to ask clients to justify why such a change is important and how such a change would improve their lives. At the very least, the leader should repeatedly ask whether a given change is still important to the client, and the members should ask each other this same question.

Even if clients think the new behavior is important, they

should consider whether it is valued by their social networks. One woman wanted to learn to refuse, assertively, her boss's excessive demands on her. It was a hierarchical organization in which she had very little power. Every attempt to assert herself was met with rebuke not only by her immediate boss but by her co-workers. (Although not all clients may have this option, she decided after consultation with the group to look for employment elsewhere.) Sometimes, the priority a client places on a goal overrides all other considerations. For example, Wilma reported that she was being sexually harassed at her job. Despite the possibility of losing the job and the difficulty in finding a new one, and the pressure from her mother "not to make waves," she lodged an official complaint. She did lose her job, but she felt the risk was worth taking.

Focus on behaviors likely to be reinforced in the real world. If a behavior is considered important in one's social network, it is also likely to be reinforced. The woman who was rebuffed every time she tried to be assertive not only failed to receive reinforcement, but was punished for her initiative. It is unlikely that her assertive behavior would be maintained if no other principles were operating. In a group of abusive men, several men selected paying more positive attention to their wives as a target behavior. This behavior was greatly appreciated by the wives, who responded with behavior that reinforced the men (positive communication, showing interest in their work, and so forth). As a result the behavior was maintained. In another group, at least one member reported the attention he paid to his wife was met with suspicion and doubt (probably for good reason). In this case, his target behavior was unlikely to be maintained without further adjustment.

3. *Teach positive self-talk.* As we pointed out in Chapter Nine, one skill that most clients lack is positive self-talk. Because the supportive environment and reinforcement found in the group setting end somewhat abruptly at the end of treatment and because these conditions often do not exist in the client's life outside the group, training clients to evaluate their achievements positively and to talk themselves through difficult situations is an essential component of a generalization program. Clients are taught these skills through exercises, cognitive modeling, and rehearsal. Details and examples of these procedures are found in Chapter Nine.

Positive self-talk, however, should be realistic. In one group of depressed and phobic patients, the positive statements were clearly untrue. As a result, most members found the exercise trivial, Pollyannaish, and upsetting. A more gradual indoctrination in positive self-talk, with the leader modeling throughout treatment, might have been more appropriate.

4. *Teach the general principle.* By the time a group approaches termination, most members have learned behaviors they can apply in a number of situations. Toward the end of the sessions, it becomes crucial for the members to draw patterns for themselves of the procedures they have learned, and to develop for themselves general principles that guide them in the determination of what they can do when new problems arise.

It is impossible to train clients to deal effectively with every situation they might face. At some point they will have to leap from the specifics they have learned and apply the general principle. For example, a client learned to handle his middle school child who came home late at night, well after curfew. The parent learned to set strict limits on a contractual basis to replace his weak "don't do it any more." He also increased reinforcement on a continuing basis for the child's achievements in keeping his room clean and doing his homework. The group leader asked the group if they could think of other situations in which firm limits were appropriate. They listed a few situations. The leader then asked the members to note when these situations arose and bring them up for discussion in the group. The group leader then noted that setting a few firm limits, expressed assertively and backed up with contingencies, in areas of concern to the parent, against a background of ongoing reinforcement, is useful in dealing with the young adolescent.

Stokes and Baer (1977) refer to "mediated generalization," which is operative when clients are taught skills to mediate performance of the target behavior in the real world. Clients can be trained to take cues into the real world to remember the content of the desired behavior and/or the conditions under which it should occur. One example of mediated generalization training is taken from an anger control group: The members were instructed to say "Cool it!" and "Relax" to themselves when they began to feel angry. The members practiced the procedure using the acronym

"Rel-ci." Each person was trained first to recognize the specific physiological events that occurred when he felt angry: headache, clenched teeth, difficulty in breathing. These became the cue for the cognitive response. The cue then mediated the relaxation response in the real world.

Stokes and Baer (1977, p. 361) recommend that clients be instructed to try out generalized behaviors in the real world, and when they provide evidence of success, they should be reinforced. There are two ways to reinforce. One, self-reinforcement, is practiced covertly in the group. The second, group approval, occurs when the client reports back to the group.

Clients can also be taught the general principle through the exercise in Exhibit 5, which is distributed to the members a week before its use so that they can prepare. Members are encouraged to prepare with buddies.

Although useful, this exercise was somewhat confusing to less well educated clients in a divorce adjustment group and an

---

Exhibit 5. Seeing the Larger Pattern: An Exercise.

Purpose

By the end of this session each member will be able to describe (1) patterns of situations that the member finds difficult or stressful and (2) cognitive, affective, and behavioral patterns of responses to stressful or otherwise difficult interpersonal situations.

Rationale

Each client will review all situations he or she has handled in group until that meeting, and to prepare a five-minute summary to present to the group.

Steps

1. Each member will briefly present the review to the group and will note (a) patterns in the situations that he or she finds difficult or stressful and (b) patterns in responses (cognitive, emotional, and/or behavioral) across several situations.
2. Other group members and the leader will suggest to the member additional patterns, as well as newly developing changes in earlier patterns.
3. Finally, the group will focus on the general principles that seem to be guiding the successes the client is having in the real world.
4. Each member will serve as discussion leader for another client.

---

anxiety management group. It may be necessary, under such conditions, to simplify the wording or break the exercise down into several exercises to slow the pace.

5. *Teach clients to apply systematic problem solving.* As indicated throughout this book, problem solving is a set of cognitive skills essential to learning more effective coping strategies. If problem-solving skills are sufficiently well learned, they can be used to solve problems outside the group. To train people to use their problem-solving skills in this way, an exercise is administered to clients requesting that they observe and record new problems that occur between sessions and describe how they used their problem-solving skills to deal with these previously undiscussed events. This exercise has been used primarily between the last regular session and a booster session, since an extended period is necessary to carry out the assignment.

6. *Teach independent behavior.* Before clients can take control of their own lives, they must practice independent behaviors in the group. To this end, members should be involved, as extensively as possible, in the treatment process, for example, in selecting their own treatment goals, performing leadership functions in the group, providing responsible feedback to others in the group, choosing treatment procedures that they deem most suitable for their problem, and designing their own extragroup and post-treatment tasks.

Throughout this book we have demonstrated how clients can be involved in such decisions. As clinicians, we have observed that homework designed by the clients is more likely to be completed than homework assigned by the leader. Interventions selected by clients are more likely to be carried out than those imposed on them. We have noted that goals formulated by the clients are more likely to be achieved. We have also seen that the act of giving feedback, especially if it is acted on by peers, is a source of satisfaction and increases self-esteem. Furthermore, as Yalom (1985) points out, one curative factor in groups is the manifestation of altruism; feedback, if properly delivered, is an expression of altruism. Yalom views involvement in any phase of treatment, which empowers the client, as another curative factor.

Obviously, a leader does not abdicate leadership. The delegation of responsibility is a gradual, but constant process. As members demonstrate basic skills in leadership, they are given increasing opportunities to practice the skills.

One way in which members are involved is by developing their own goals. Kelley and Stokes (1984) evaluated the strategy of goal setting on the academic productivity of eight economically disadvantaged high school dropouts between the ages of sixteen and twenty-one. Students wrote their own work contracts without teacher feedback and were paid contingent on contract completion. The results indicated that goal setting for response maintenance proved effective.

In an eight-session assertiveness training group for secretaries in a large governmental department, the leader had the members plan for and lead the last four sessions (a manual was used as a point of departure). The members evaluated every session and asked for specific changes in the program. Changes were made if the other group members agreed. At the end of the third session, each member formulated her own goals and interventions with consultation, only, from the leader and the group. Rather than being assigned extragroup tasks, members selected tasks from a list of recommendations. On the postsession questionnaire, members consistently rated their independence between 6 and 7 on a 7-point scale.

Principles of Multiple Trials and Variation

The leader is able to vary the training program in many ways and thus provide the group different learning experiences. This variation is based on several principles.

1. *Provide varied examples.* To prepare the client to handle unpredictable problem situations in the real world, during or after termination of the group, many varied examples are introduced to illustrate each principle or technique. The leader also asks members for examples from their own experience. Often, the leader will introduce a topic one week and, as an extragroup task, ask members to seek examples between sessions.

The availability of many examples allows the parameters of the principle to be more clearly delineated. Moreover, the cues that correlate with reinforcement eventually gain control over the associated behaviors (that is, the behavior appears in the presence of the cues.) Variation, therefore, tends to expand the cues under which the behavior is reinforced (Goldstein, Heller, and Sechrest, 1966). This, in turn, increases the likelihood that a variety of cues, rather than just those associated with the group and the group leader, will elicit the desired behaviors and, hence, are more likely to generalize to the natural environment and be maintained over time.

Real-life problem situations vary a great deal. The significant others change, the content of interactions changes, and the environments in which these situations arise change. The content of problem situations used in treatment should also be varied. The group leader may incorporate variety in a number of ways. Real-life situations can be generated through situational analyses, as described in Chapter Four. Situations may also be obtained from the weekly diaries kept by the members. These situations are then used as the content of group roleplays or problem-solving sessions, as cards in a board game, or as the theme of a group exercise.

2. *Provide many modeling and practice trials.* One consequence of variation is the opportunity it provides for multiple trials. One-trial learning is possible but highly unlikely. For the most part, multiple trials are required in treatment. Therefore, wherever possible, multiple models are presented, situations are frequently rehearsed, and reinforcement is given on frequent occasions in response to a given situation. One member of a parent group complained, "You know that situation where I was supposed to sit down with my kid and work out a contract. I roleplayed it once in the group; I still wasn't able to do it with my kid." The leader then provided the member many opportunities to practice. He arranged that she would roleplay the situation on landing on the roleplay square in a board game. She roleplayed several variations on the same situation during the meeting. She roleplayed the negotiation process several times with her buddy between sessions. The client then modeled, for someone else, a similar situation. She was able to practice it a total of ten times; after the next session, she reported success in negotiating a reasonable contract with her child.

The more similar the problems of the members of the group, the greater the opportunity for both multiple models and multiple rehearsal. In fact, one client's rehearsal is frequently a model for other members of the group with the same problem situation. More heterogeneous groups provide fewer opportunities for multiple trials in the same period of time, which argues against a high level of heterogeneity in group therapy.

This principle implies that it is usually more effective, in terms of what is actually learned, to focus on a few important cognitions or overt skills and related problem situations than to treat too many problem situations, especially if time is limited (for example, six to eight one-hour sessions).

3. *Vary the treatment media.* As the group progresses, the program media are varied: board games, nondirective discussions, field trips, and different group exercises are used not only to change learning cues, but also to increase members' interest in the group and group cohesion. Most individuals have unique learning patterns. Reliance on one medium such as roleplays may not be suitable to some clients. The availability of a variety of media increases the likelihood that every client will find a suitable medium. It is also our experience that groups that adhere rigidly to one pattern tend to show a drop in attraction to the group. In most of the groups we lead, each meeting is characterized by common elements and by different elements that change week to week. Variation in programs is also one way to increase the level of difficulty and to prepare for uncertainty.

4. *Vary the level of difficulty.* It is not sufficient to vary the exemplars used in treatment; their complexity should also be increased. Early in treatment, the tasks must be simple, so that success is achieved. Success is a powerful reinforcer. But, as the real world is complex and demanding, to prepare adequately, clients must eventually be assigned complex tasks. For example, in a group of elderly clients who complained of anxiety and isolation and who were observed to have very poor communication skills, the initial task assigned to the group was to learn the names of the other people in the group. The extragroup task was to call one of the other members and discuss the group. Clients rehearsed the call in the group. Later in-group tasks were to observe and comment on a roleplay by the leaders. It was not until the third session that the members themselves roleplayed a single response to a situation in

which the antagonists were played by the leaders. In the fifth session, the members roleplayed both roles, which involved them in interaction in simulated situations of concern to them. In the sixth session, they agreed to try out the newly learned behaviors in the real world prior to the seventh session. They discussed their experiences with each other at the seventh session.

5. *Vary the degree of predictability.* The real world is often very uncertain, and thus it is necessary to incorporate unpredictability into the situations practiced in the group setting. One way to prepare clients for uncertainty is to vary the program elements. Another way is to introduce entirely new situations to which different cues are attached and require clients to respond without preparation. These new situations may be introduced at any time in the course of the program. The danger in the early sessions is that the clients may feel overwhelmed and the procedure may become aversive. For this reason, spontaneous roleplays are usually restricted to later sessions, when clients have had a great deal of roleplay experience and the relationship to the leader as reinforcing person has been established.

One unpredictable element in the real world is the degree of acceptance by others of changes that were realized in the group. Clients expect the world to be sympathetic and are deeply disappointed when those expectations are not realized. Unexpected responses by significant others are roleplayed for the client and discussed in the group. Former members often provide rich anecdotal accounts of similar unsympathetic responses as a means of tempering expectations.

6. *Vary, but make it real.* Examples, as well as other structural elements of treatment programs, should be varied so as to simulate more nearly the conditions of the real world. Use of props in roleplaying, longer roleplays, and multiperson roleplays are useful techniques. Members similar to the real antagonists may enhance the use of the roleplay. Some groups, especially during the last meetings, meet in living rooms or in cafes. The homework assignment goes the furthest in simulating real-world conditions because it is carried out in the real world. The group exposure method also takes advantage of this principle.

Another way to simulate the real world is to fade treatment

cues. Reinforcement schedules are thinned, because reinforcement in the real world is intermittent at best. Leader instructions are reduced in frequency. Responsibility for treatment planning is delegated to the members. Group conflict is eventually left to the members to resolve.

7. *Prepare for setbacks.* The group leader should, in varying the program, introduce situations in which a setback might occur. Setbacks are so common that they constitute a regular topic in the last few group sessions. Often case studies are used to deal with this issue. The leader of a group of alcoholics related the case of a person who had quit drinking. One day the stressors in this man's life overwhelmed him; he dropped out of the group, claiming, when he was called, that he was a failure. The members discussed how they would feel in such a situation and brainstormed about what they could do about it. Then each group member had to imagine what would be a setback for him or her and how to respond to such a setback.

Former clients may be brought in to discuss their setbacks and what they did about them. Mathews, Gelder, and Johnston (1981) used individual setback lists for clients in their agoraphobia groups. These lists included instructions for coping with setbacks. The clients were instructed to face the anxiety-producing situation as soon as possible, to rehearse many times the steps that gave them difficulty in that situation, to brush up on the coping instructions, and to remind oneself of previous gains. In addition, Jansson, Jerremalm, and Ost (1984) warned their agoraphobic patients about high-risk situations, such as holidays, sickness, and conflicts with co-workers or spouses, to prepare them in the use of setback strategies in those situations. Jansson and colleagues (1984) found that patients who received such preparation for setbacks improved on 34 percent of the items on the Behavior Approach Test (BAT) at pretest and on 76 percent at post-tests and that these improved scores were maintained at the six-month follow-up. In summary, three strategies are employed to prepare clients for setbacks, all of which can be used in the group: case studies, models who have handled setbacks before, and the setback list.

8. *Prevent relapses.* Conditions such as those that cause setbacks are likely to lead to relapse. If clients can be trained to

identify and to deal with these conditions as they arise, the actual relapse may be avoided (Marlatt and Gordon, 1980). Some modest empirical support for this assertion is provided by Chaney, O'Leary, and Marlatt (1978). Such a procedure lends itself to group training. For example, several members in a drug abuse group pointed out that in the past, they had relapsed when the pressure at work became too great. Others found it especially difficult when they received a great deal of criticism from their partners. The group members looked at the different situations and agreed that a need to be approved of by everyone in their lives (an illogical assumption articulated by Ellis, 1977) was a dominant theme, so this was worked on as a form of relapse prevention. Members learned to use criticism as a cue indicating that they worked hard to cope with the pressures of the world and no one could or needed to be perfect. Criticism was simply one way of learning and growing on the job. The members also learned how to accept criticism through the modeling sequence and practiced responding to criticisms voiced by the other members of the group.

Stuart (1980, p. 378) recommends the use of "what-if" exercises to families he works with, as part of the maintenance skill-building package. Based on the examples presented by Stuart, we developed the following "what-if" exercise for groups. In the eighth session of a ten-week divorce adjustment group, the leader presented the following situations to the members one at a time.

You are at a dance for singles (or a bar). You are alone. Suddenly your ex-spouse enters the room: she or he is also alone. All those terrible feelings are aroused. How should you handle this situation?

Your ex-spouse telephones you; he or she wants "just to talk, nothing in particular." You feel clutched as if you were falling apart. You thought you had already adjusted to the separation.

A parent group was presented with the following situation:

Your adolescent child has been doing great for a month. Suddenly, he comes home smelling of alcohol at four in the morning, shouting at the top of his lungs that he can't stand it any more. You feel you have failed him. All the emotions experienced six months ago are suddenly resurrected.

The members wrote down their ideas and, after a brief discussion, roleplayed either cognitively or behaviorally several solutions to the problem situations. The discussion should lead to a summarization of general principles that can guide the members in similar situations. In the divorce adjustment group, the examples presented by the leaders made members think of other potential situations that might overwhelm them. Another session was added just to handle these potentially difficult situations, as a means of relapse prevention.

Training Beyond the Boundaries of the Group

In Chapter One, it was noted that in the multimethod group approach, one of the strategies for change is the extragroup method. Thus far, we have discussed what the group leader does within the structure of the group to facilitate the generalization of change. Effective generalization, however, cannot occur unless the group leader is intimately aware of events occurring in the client's natural environment and even becomes involved in the change. Several extragroup strategies are available.

1. *Make booster sessions and maintenance groups available.* Booster sessions are an opportunity to review, update successes and failures, and keep members accountable for changes or lack thereof, for an extended period. New problems may be dealt with as well. The first booster session is often held two months after group termination and the second, four to six months later. Some members drop out of the group before the first booster session, so usually several similar groups are combined. Although research on booster sessions with adults has not been encouraging (for example, Ashby and Wilson, 1977, with obese adult women, and Maletzky, 1977), Kazdin (1982) did demonstrate with children the efficacy of booster sessions in maintaining and even increasing gains made in the group. In most of these studies, the methodological weaknesses (for example, insufficient power to reject the null hypothesis)

prevent us from claiming that booster sessions are effective. Another reason for the lack of clarity of the results may be the small number of booster sessions used in any of the studies done thus far. Two or three booster sessions may simply not be enough to show a significant gain compared with a control group.

The maintenance group, an extended series of sessions, is usually based on the principles established in the first part of this chapter. These groups meet less frequently, usually once a month, and are less structured than treatment groups. The group leader acts as consultant to the group. Members serve as discussion leaders. For the most part, the members determine their own agendas, although problem situations, usually more complex than those in the regular treatment group, are also discussed. The maintenance group tends to be larger than the treatment group and is composed of people who are not yet ready to sever ties with the treatment program or who cannot find support in their environment for their newly learned life-style.

2. *Plan follow-up contacts.* Gambrill (1983, p. 387) recommends the use of follow-up contacts after termination of treatment. She reasons that as in booster sessions, "anticipation of this meeting may serve as a reminder to use skills that have been learned and as support for their use." In our groups, we have found it difficult to attract 50 percent of the original membership at a given booster session. A larger number of clients can be reached through individual follow-up. In the ideal solution, members organize a set of booster sessions at their last regular treatment session. The calls made to remind people of the booster session may be opportunities for individual follow-up interviews, if the members are willing.

Such a plan was implemented in a stress management group. All of the members voiced a willingness to attend the booster session. A fee was collected in advance to cover expenses. When the phone calls were made to remind members of the booster session, nearly 60 percent of clients had either moved away or had other things to do. Those who had alternative plans made a telephone appointment to review what had happened in the booster session and to review their successes in the three months since termination of the group. Even though a fee had been paid and an appointment made, 20 percent of the group were not available when the appointed phone call was made. Those who did respond to the telephone appointment found it very helpful and requested other appointments for which they were willing to pay in advance. Though clearly not for everyone, the follow-up telephone contact is extremely useful to some.

3. *Encourage membership in socioeducational and self-help groups.* Another variation of the maintenance group is membership in existing groups that do not have a therapeutic focus. For example, members of one weight control group decided, prior to termination of the group, to join Weight Watchers. The first few Weight Watchers sessions and the last few treatment group sessions overlapped, so that the members could be helped to deal with the new philosophy and any other social problems incurred by membership in the new organization. Other self-help groups that members have joined are Alcoholics Anonymous, Batterers Anonymous, and various groups for the recently divorced.

Sociorecreational groups include dance classes, bowling clubs, friendship groups, art groups, and practically everything a community center has to offer. Joining just before termination of the therapy group is extremely important in preventing failures or even difficulties that the clients are unable to handle without help. Members of a therapy group for the elderly took field trips to the local Y and other organizations serving the elderly. They had practiced their interview skills in the groups beforehand to discover whether their interests could be met. In the fifth-to-the-last therapy group session, the members were asked to describe the group or organization they had joined, and in the next two sessions, they described what happened at the first meeting of the new group.

4. *Work with others outside the group.* In groups in which the problems are quite severe, such as schizophrenic groups, it is not unusual for the leader to work with staff of other social agencies or with significant others (spouses, parents, children). It may be necessary for the leader to contact landlords when difficulties arise that the member is not yet ready to handle alone. Such contacts are always made with the knowledge and approval of the client. The client should handle such situations alone as soon as possible.

In some cases, significant others form groups, such as groups for siblings and spouses of schizophrenics. Al-Anon is a group for relatives of alcoholics. It is clear that for many clients, group therapy is not sufficient to bring about even minimal change. The cooperation of many others may be required. The nature and complexity of such extragroup contacts can only be acknowledged here. When problems arise, they can be dealt with by the group leader, functioning in the role of client advocate and broker of service. (See Toseland and Rivas, 1984, for a more detailed description of various extragroup approaches.)

5. *Modify the social network.* In many cases, the social networks of our clients are either too limited or not able to meet their needs, especially those needs related to generalization of changes. One way to deal with this is to examine the clients' social networks in the group in light of the needs being served, and to problem solve methods of modifying that network. Kirkham and others (1986), in working in cognitive-behaviorally oriented groups of parents of handicapped children, encouraged the clients to broaden their social networks. Parents learned to identify the people in their social networks and the support they received from each person. Then, each client, with the help of a "buddy" from the group, devised a plan to modify the social network so that it would better meet personal needs for social support outside the group.

6. *Act as advocate.* In many groups, the leader may have to act as advocate on behalf of the clients to other social agencies. One man from a family violence group had lost visitation rights with his child. He had worked extremely hard in the group and had demonstrated skill in handling his anger in a relationship he had recently entered. As a result of the testimony of the group leader, the man was permitted supervised contacts with his child. As a consequence of the contact with his child, he made rapid gains in the group.

A parent group advocated at the county social services on behalf of one member who had been trying to adopt a handicapped foster child. They wrote dispositions on what the client had done to upgrade her parenting skills, described the plan she had developed for further refining her skills, and told about the specific nature of the support she would receive from the group for carrying out that plan.

Kirkham (1988) reports how she integrated social advocacy

into her parent-skill-training groups. These projects included a manual for professionals on what to say and what not to say to parents of handicapped children, a list of suggestions on how physicians should interview such parents, and a resource book for parents of handicapped children.

7. *Take treatment into the community.* It is far easier to transfer learning from the therapeutic setting to the real world if the treatment actually occurs in the real world. For practical reasons, this is not always possible. The group exposure method is one way; members accompany each other to social events under increasingly difficult conditions. Occasionally, group sessions are held at restaurants, community centers, bowling alleys, bars, dances, and other locations where the actual problem occurs. If, as we assume, the learning is associated with the cues under which the behavior is learned, treatment in the real world would increase the variety of cues under which the behavior is learned. When treatment occurs in the community, the leader either is present for only a part of the meeting or is present for the entire meeting but as a consultant. In this way, the clients are given the responsibility of handling their own problems as preparation for termination of the group. The best examples of group exposure are found in those groups where the members together face phobic situations in the real world after brief in-group preparation.

Of course, group therapy in settings with limited supervision is not without problems. Unsupervised meetings may result in establishment of antitherapeutic norms. Buddies may not have the leadership skills necessary to help one another. There exist many diversions in the outside world to keep members off-task. Moreover, organizational restraints often restrict the institution of such practices. Nevertheless, it appears to us that in future development of the multimethod approach, greater attention must be paid to training in the external environment.

Putting It All Together

One way to unite the preceding principles to is to list, prior to group termination, all the principles presented in the course of the program. Some new principles may be introduced. All the principles are briefly reviewed. The members are asked to design for themselves, either as a home or an in-group exercise, a plan to prepare them for life after the group. Members then evaluate each other's plans and modify their plans on the basis of the evaluations. The following generalization exercise has been evaluated very highly by members in our groups.

Exhibit 6. Transfer and Maintenance of Change: An Exercise.

Purpose

By the end of this exercise, you will have devised a personal transfer of change and maintenance plan.

Rationale

Transfer-of-change techniques help you learn to apply what you have learned in group to problem situations outside the group. Actually, we have already used many of these techniques. Without transfer of change, the group experience would simply be an interesting exercise with no application to your life.

Maintenance-of-change techniques help you to preserve the positive gains you have made in group. The aim is to make the skills you have learned in the group have a lasting benefit, after the group is completed. Sometimes, people find it hard to keep their newly learned skills sharp without an active plan for maintaining those skills. This exercise is designed to help you formulate such a plan.

Steps

Keeping the skills you have learned sharp, improving your performance, and applying what you have learned in the group to other situations take work, but are important. These steps can lead you to a follow-up plan:

A. Become familiar with the techniques available to you:
    1.   Focus on behaviors and situations considered important in the real world.
    2.   Focus on behaviors likely to be reinforced in the real world.
    3.   Practice positive self-talk.
    4.   Learn the general principle.
    5.   Practice independent behavior.
    6.   Practice with varied examples.
    7.   Observe many models and practice many times.
    8.   Practice situations with different levels of difficulty.
    9.   Prepare for setbacks.
    10. Prevent relapses.
    11. Train yourself beyond the boundaries of the group.
    12. Attend booster sessions and maintenance groups if available.
    13. Plan follow-up contacts with buddies or staff.

14. Join socioeducational and self-help groups.
15. Work with your significant others outside the group.
16. Take your own treatment into the community. Keep a diary of successes and problem areas.
17. Periodically review the techniques you have learned.
18. Review the techniques and decide which ones could work for you.

B. Develop a specific, *realistic* plan including only those techniques you plan on using.

Exercise

1. Each member should devise a plan prior to the meeting in which the rest of the exercise takes place. (It may also be done in the meeting.)
2. At the meeting, break up into pairs to discuss and refine plans.
3. Share plans with the entire group.
4. The group helps in evaluation of each member's plan. Is it complete? Is it realistic? How can group members help each other to maintain change?

Using this exercise, three members of a group devised the following plan:

Each person prepared a setback list. They rehearsed the potential setback situations. These situations were sprung on members without warning by other group members. Each member joined an interest group at the Y. One parent who had difficulty in controlling her anger joined Parents Anonymous. They agreed to contact each other once a week to tell each other how they were doing. In emergencies or if setbacks actually occurred, they agreed to call the leader. All three decided to adjust their social support network by spending more time with a sympathetic friend, and one decided to reduce time spent with overanxious family members who added stress.

Preparing for Termination

In contrast to many other forms of group therapy, preparation for termination consists largely of planning to continue carrying out a target behavior when the group terminates. We acknowledge that members often become very attached to the group experience and the group members, even in short-term groups. Some view termination as a painful experience. As the group approaches termination, there may be a recurrence of maladaptive behaviors, a sudden increase in dependence on the group leader, emergence of new complex problems for which time is not available, and a focus on social activities.

Often, these problems can be avoided if the members are given greater responsibility for group activities and their own individual treatment programs. By helping members to establish and strengthen social networks in the community, the leader abdicates her or his central role in their lives. If relationships outside the group become stronger than those within the group, the leader has accomplished his or her task. If not, work remains.

When prophylactic measures do not work and manifestations of dependence remain strong as the group approaches termination, the group leader can deal with the situation as a group problem to be considered by the members. Often, simple discussion is sufficient. A strategy commonly used to weaken bonds between group members is to have each member invite a nonmember to a group meeting and describe the nature of the group. To maintain confidentiality, only general problems and strategies are discussed.

In general, in groups meeting ten sessions or fewer we have not frequently observed emotional ties so great that members were upset at the thought of leaving. Usually, termination is more like graduation; members are excited about doing things on their own. Most of the strategies described in this section are initiated in longer-term groups.

Conclusions and Summary

Two basic assumptions are made in this chapter: (1) generalization does not occur unless it is planned for and (2) no one procedure is universally effective in helping members to achieve maintenance and transfer of change to the real world. Use of a battery of strategies is advocated. The major principles that guide planning for generalization are outlined. Although these principles and the related strategies are discussed near the end of the book, their importance should not be lessened. Since the success of a group is measured by the success of its members in altering their behavior and cognitions in problematic situations in the real world, it is only through careful planning and incorporation of these principles that the benefits of the group will be maintained over the long term.

FOURTEEN

The Multimethod Approach in Action

with Randy Magen

To provide an overview of the multimethod approach, we present a case study of a typical group, a stress management group, in this chapter. We focus on the tasks of the group leader, the group interventions, the data collection procedures, and the generalization strategies used over the ten sessions. We include brief excerpts from all ten sessions and the pre- and postgroup interviews. The strategies and principles covered in this book are noted parenthetically where appropriate.

How the Group Began

An agency that served its clients primarily through group programs decided to include as clients those suffering from stress disorders. Trained and interested leaders were available, and the need in the community was made apparent by the number of people who had already referred themselves. Other clients were recruited by means of public service advertisements in the local newspaper.

Those who called the agency received a brief description of the program and how it would be carried out. The telephone interviewer explained that the groups would meet for two hours once per week for ten weeks. Costs and other conditions of mem-

Note: This chapter was coauthored by Randy Magen and Sheldon D. Rose.

bership were also clarified. The applicant was informed that the group had four major components: relaxation training, social skill training, cognitive restructuring, and group exercises. Members would be provided selected readings and would have the opportunity to examine and work on specific stress problems of concern to them. If the caller was interested, an appointment was made for an individual pregroup interview that would last about an hour. Further information was provided in this interview. The client was tested with the measures described later and interviewed to determine the specific parameters of the stress. The interviewer also explored situations the client wanted to work on in the group. The following interviewees agreed to come to the stress management group being offered at that time. (The specific information was gathered at the pregroup interview.)

Jerry L. found out about the stress group in the classified section of the local newspaper. He is a 36-year-old construction supervisor, has been at his current job for the past six years, and is considering making a change either in his profession or where he lives. Jerry is considering a job change because he usually is assigned more work than he has time to complete. Another reason is that his co-worker often criticizes the way he does his job. Jerry acknowledges that he rarely handles criticism well. He says that he constantly feels stressed out, is fatigued, and suffers from headaches as a result of this work-related pressure.

On the bulletin board in her physician's waiting room, Ellen M. noticed a poster recruiting members for a stress management group. Ellen reported in the group that she has been managing a clothing store for the past 12 years. Until recently, she had lived alone, a situation with which she was content. Last month, Ellen's 15-year-old grandchild came to live with her. Ellen's peaceful rural life has been shattered by loud music, phone calls, and the responsibilities of caring for a teenage girl. Ellen told the interviewer that she feels a great deal of stress from having to deal with her grandchild.

Susan B.'s friend, noting her inability to handle the transition from high school to the working world, told her about the stress management group. Susan had graduated from high school two years earlier. Since graduation, she had been working as a secretary for an insurance company. Many of Susan's friends moved away or went off to college. Susan's two older siblings are both married and have children. Susan feels alone in the world and wonders if she will ever fall in love. She does not like her job but does not know what to do about it.

Jim W.'s social worker at Catholic Social Services referred him to the stress management group. Jim works on the line at a factory. His wife of 14 years recently moved out and is divorcing him. Jim feels depressed and nervous. The effect of the divorce seems to have resulted in constant stomach aches and feelings of uneasiness. He has little idea of what to do with his life.

Rosemary M., who also read about the group in the newspaper, is a homemaker. She has a husband and two daughters. Now that her children are older and need her less, she feels bored with life. The stress of this period in her life has left Rosemary without purpose and with a sense of hopelessness. She also complains of increasing insomnia.

Janet A. noticed a poster in her dormitory advertising a stress management group. Janet is an undergraduate student at the university. Every semester she feels so much anxiety that she fails to complete most of her assignments. She has dropped more classes than she has completed. Janet has been told by her advisor that if she does not complete her work, she will not be permitted to finish college. This threat adds to her inability to function.

Assessment

Since all the assessment interviews were structured similarly, we focus on Jerry's pregroup interview. On arrival, Jerry asked more about the group. After his questions were answered, he was given three paper-and-pencil assessment instruments—the Profile of Mood States (POMS) (McNair, Lorr, and Droppleman, 1971), the Symptom Check-List-Revised (SCL-90-R) (Derogatis, 1982), and the Hassles Scale (Kanner, Coyne, Schaefer, and Lazarus, 1981)—to estimate level of stress and coping skills. Jerry took about twenty-five minutes to complete the three tests.

After Jerry completed the Hassles Scale, the group leader, Lydia, discussed those items that were scored "3" (that is, occurred often). Some of Jerry's "often occurring" hassles included "too many responsibilities, trouble relaxing, problems getting along with fellow workers, not liking fellow workers, being dissatisfied with job, worrying about decision to change jobs, and being concerned about getting ahead." The discussion of these hassles revealed that Jerry was feeling pressured by work and by his partner. Jerry readily identified these as two issues he would like to deal with in the group. (The reader should note that the tests were used not only to obtain a score, which was later used to evaluate outcome for Jerry and the group, but as a point of departure for determining specific situations on which to focus interventions in the ensuing weeks.)

To assess Jerry's ability to use the group effectively, Lydia asked him about his previous experiences as a member of groups. Lydia inquired how Jerry felt about talking and sharing his problems with six to eight strangers. In addition, Lydia asked about Jerry's specific social skills and skill deficits and the situations in which these skills were manifested. Jerry stated that he had participated in several discussion groups at his church. He added that he had been in a weekend encounter group that he did not like, although he did feel it opened him up a little. He remarked that he might be hesitant at first in talking with strangers, but once others began to talk, he thought that he would have little trouble participating. (On the basis of Jerry's successes in past groups and his avowed willingness to participate, the leader concluded that Jerry could effectively use the group but would have to be eased in slowly at the beginning.)

Finally, Lydia reviewed with Jerry the treatment contract, which covered extragroup tasks, types of interventions, attendance, promptness, and other issues (see Chapter Two). Jerry asked how much time the extragroup tasks would take. Lydia responded that because they were negotiated, it would be up to him. Both Jerry and Lydia signed the contract.

Prior to the first session, the group leader examined the assessment data on all clients. She redesigned the format of the ten-session group based on the common need for the modeling sequence to enhance social skills and the expressed need for relaxation training to help cope with minor stressors. Although these two elements were to be given proportionately greater emphasis, no interventions from the general format were dropped.

Group Sessions

The ten group sessions could be roughly divided into three phases. The early phase continued the orientation and assessment begun in the pregroup interview. In addition, group cohesion was built up, and basic training in dealing with stress was initiated. Provision of information and skill training were continued in the second or middle phase. Clients began to identify and work on their own unique problems. In the final phase, clients focused on more complex stress situations and began to prepare to transfer what they had learned in the group to the real world.

The Initial Phase: Sessions One Through Three. In the first session, the leader's goals were for group members to learn about each other, to increase their attraction to one another (group cohesion), and to continue to identify and further clarify their target problems. For the first exercise, members broke into pairs and took turns interviewing each other for two minutes each. Suggested interview questions were put on the chalk board as a means of reducing anxiety. When members returned to the large group, they introduced their partners. Their partners reminded them when they forgot anything. These introductions were accompanied by some joking and laughter. (Introducing one's partner rather than oneself is likely to reduce initial anxiety. Moreover, this exercise elicited the active participation of all members within a few minutes in the first session. Broad participation, as well as a snack at the midgroup break, is likely to increase group cohesion.)

After a minilecture on the nature of stress and stressors, the members completed an individual checklist to identify their specific physical cues of stress. First Lydia, as a model, and then the members, one at a time, summarized their unique physical stress responses before the group. After the break in which decaffeinated (!) coffee and soft drinks were served, each member described a stressful situation recently encountered and the response to it. (During both exercises, Lydia noted that Rosemary and Ellen chatted with each other but did not participate in the general group discussion, except when called on.)

To prepare for the next week, Lydia suggested two extra-group tasks. In the first, members would monitor their daily stress levels on a 10-point scale. The second task was to record their physical cues when feeling high levels of stress. When the members agreed to these suggestions, Lydia asked them to report on their monitoring at the beginning of the next session. Lydia mentioned that because self-monitoring was probably not a common experience for them, they might require a system to remind them. Jerry, who stated that he never forgot anything, was the only one who did not develop such a system. (It should be noted that to increase the likelihood of compliance, extragroup tasks were negotiated rather than assigned and use of a self-monitoring system was encouraged.)

At the end of the first session, Lydia distributed and explained the postsession questionnaire, which is used to collect the members' perceptions of the session. Three of the questions asked were (1) How useful was this session? (2) How supportive were the other members? and (3) How close do you feel to other members? Although these questions were answered with numbers on a 6-point scale, two other questions were open-ended: What did you find most useful about this session? and What did you find least useful or would like to have changed? As the group ended, Lydia noted how hard the members had worked and looked forward to the next session. (The leader in the early sessions attempts to find every opportunity to reinforce the real achievements of individuals and the group.) Ellen said she would bring cookies next week to enliven the break. Lydia chatted informally with the members as they slowly departed.

As members arrived for the second session, Lydia purposely sat between Rosemary and Ellen to encourage them to talk to others in the group. She chatted with both while the others arrived. Lydia praised those who were present for their punctuality and started the session on time to establish promptness as a norm, even though Jerry and Janet had not yet arrived. As they trickled in, Lydia smiled, indicated the free seats to them, and said "we've just started." (Apparently, by reinforcing those who were on time and not commenting on the tardiness of the latecomers, the norm was established. For the remaining sessions all but one person arrived on time.)

In session two, after Rosemary read the agenda, Lydia briefly summarized the postsession evaluations from the first group meeting. Lydia remarked that group members had given the group a 3.8 on a 6-point scale for usefulness. A few of the members' written responses to the open-ended questions were read aloud. Lydia stated that one member remarked that he had found learning about other people in the group helpful. Another member wrote that Lydia had used some technical words that she did not understand. In response, Lydia asked the group if there were any specific terms she had used the previous week that could be clarified. No one responded. Lydia stated that she would attempt to use clearer language in the future. She also encouraged members to stop her when something was unclear. (Several principles should be noted here. First, if evaluations are to be used, they must be commented and acted on. Second, by using feedback, the leader provides opportunities for the members to assume increasing responsibility for structuring the group. Third, by having the members read the agenda and encouraging them to ask questions, the leader decreases her activity and increases participation by the members.)

The next agenda item, as in all sessions, was review of the tasks performed between sessions. Lydia asked members to state what parts of the extragroup tasks they had completed. Three members responded that they had written down physical stress cues in their diary and five members remarked that they had monitored their stress levels, though not every day. Jerry said he was too busy to do any of it. As each person mentioned an achievement, Lydia offered praise, giving little attention to those who did not complete tasks.

Next, Lydia noted that most people did some part of the task. She then remarked that homework is not something one does on a regular basis when no longer in school. Members expressed a variety of other reasons for not doing the homework completely: "having a busy week," "not remembering," and "not understanding what I was supposed to do." Jerry, in particular, noted that he should have developed a reminder system for himself, as he was more forgetful than he thought. Once the obstacles were identified, Lydia asked for suggestions as to what members could do to overcome them. Many ideas were generated. One was that each member could call another group member between sessions to remind him or her to do the homework. In line with another idea, Lydia would spend the last ten minutes of every session explaining the task and responding to questions. All the suggestions were evaluated and the two mentioned here were selected by the group to be implemented. (Note that as in most groups, homework completion rates were low at the second session and required attention; in this case, the leader made use of group problem solving rather than attempt to solve the problem herself.)

One additional theme of session two was introduction to relaxation training. After a brief review of the use of relaxation to cope with stress, Lydia cautioned members about muscle spasms, medications, and other factors that in combination with relaxation, might result in negative side effects. Lydia then led the group through progressive muscle relaxation in which she had them alternately tense and relax muscle groups. The group members were asked to rate their tension before and after the exercise. After the relaxation practice, members discussed their response to the exercise and several agreed to try relaxation at home. At the end of the session other homework assignments were negotiated in pairs and then read to the group. Finally, the members completed the postsession questionnaire. As they drifted out of the room, they talked informally with each other.

The third session was similar in many respects to the second. As Lydia reviewed the experience with the extragroup tasks, she noted enthusiastically that almost everyone had completed the tasks. Lydia also informed the members that their evaluations of the group had gone up dramatically this week. Several members noted that they could better understand what happens in this kind of group and how it might help them. Two people expressed their enthusiasm for relaxation in particular. Lydia concluded the evaluation by saying that she was pleased that each person was finding his or her own way of making the group useful.

Lydia then introduced a new group exercise designed to help members identify and change those thoughts that seemed to increase stress, such as putting oneself down or making a catastrophe of an insignificant event (self-defeating thoughts). As this exercise involved assimilation of a great deal of information, Lydia supplemented the instructions with a handout explaining the exercise and wrote down the important points on the chalk board. Lydia began the exercise by providing a rationale to show the link between self-defeating thoughts and stress. This rationale also demonstrated how a person can replace self-defeating with self-enhancing thoughts. (In the dissemination of information, the leader made use of a number of didactic strategies, audiovisual aids and demonstrations, brief lectures with ample opportunity for questions, and handouts to supplement the lecture. This, like all lectures, was held to a maximum of five minutes to maintain members' attention.

Lydia modeled a number of different types of self-defeating thoughts, which were identified and discussed by the members. For example, one type of self-defeating thought is "absolutizing." Lydia said "One of the things I have often said to myself just before a meeting is, 'I'll never be able to explain that concept understandably.'" After the group discussed why this statement might be self-defeating, Lydia demonstrated how she would stop it. She would yell "Stop!" to herself. She then immediately replaced her earlier statement with "Clear explanations are sometimes difficult for me; but if I take my time and check to see whether people understand, I can do a better job of explaining concepts." Next, the members discussed how the latter statement was more effective and honest than the first. (To increase self-disclosure the leader modeled self-disclosure. In addition, she involved the members by having them discuss her self-statements, which was less threatening than discussing their own.)

The members were asked to read a list of ten different self-statements (see Chapter Nine), after which they took turns identifying the statements as either self-defeating or self-enhancing and changing the self-defeating to self-enhancing statements. After the ten statements had been reviewed and modified, each member was asked to contribute a personal self-defeating statement.

Rosemary: When I start to worry at night, I say to myself, "I'll never be able to sleep—there's nothing I can do about it."

Janet: Sometimes when I'm studying, I think I'm just too dumb to do this kind of work. I should drop out of college.

Jim: I keep thinking, "I failed with my wife; I'll probably fail with every other woman I come into contact with." Sometimes I add, "My life is finished."

Susan: Today I just met a new guy at the office, and I said, as usual, "No sense talking to him. He won't like me, anyway."

Jerry: I can't think of one at all. While the others were talking I kept worrying about it. I don't know why it is, but when anyone asks me to do something, I always freeze.

Group Leader: Can anyone find a self-defeating statement in what Jerry just said? [Occasionally, members are not able to come up with a self-disclosing response during an exercise. Usually, the leader acknowledges the difficulty and goes on. In this case, the self-defeating statement was obviously implied, so the leader involved the group in helping Jerry find it.]

After each of these statements, the other members pointed out why the given statement was self-defeating and brainstormed about how to replace it. For example, Rosemary replaced her "I'll never be able to sleep" with "It may be difficult for me to sleep, but if I relax it sometimes helps a lot." (Throughout this and most exercises, the leader praised members on their work, for example, for successfully identifying and changing self-statements, for giving feedback to others, and for raising good questions. In addition, the leader constantly involved members by encouraging them to take responsibility for reinforcing and providing constructive feedback to each other.)

Session three ended as did the earlier sessions with additional relaxation practice, group task planning, and a postsession questionnaire. To prepare for session four, Lydia carefully explained the principles of problem solving. For the extragroup task, all the members agreed to record specific stressful situations in which they were dissatisfied with the way they coped. Lydia handed out the criteria for selecting a stressful situation (see Rose and others, 1985, pp. 34–35) and provided the members with examples of situations that met these criteria.

At this meeting, Lydia noticed that Rosemary and Ellen were addressing most of their comments to the group at large even though they sat together. During the session, Jerry was somewhat reluctant to talk about himself although he had comments for the others. (Unless the lack of self-disclosure is persistent by one person or characterized by several group members, the leader would not act on such observations; however, should it persist or include more than one person, the leader might deal with it as a group problem.)

The Intermediate Phase: Sessions Four Through Seven. In the fourth session, after review of the previous week's data, the monitoring of extragroup tasks, and the rate of completion (which continued to be high), Lydia provided a feedback exercise. After breaking into pairs, each member wrote down one specific thing that his or her partner had done well in the group, and one specific thing the partner might do differently. Using general feedback criteria (see Chapter Eight) as a guide, they provided their partners first with positive feedback, then with constructive negative feedback. Each member was evaluted with respect to how well the criteria had been met.

After this exercise, Lydia talked briefly about the relationship between stress and unsatisfactory performance in interpersonal situations. She provided the group with some examples and members came up with some of their own examples. Then Lydia described how one can learn concrete skills in handling difficult situations by getting ideas from others, by demonstration, by practice, and by feedback. She noted that they would be doing a lot of roleplaying demonstrations and practice in the group from now on. Lydia then suggested that they look at the stressful situations they had observed during the week.

Each member had the opportunity to present and to deal systematically with his or her own problematic situations. Jerry brought up a situation even though he had not agreed to the previous week. (Some clients function better if they feel free to do what they want.) The problem-solving and modeling process is exemplified by Rosemary's situation.

Rosemary: I was speaking with my mother the other day and was upset with what she said. You should know that we don't see eye to eye on many things, particularly child rearing. I wonder if you could tell me what I could do to get my mother to stop telling me how to raise my children?

Group Leader: Does anyone have any questions that might help us see the situation more clearly?

Jerry: What did your mother say exactly?

Rosemary: We were talking on the telephone, and out of the clear blue sky (can you imagine?) she said it was wrong that I allowed the children to eat their meals while they watched television.

Ellen: What did you say to your mother after her advice?

Rosemary: I told her that things have changed since she raised me and that she doesn't understand. That always seems to stop her advice but then she sounds angry and I end up feeling guilty. [Several other questions were asked: "How often do you talk to your mother?" "Is this a common exchange?" "Do others in your family have the same difficulty?" These resulted in greater specification of the problem.]

Susan: Rosemary, I wonder if you could tell us when the "critical moment" occurred.

Group Leader (noting that Rosemary looks confused):   Why doesn't someone explain what the critical moment is? Some people may have forgotten.

Susan: Isn't it the point in time when you are faced with a situation and have a choice of how to respond?

Janet: Yeah, the point at which you wished you had done something different.

Rosemary: I remember now. I guess my critical moment was after she said, "You shouldn't allow your children to eat their meals while watching television. I never did."

Now that Rosemary, with the help of the group, had identified the concrete situation, the response, and the critical moment, the next step was goal setting.

Susan: Rosemary, could you tell us what you would like to have achieved in this situation?

Rosemary: I want to get my mother to stop telling me what to do about my kids.

Group Leader: Who is this a goal for, I wonder?

Ellen: I think it's a goal for Rosemary's mother. I do that all the time. I want everyone else to change when it's me that has to do the work.

Rosemary: You're right. I guess my goal for myself is to let my mother know how I feel on this issue. Can you believe it, I've never told her?

Note that in the preceding dialogue, the group leader guided the discussion while maximizing member participation by asking questions rather than providing answers. Once the goal had been established and accepted by Rosemary, she was then encouraged to state specifically what she could do or say differently to achieve that goal.

Susan: Rosemary, what do you want to tell your mother? Use that phrase we were told to use, "State a feeling and make a request." [Note that Susan is beginning to assume a leadership role. The group leader usually encourages this unless the given member discourages active participation among others; however, if possible, the leader encourages more than one person to assume a variety of leadership functions.]

Rosemary: I want to tell my mother I am angry and ask her to not give me advice . . . that is, unless I ask for it [laughing].

The next step in the behavioral rehearsal process was for Rosemary to evaluate the risks involved in stating her feelings and making this request. The members then brainstormed about alternative responses Rosemary could make to her mother.

Jerry: Maybe you could tell her that her advice pissed you off and that you really don't need it.

Rosemary: Oh, I could never say that to my mother.

Group Leader: Remember, group, we don't evaluate brainstorm ideas—any suggestion is valuable. Who hasn't given an alternative? How about you, Ellen? What would you say?

Ellen: I might tell her that she was a good mother and did a fine job raising me and that I had to do what worked for me.

After two minutes of brainstorming, Susan asked Rosemary to pick out something she could say to her mother that met her goal.

Rosemary: I think I could say, "Mom, sometimes I feel incompetent when you give me advice, especially since I usually have ideas of my own. It's important to me to stand on my own two feet and find my own way of doing things. I know this will be difficult for you, Mom, but I really don't want you to give me advice unless I ask for it, OK?"

Practicing the alternative response was the next step in the modeling sequence. Ellen volunteered to roleplay Rosemary's role and Rosemary played her mother. When they finished, Lydia asked Rosemary if she wanted to repeat the statement in the way Ellen had said it. Rosemary responded that she liked it a lot and would be willing to try it out herself, with Ellen playng the role of the mother.

After Rosemary practiced the response in a roleplay, the group provided her feedback on the performance.

Susan: What did you like about what you did in that roleplay?

Rosemary: Not much . . . well, I guess I told her how I felt. That would be an improvement over how I usually handle it.

Group Leader: It's important that you see improvement, Rosemary, and I do, too. What did others like about Rosemary's roleplay?

Jim: Well, Rosemary looked directly into Ellen's, I mean her mother's, eyes.

Janet: She made a request for change.

Group Leader: Tell Rosemary what she specifically said that was a request? [The leader shapes more specific feedback while helping people give their feedback directly to the person involved.]

Janet: Rosemary, you told your mother to wait until you asked her to give advice, and I think you did it gently.

When the members had finished giving both positive and negative feedback, Lydia asked Rosemary to rehearse one more time. Lydia complimented Rosemary on the quality of the roleplay and commented on Susan's and Ellen's active participation in the roleplaying. She also said that she was "impressed by the excellent comments" of the other members and noted how well they adhered to the feedback criteria. At the same meeting, Jim's and Janet's situations were handled. Because the time needed to get through all their situations was not available, Lydia asked if they could continue next week.

Lydia reviewed the problem-solving steps, in particular the modeling sequence. (The leader continues to teach the general principles after the group has had experience with the sequence, to enhance the generalization of change. The frequent use of review is an important leadership function.) She then ended session five in the same manner as the four previous sessions, with relaxation practice, group task negotiations, and completion of the postsession questionnaire. As their extragroup task, most members decided to see how many other stress situations they could come up with in addition to the one they were working on. Everyone committed themselves to practicing relaxation at least ten minutes a day. Ellen, in addition, decided to roleplay her situation several times into a tape recorder to get it down perfectly.

After the meeting, because she had noted that Janet's evaluation of the group had gone down dramatically, Lydia called Janet. Janet said that she was thinking of not returning to the group. Lydia listened to her concerns. She wondered aloud whether Janet may have felt too much pressure after last week's roleplay. Janet admitted that the group was going too fast for her and it was making her anxious; she had had the same trouble in another group she had been in. (The leader may have made a mistake in not using "warmups" before roleplaying to accustom members to roleplaying. Examples of warmups are roleplaying neutral situations, playing a game of charades, and so forth.)

Lydia noted that perhaps others were feeling the same way and suggested that this was a problem that could be talked about in general in the group. Janet thought this was a good idea and said she felt better about coming back to the group next week. She was glad Lydia had called. (The preferred procedure when identifying group problems is to present the problem to the entire group. In this case, the leader was concerned that Janet would drop out before the problem could be brought up in the group. However, after talking to Janet, the leader still had the option of bringing the problem to the group in the event that the concern was shared by more than one member.)

In the sixth session, after review of the extragroup tasks and evaluations, which had dropped slightly, Lydia stated that a few people were concerned that the group was going too fast or putting too much pressure on them to change. In the discussion several members agreed, although Jim noted that he needed pressure to change. Jerry laughed as he agreed with Jim, "I'm finally ready to talk about myself." After further discussion, the members agreed that everyone should go at his or her own pace without pressure from anyone. They also suggested that members could back off on any exercise that was too difficult for them to handle. Jim reminded the group that if they took too much pressure off themselves, "they probably wouldn't get much from the group." Janet listened intently to the discussion, occasionally nodding agreement but saying nothing. The rest of the session dealt with the stressful situations not discussed and rehearsed the previous week. Jim and Ellen had time to deal with a second situation. The evaluations were extremely high at the end of this session and all comments were positive. (It is not uncommon for mere discussion of a group problem to result in an increase in group cohesion.)

During the seventh and eighth sessions members continued to handle stressful situations, but added cognitive elements to the behavioral roleplays. For example, Janet told of a situation in class where the instructor called on her and she panicked, telling herself "I'm too dumb to answer any question." The members suggested that because she usually knows the answers to questions in class and in this group, when called on, she might instruct herself to take a deep breath and relax and to repeat the question in her mind. Before class, she would prepare herself to say, "I know the answers to almost all questions asked and it's not so terrible to make a mistake." Jim then cognitively modeled what she had to say. This was followed by her own cognitive rehearsal (in a stage whisper) combined with an answer to the question aloud in a behavioral rehearsal. In the final practice, everyone in the group asked her one question as if she were in class. (Janet had provided the members with the questions.) She stood up and answered them while silently reassuring herself of her ability to answer. Her success was met with wild applause from the group.

These sessions also ended with extragroup task planning and session evaluations. In these extragroup tasks, the members actually tried out the behaviors and cognitions learned in the group much more frequently than in the earlier sessions. In addition, most members continued to practice relaxation and to note their successes and failures in handling stress.

The Final Phase: Sessions Nine and Ten. During the final phase, the emphasis was placed on reviewing the skills that had been taught and planning for dealing with stress after the group ended. In session nine, Lydia suggested some extragroup tasks that would help members think of how they could maintain the skills they had learned during the previous eight weeks. Lydia prepared them for the task of maintenance and generalization with the following presentation.

There are limits to how much people can change after twenty hours of stress management training. Although the

extragroup tasks extend the power of the group during its ten-
week course, without planning for the maintenance of skills
after the group ends, any benefits of stress management
training would greatly diminish over time.

The members discussed, one at a time, the principles of
transfer and maintenance of change (see Chapter Thirteen). Lydia
suggested, as an extragroup task, that they use the principles to
develop a personal maintenance plan which would be the focus of
the last session. Everyone agreed to try it out.

At the beginning of the tenth session the members reviewed
each other's plan. There were a variety of ideas. Jim planned to read
several books on assertiveness and stress management; he had even
purchased two the previous week. Ellen was going to maintain
contact with Susan as well as keep a diary of stress situations and
how she handled them. She was going to continue her new regimen
of walking two miles a day, and Susan would accompany her. Susan
had already joined a church group in which she planned to try out
the assertive techniques she learned in the group. She was considering joining an assertiveness training group to bolster her newly
learned skills. Rosemary decided together with her husband to enter
marital counseling, something the members had suggested earlier.
Janet was going to join a yoga class to improve her relaxation. Jim
felt he should join another stress group. "I passed this one, but just
barely," he joked.

Jerry asked whether any of the others might not be interested
in a booster session in three months. They could discuss how they
had used their stress management skills, refresh any skills that had
been forgotten, and do problem solving. Most of the members were
willing to attend and Lydia noted that she and the agency would be
happy to cooperate with such a plan. Jerry and Ellen agreed to help
organize it. The most important purpose of the booster session, they
agreed, would be to see how well they were carrying out their
maintenance plans. (As pointed out in Chapter Thirteen, a focus on
development of a maintenance plan, public commitment to the
maintenance plan, and monitoring of the plan in a booster session
contribute to implementation of the plan.)

Lydia commended the members for their hard work in

developing these plans. She organized the following closing exercise. Each member distributed to every other member a note on which was written one positive comment. The members were not to read the notes until they went home. Thus, the group ended with the exchange of tangible positive feedback.

At the end of the tenth session, the members were asked to retake the three assessment tests from the pregroup interview, to assess individual gains in stress management skills. Lydia arranged to meet with the members individually during the week following the last session to inform them of the test results. At that postgroup meeting, members would be able to provide Lydia with feedback about the program.

Summary

In this ten-session group, the leader implemented the paradigm discussed in this book from organization and assessment through maintenance of change. She used a wide variety of assessment and intervention procedures, including the modeling sequence, reinforcement, cognitive restructuring, self-instructional training, and relaxation training. The leader dealt with group problems before they arose, for example, the negative subgrouping by Rosemary and Ellen, a drop in group cohesion, and low productivity. She encouraged broad participation through the formation of subgroups and the use of exercises and was careful to involve members wherever possible in leadership functions and decision making. The leader brought her warmth, her interviewing skills, and her humor to the group. She encouraged self-disclosure but protected clients from too much too soon. She opened herself up to criticism and accepted it without becoming defensive. She acknowledged her mistakes. At the same time she kept the group moving and provided a flexible structure while the focus on improving coping skills was maintained. She recorded data and used them for evaluation and to improve practice.

This group is typical of the many multimethod groups we have dealt with through the years. No two groups are exactly the same even when they have the same general purpose. They vary with respect to specific purpose, composition, primary means of intervention, assessment strategies, and in every other aspect. They hold in common a focus on problem solving, goal orientation, cognitive-behavioral interventions, diverse approaches for diverse phases, and coping skill training. Of equal importance is the use of the group as a major tool of assessment, intervention, and generalization in the treatment process.

References

Alberti, R. E., and Emmons, M. L. *Your Perfect Right.* (5th ed.) San Luis Obispo, Calif.: Impact Publishers, 1985.

American Psychiatric Association. *Diagnostic and Statistical Manual of Mental Disorders.* (3rd Rev. ed.) (DSM-III-R), Washington, D.C.: American Psychiatric Association, 1987.

Anderson, M. P. "Imaginal Processes: Therapeutic Applications and Theoretical Models." In M. J. Mahoney (ed.), *Psychotherapy Process: Current Issues and Future Directions.* New York: Plenum, 1980.

Antonuccio, D. O., Lewinsohn, P. M., and Steinmetz, J. Identification of therapist differences in a group treatment for depression. *Journal of Consulting and Clinical Psychology,* 1982, *50,* 433–435.

Ashby, W. A., and Wilson, G. T. "Behavior Therapy for Obesity: Booster Sessions and Long-Term Maintenance of Weight Loss." *Behavior Research and Therapy,* 1977, *15,* 451–463.

Ausubel, D. P. *The Psychology of Meaningful Verbal Learning.* New York: Grune & Stratton, 1963.

Azrin, N. H, Flores, T., and Kaplan, S. J. "Job-Finding Club: A Group-Assisted Program for Obtaining Employment." *Behaviour Research and Therapy,* 1975, *13,* 17–27.

Bandura, A. *Principles of Behavior Modification.* New York: Holt, Rinehart & Winston, 1969.

Bandura, A. *Social Learning Theory.* Englewood Cliffs, N.J.: Prentice-Hall, 1977a.

Bandura, A. "Self-Efficacy: Toward a Unifying Theory of Behavioral Change." *Psychological Review,* 1977b, *84,* 191–215.

Barlow, D. H., Hayes, S. C., and Nelson, R. M. *The Scientist Practitioner.* Elmsford, N.Y.: Pergamon Press, 1984.

Bates, P. E. "The Effect of Interpersonal Skills Training on the Acquisition and Generalization of Interpersonal Communications Behaviors by Moderately/Mildly Retarded Adults." Unpublished doctoral dissertation, University of Wisconsin-Madison, 1978.

Beck, A. T. *Cognitive Therapy and Emotional Disorders.* New York: International Universities Press, 1976.

Beck, A. T., Mendelson, M., Mock, J., and Erbaugh, J. "An Inventory for Measuring Depression." *Archives of General Psychiatry,* 1961, *4,* 561-571.

Bednar, R., and Kaul, T. "Experiential group research." In S. Garfield and A. Bergin (eds.), *Handbook for Psychotherapy and Behavior Change.* (3rd ed.) New York: Wiley, 1985.

Belfer, P. L., and Levendusky, P. "Long-Term Behavioral Group Psychotherapy: An Integrative Model." In D. Upper and S. M. Ross (eds.), *Handbook of Behavioral Group Therapy.* Pp. 119-144. New York: Plenum, 1985.

Bellack, A., Hersen, M., and Turner, S. "Generalized Effects of Social Skills Training in Chronic Schizophrenics: An Experimental Analysis." *Behavior Research and Therapy,* 1976, *14,* 391-398.

Berger, R. M. "Interpersonal Skill Training with Institutionalized Elderly Patients." Unpublished doctoral dissertation, University of Wisconsin-Madison, 1976.

Bergner, M., Bobbitt, R. A., and Pollard, W. E. "The Sickness Impact Profile: Validation of a Health Status Measure." *Medical Care,* 1976, *14,* 56-67.

Bernstein, D. A., and Borkovec, T. D. *Progressive Relaxation Training: A Manual for the Helping Professions.* Chicago: Research Press, 1973.

Biddle, B. J., and Thomas, E. J. *Role Theory: Concepts and Research.* New York: Wiley, 1966.

Bion, W. P. *Experiences in Groups.* New York: Basic Books, 1959.

Bloch, S. "Patients' Expectations of Therapeutic Improvement and Their Outcomes." *American Journal of Psychiatry,* 1976, *133,* 1457-1459.

Bloom, M., and Fischer, J. *Evaluating Practice: Guidelines for the Accountable Professional.* Englewood Cliffs, N.J.: Prentice-Hall, 1982.

Brierton, D., Rose, S. D., and Flanagan, J. "A Behavioral Approach to Corrections Counseling." *Law in American Society,* 1975, *4,* 10–16.

Campbell, D. T., and Stanley, J. C. *Experimental and Quasi-Experimental Designs for Research.* Skokie, Ill.: Rand McNally, 1963.

Carrington, P. *Clinically Standardized Meditation (CSM). Instructor's Manual.* Kendal Park, N.J.: Pace Educational Systems, 1978a.

Carrington, P. *Learning to Meditate: Clinically Standardized Meditation (CSM). Course Workbook.* Kendall Park, N.J.: Pace Educational Systems, 1978b.

Carson, W., and Deschner, J. "Using Videotaped Vignettes in Group Anger Control Training Research." Paper presented at the Third Annual Symposium of Empirical Group Work Practice, Chicago, 1987.

Cartwright, D., and Zander, A. *Group Dynamics: Research and Theory.* (3rd ed.) New York: Harper & Row, 1968.

Cautela, J. R., and Groden, J. *Relaxation: A Comprehensive Manual for Adults, Children, and Children with Special Needs.* Champaign, Ill.: Research Press, 1978.

Chaney, E. F., O'Leary, M. R., and Marlatt, G. A. "Skill Training with Alcoholics." *Journal of Consulting and Clinical Psychology,* 1978, *46,* 1092–1104.

Christoff, K. A., and Kelly, J. A. "A Behavioral Approach to Social Skills Training with Psychiatric Patients." In L. L'Abate and M. A. Milan (eds.), *Handbook of Social Skills Training and Research.* Pp. 361–387. New York: Wiley, 1985.

Clark, K. W. "Evaluation of a Group Social Skills Training Program with Psychiatric Patients: Training Viet Nam Era Veterans in Assertion, Heterosexual, and Job Interview Skills." (Doctoral Dissertation, University of Wisconsin-Madison, 1974.) *Dissertation Abstracts International,* 1975, *35,* 4642B. (University Microfilms No. 74-28, 795)

Cormier, W. H., and Cormier, L. S. *Interviewing Strategies for*

Helpers: Fundamental Skills and Cognitive Behavioral Interventions. (2nd ed.) Monterey, Calif.: Brooks/Cole, 1985.

Costell, R., and Koran, L. "Compatibility and Cohesiveness in Group Psychotherapy." *The Journal of Nervous and Mental Disease,* 1972, *155* (2), 99–104.

Coyne, J. C. "A Critique of Cognitions as Causal Entities with Particular Reference to Depression." *Cognitive Therapy and Research,* 1982, *6,* 3–13.

Cragan, M. K., and Deffenbacher, J. L. "Anxiety Management Training and Relaxation as Self-Control in the Treatment of Generalized Anxiety in Medical Outpatients." *Journal of Counseling Psychology,* 1984, *31* (2), 123–131.

Cytrynbaum, S., Ginath, Y., Birdwell, J., and Brandt, L. "Goal Attainment Scaling: A Critical Review." *Evaluation Quarterly,* 1979, *3,* 5–40.

D'Alelio, W. A., and Murray, E. J. "Cognitive Therapy for Test Anxiety." *Cognitive Therapy and Research,* 1981, *5,* 299–307.

Deffenbacher, J. L., and Hahnloser, R. M. "Cognitive and Relaxation Coping Skills in Stress Inoculation." *Cognitive Therapy and Research,* 1981, *5,* 211–215.

Delange, J. "Effectiveness of Systematic Desensitization and Assertive Training with Women." Doctoral dissertation, University of Wisconsin-Madison, School of Social Work, 1976.

Derogatis, L. "Self-Report Measures of Stress." In L. Goldberger and S. Breznitz (eds.), *Handbook of Stress: Theoretical and Clinical Aspects.* New York: Free Press, 1982.

Dies, R. "Group Therapists Self-Disclosure: An Evaluation by Clients." *Journal of Counseling Psychology,* 1973, *20,* 344–348, 1973.

Dies, R., and Cohen, L. "Content Consideration in Group Self-Disclosure." *International Journal of Group Psychotherapy,* 1976, *26,* 71–88.

Drescher, S., Burlingame, G., and Fuhriman, A. "An Odyssey in Empirical Understanding." *Small Group Behavior,* 1985, *16* (1), 3–30.

D'Zurilla, T. J. *Problem-Solving Therapy: A Social Competence Approach to Clinical Intervention.* New York: Springer, 1986.

D'Zurilla, T. J., and Nezu, A. "Social Problem Solving in Adults."

In P. C. Kendall (ed.), *Advances in Cognitive-Behavioral Research and Therapy.* Vol. 1, pp. 201–274. New York: Academic Press, 1982.

Edleson, J. L., Miller, D. M., and Stone, G. W. *Counseling Men Who Batter: Group Leader's Handbook.* Albany, N.Y.: Men's Coalition Against Battering, 1983.

Edleson, J. L., Miller, D. M., Stone, G. W., and Chapman, D. G. "Group Treatment for Men Who Batter." *Social Work Research and Abstracts,* 1985, *21* (3), 18–22.

Edleson, J. L., Witkin, S. L., and Rose, S. D. "The Recruitment Process: An Initial Investigation." *Journal of Social Service Research,* 1979, *2,* 405–414.

Eisler, R. M. "The Behavior Assessment of Social Skills." In M. Hersen and A. S. Bellack (eds.), *Behavioral Assessment: A Practical Handbook.* Elmsford, N.Y.: Pergamon, 1976.

Ellis, A. *Humanistic Psychotherapy.* Pp. 237–242. New York: McGraw-Hill, 1974.

Ellis, A. "The Basic Clinical Theory of Rational-Emotive Therapy." In A. Ellis and R. Grieger (eds.), *Handbook of Rational-Emotive Therapy.* New York: Springer, 1977.

Emmelkamp, P.M.G. *Phobic and Obsessive-Compulsive Disorders: Theory, Research and Practice.* New York: Plenum, 1982.

Emmelkamp, P.M.G., and Kuipers, A.C.M. "Agoraphobia: A Follow-up Study Four Years after Treatment." *British Journal of Psychiatry,* 1979, *134,* 352–355.

Emmelkamp, P.M.G., and Kuipers, A.C.M. "Behavior Group Therapy for Anxiety Disorders." In D. Upper and S. M. Ross (eds.), *Handbook of Behavior Group Therapy.* New York: Plenum, 1985.

Emmelkamp, P.M.G., and Van der Hout, A. "Failure in Treating Agoraphobia." In E. B. Foa and P.M.G. Emmelkamp (eds.), *Failures in Behavior Therapy.* New York: Wiley, 1983.

Everly, G. S. "A Technique for the Immediate Reduction of Psychophysiologic Stress Reactivity." *Health Education,* 1979a, *10,* 44.

Everly, G. S. "A Psychophysiologic Technique for the Rapid Onset of a Trophotropic State." *IRCS Journal of Medical Science,* 1979b, *7,* 423.

Everly, G. S., and Rosenfeld, R. *The Nature and Treatment of the Stress Response: A Practical Guide for Clinicians.* New York: Plenum, 1981.

Festinger, L. "A Theory of Social Comparison Processes." *Human Relations,* 1954, *7,* 117–140.

Fiedler, F. E. *Leadership.* Morristown, N.J.: General Learning Press, 1971.

Fielding, J. "Verbal Participation and Group Therapy Outcome." *British Journal of Psychiatry,* 1983, *142,* 524–528.

Flowers, J., Booraem, C., and Hartman, K. "Client Improvement on Higher and Lower Intensity Problems as a Function of Group Cohesiveness." *Psychotherapy: Theory, Research, and Practice,* 1981, *18* (2).

Flowers, J., and Schwartz, B. "Behavioral Group Therapy with Clients with Homogeneous Problems." In S. Ross and D. Upper (eds.), *Handbook of Behavioral Group Therapy.* New York: Plenum, 1985.

Flowers, J. V. "Behavioral Analysis of Group Therapy and a Model for Behavioral Group Therapy." In D. Upper and S. M. Ross (eds.), *Behavioral Group Therapy.* Champaign, Ill.: Research Press, 1979.

Galinsky, M. J., and Schopler, J. H. "Structuring Co-leadership in Social Work Training." *Social Work with Groups,* 1980; *3* (4), 51–64.

Gambrill, E. D. *Casework: A Competency-Based Approach.* Englewood Cliffs, N.J.: Prentice-Hall, 1983.

Gambrill, E. D., and Richey, C. A. "An Assertion Inventory for Use in Assessment and Research." *Behavior Therapy,* 1973, *6,* 550–561.

Garvin, C. D. *Contemporary Group Work.* Englewood Cliffs, N.J.: Prentice-Hall, 1987.

Goldfried, M. R., Decenteceo, E., and Weinberg, L. "Systematic Rational Restructuring as a Self-Control Technique." *Behavior Therapy,* 1974, *5,* 247–254.

Goldfried, M. R., and D'Zurilla, R. J. "A Behavioral Analytic Model for Assessing Competence." In C. D. Spielberger (ed.), *Current Topics in Clinical and Community Psychology.* Vol. 1. New York: Academic Press, 1969.

Goldstein, A. P., Carr, E. G., Davidson, W. S., II, and Wehr, P. *In Response to Aggression.* Elmsford, N.Y.: Pergamon, 1981.

Goldstein, A. P., Heller, K., and Sechrest, L. B. *Psychotherapy and the Psychology of Behavior Change.* New York: Wiley, 1966.

Goldstein, A. P., and Kanfer, F. H. *Maximizing Treatment Gains: Transfer Enhancement in Psychotherapy.* New York: Academic Press, 1979.

Goldstein, A. P., and Myers, C. R. "Relationship-Enhancement Methods." In F. H. Kanfer and A. P. Goldstein (eds.), *Helping People Change—A Textbook of Methods.* (3rd ed.) Elmsford, N.Y.: Pergamon, 1986.

Goodman, G. "An Experiment with Companionship Therapy: College Students and Troubled Boy—Assumptions, Selection and Design." In B. G. Guerney (ed.), *Psychotherapeutic Agents: New Rules for Non-professionals, Parents and Teachers.* New York: Holt, Rinehart & Winston, 1969.

Hafner, R. J., and Marks, I. M. "Exposure *in Vivo* of Agoraphobics: Contributions of Diazepam, Group Exposure, and Anxiety Evocation." *Psychological Medicine,* 1976, *6,* 71–78.

Hand, I., Lamontagne, Y., and Marks, I. "Group Exposure (Flooding) in Vivo for Agoraphobics." *British Journal of Psychiatry,* 1974, *124,* 588–602.

Hartmann, D. P., and Hall, R. V. "The Changing Criterion Design." *Journal of Applied Behavior Analysis,* 1976, *9,* 527–532.

Heide, F. J., and Borkovec, T. D. "Relaxation-Induced Anxiety: Paradoxical Anxiety Enhancement due to Relaxation Training." *Journal of Consulting and Clinical Psychology,* 1983, *51,* 171–182.

Heppner, P. P. "A Review of the Problem-Solving Literature and Its Relationship to the Counseling Process." *Journal of Counseling Psychology,* 1978, *25,* 366–375.

Hewitt, J. *The Complete Yoga Book.* New York: Schocken, 1977.

Hill, W. F. *Hill Interaction Matrix.* Los Angeles: University of Southern California Youth Study Center, 1965.

Hillenberg, J. B., and Collins, F. L., Jr. "A Procedural Analysis and Review of Relaxation Training Research." *Behaviour Research and Therapy,* 1982, *20,* 251–260.

Hoehn-Saric, R., Frank, J. D., Imber, S. D., Nash, E. H., Stone, A.

R., and Battle, C. C. "Systematic Preparation of Patients for Psychotherapy: Effects on Therapy Behavior and Outcome." *Journal of Psychiatric Research*, 1964, *2*, 267-281.

Hudson, W. W. *The Clinical Measurement Package*. Homewood, Ill.: Dorsey Press, 1982.

Jacobson, E. *Progressive Relaxation*. Chicago: University of Chicago Press, 1929.

Jacobson, E. *You Must Relax*. New York: McGraw-Hill, 1978.

Jansson, L., Jerremalm, A., and Ost, L. G. "Maintenance Procedures in the Behavioral Treatment of Agoraphobia: A Program and Some Data." *Behavioral Psychotherapy*, 1984, *12* (2), 109-116.

Jayaratne, S. L., and Levy, R. L. *Empirical Clinical Practice*. New York: Columbia University Press, 1979.

Kanfer, F. H., and Gaelick, L. "Self-Management Methods." In F. H. Kanfer and A. P. Goldstein (eds.), *Helping People Change: A Textbook of Methods*. (3rd ed.) Elmsford, N.Y.: Pergamon, 1986.

Kanner, A. D., Coyne, J. C., Schaefer, C., and Lazarus, R. S. "Comparisons of Two Modes of Stress Measurement: Daily Hassles and Uplifts Versus Major Life Events." *Journal of Behavioral Medicine*, 1981, *4*, 1-39.

Kaul, T., and Bednar, R. "Experiential Group Research." In *Handbook for Psychotherapy and Behavior Change*. (3rd ed.) New York: Wiley, 1985.

Kazdin, A. E. "Symptom Substitution, Generalization, and Response Covariation: Implications for Psychotherapy Outcome." *Psychological Bulletin*, 1982, *91*, 349-365.

Kelley, M. L., and Stokes, T. F. "Student-Teacher Contracting with Goal Setting for Maintenance." *Behavior Modification*, 1984, *8* (2), 223-244.

Kelly, G. A. *The Psychology of Personal Constructs*. New York: Norton, 1955.

Kelly, G. A., Wildman, B. G., and Berler, E. S. "Small Group Behavioral Training to Improve the Job Interview Skills Repertoire of Mildly Retarded Adolescents." *Journal of Applied Behavior Analysis*, 1980, *13*, 461-471.

Kiresuk, T. J., and Garwick, G. "Basic Goal Attainment Scaling

Procedures." In B. R. Compton and B. Galaway (eds.), *Social Work Processes*. Homewood, Ill.: Dorsey Press, 1979.

Kirkham, M. A. "Life Skills Training with Mothers of Handicapped Children: A Two Year Follow-up Study." Unpublished Doctoral Dissertation, University of Washington, 1988.

Kirkham, M. A., Schinke, S. P., Schilling, R. F., II, Meltzer, N. J., and Norelius, K. L. "Cognitive-Behavior Skills, Social Supports, and Child Abuse Potential among Mothers of Handicapped Children." *Journal of Family Violence*, 1986, *1* (3).

Kirshner, B., Dies, R., and Brown, A. "Effects of Experimental Manipulation of Self-Disclosure on Group Cohesiveness." *Journal of Consulting and Clinical Psychology*, 1978, *46* (6), 1171–1177.

Klein, A. *Effective Group Work*. New York: Association Press, 1972.

Langer, E. J., and Rodin, J. "The Effect of Choice and Enhanced Personal Responsibility for the Aged: A Field Experiment in an Institutional Setting." *Journal of Personality and Social Psychology*, 1976, *34*, 191–198.

Lazarus, A. A. "Behavior Rehearsal vs. Nondirective Therapy vs. Advice in Effecting Behavior Change." *Behavior Research and Therapy*, 1966, *4*, 209–212.

Lazarus, R. S. "The Stress and Coping Paradigm." In C. Eisdorfer, C. Cohen, and A. Kleinman (eds.), *Conceptual Models for Psychopathology*. New York: Spectrum, 1980.

Levitt, J. L., and Reid, W. J. "Rapid-Assessment Instruments." *Social Work Research and Abstracts*, 1981, *17* (1), 13–20.

Levy, R. L. "Relationship of an Overt Commitment to Task Compliance in Behavior Therapy." *Journal of Behavior Therapy and Experimental Psychiatry*, 1977, *8*, 25–29.

Levy, R. L., and Clark, H. "The Use of an Overt Commitment to Enhance Compliance: A Cautionary Note." *Journal of Behavior Therapy and Experimental Psychiatry*, 1980, *11*, 105–107.

Levy, R. L., Yamashita, D., and Pow, G. "Relationship of an Overt Commitment to the Frequency and Speed of Compliance with Decision Making." *Medical Care*, 1979, *17*, 281–284.

Lewin, K. *Field Theory in Social Science*. New York: Harper & Row, 1951.

Lewinsohn, P. M. "Clinical and Theoretical Aspects of Depression." In K. S. Calhoun, H. E. Adams, and K. M. Mitchell (eds.), *Innovative Methods in Psychopathology.* New York: Wiley, 1974.

Lewinsohn, P. M., Sullivan, M. J., and Grosscup, S. J. "Changing Reinforcing Events: An Approach to the Treatment of Depression." *Psychotherapy: Theory, Research and Practice,* 1980, *17,* 322-334.

Lewinsohn, P. M., Weinstein, M., and Alper, T. "A Behavioral Approach to the Group Treatment of Depressed Persons: A Methodological Contribution." *Journal of Clinical Psychology,* 1970, *26,* 525-532.

Lieberman, M., Yalom, I., and Miles, M. *Encounter Groups: First Facts.* New York: Basic Books, 1973.

Linehan, M. M., and others. "Group Versus Individual Assertion Training." *Journal of Consulting and Clinical Psychology,* 1979, *47,* 1000-1002.

Lloyd, M. E. "Selecting Systems to Measure Client Outcome in Human Service Agencies." *Behavioral Assessment,* 1983, *5,* 55-70.

Locke, E. A., Shaw, K. N., Saari, L. M., and Latham, G. P. "Goal-Setting and Task Performance, 1969-1980." *Psychological Bulletin,* 1981, *90,* 125-152.

Lott, A. J., and Lott, B. E. "Group Cohesiveness as Interpersonal Attraction: A Review of Relationships with Antecedent and Consequent Variables." *Psychological Bulletin,* 1965, *64,* 259-309.

Lyles, J. N., Burish, T. G., Korzely, M. G., and Oldham, R. K. "Efficacy of Relaxation Training and Guided Imagery in Reducing the Aversiveness of Cancer Chemotherapy." *Journal of Consulting and Clinical Psychology,* 1982, *50,* 509-524.

McFall, R. M., and Marston, A. R. "An Experimental Investigation of Behavioral Rehearsal in Assertion Training." *Journal of Abnormal Psychology,* 1970, *76,* 295-303.

McGovern, K. B. and Jensen, S. H. "Behavioral Group Treatment Methods for Sexual Disorders and Dysfunctions." In D. Upper and S. M. Ross, eds., *Handbook of Behavioral Group Therapy.* New York: Plenum Press, 1985.

McNair, D. M., Lorr M., and Droppleman, L. F. *Profile of Mood*

States. San Diego, Calif.: Education and Industrial Testing Service, 1971.

MacPhillamy, D. and Lewinsohn, P. M. "Depression as a Function of Levels of Desired and Obtained Pleasure. *Journal of Abnormal Psychology,* 1974, *83,* 651–657.

Mahoney, M. J. *Cognition and Behavior Modification.* Cambridge, Mass.: Ballinger, 1974.

Maletzky, B. M. "Booster Sessions in Aversion Therapy: The Permanancy of Treatment." *Behavior Therapy,* 1977, *8,* 460–463.

Marlatt, G., and Gordon, J. "Determinants of Relapse: Implications for the Maintenance of Behavior Change." In P. Davidson (ed.), *Behavior of Medicine: Changing Health Lifestyles.* New York: Brunner/Mazel, 1980.

Mash, E. J., and Terdal, L. G. *Behavior-Therapy Assessment: Diagnosis, Design, and Evaluation.* New York: Springer, 1976.

Mash, E. J., Terdal, L., and Anderson, K. "The Response-Class Matrix: A Procedure for Recording Parent-Child Interactions." *Journal of Consulting and Clinical Psychology,* 1973, *40,* 163–164.

Mathews, A. M., Gelder, M. G., and Johnston, D. W. *Agoraphobia: Nature and Treatment.* New York: Guilford Press, 1981.

Mathews, A., Jannoun, L., and Gelder, M. "Self-Help Methods in Agoraphobia." Paper presented at the Conference of the European Association of Behavior Therapy, Paris, 1979.

Maultsby, M. "Systematic Written Homework in Psychotherapy." *Rational Living,* 1971, *6,* 17–23.

Meichenbaum, D. "A Cognitive-Behavior Modification Approach to Assessment." In M. Hersen and A. S. Bellack (eds.), *Behavioral Assessment.* Elmsford, N.Y.: Pergamon, 1976.

Meichenbaum, D. *Cognitive Behavior Modification.* New York: Plenum, 1977.

Meichenbaum, D. "Self-Instructional Methods." In F. Kanfer and A. Goldstein (eds.), *Helping People Change.* Elmsford, N.Y.: Pergamon, 1986.

Middleman, R. R. "Co-leadership and Solo-Leadership in Education for Social Work with Groups." *Social Work with Groups,* 1980, *3* (4), 39–50.

Nelson, R. O., and Barlow, D. H. "Behavioral Assessment: Basic

Strategies and Initial Procedures." In D. H. Barlow (ed.), *Behavioral Assessment of Adult Disorders*. New York: Guilford Press, 1981.

Nixon, H. L. *The Small Group*. Englewood Cliffs, N.J.: Prentice-Hall, 1979.

Novaco, R. W. *Anger Control: The Development and Evaluation of an Experimental Treatment*. Lexington, Mass.: Lexington Books, 1976.

O'Donnell, C. R., Lydgate, T., and Fo, W.S.O. "The Buddy System: Review and Follow-up." *Child Behavior Therapy*, 1979, *1*, 161–169.

Osborne, J. G. *Applied Imagination: Principles and Procedures of Creative Problem Solving*. (3rd ed.) New York: Scribner's, 1963.

Patterson, G. *Families*. (2nd ed.) Champaign, Ill.: Research Press, 1975.

Paul, G. L. *Insight vs Desensitization in Psychology: An Experiment in Anxiety Reduction*. Stanford, Calif.: Stanford University Press, 1966.

Pincus, A. and Minahan, A. *Social Work Practice: Model and Method*. Itaska, Ill.: F. E. Peacock, 1973.

Piper, W. E., Montvila, R. M., and McGihon, A. L. "Process Analysis in Therapy Groups: A Behavior Sampling Technique with Many Potential Uses." In D. Upper and S. M. Ross (eds.), *Behavioral Group Therapy*. Champaign, Ill.: Research Press, 1979.

Prinz, R. J., and Kent, R. N. "Recording Parent-Adolescent Interactions Without the Use of Frequency or Interval-by-Interval Coding." *Behavior Therapy*, 1978, *9*, 602–604.

Quinsey, V. L., and Varney, G. W. "Social Skills Game: A General Method for the Modeling and Practice of Adaptive Behaviors." *Behavior Therapy*, 1977, *8*, 279–281.

Rathus, S. A. "An Experimental Investigation of Assertive Training in a Group Setting." *Journal of Behavior Therapy and Experimental Psychiatry*, 1972, *3*, 81–86.

Redl, F. "Group Emotion and Leadership." In P. Hare, E. Borgotta, and R. Bales (eds.), *Small Groups: Studies in Social Interaction*. New York: Knopf, 1955.

Reid, W. J. *The Task Centered System*. New York: Columbia University Press, 1978.

Reynolds, W. M., and Coats, K. I. "A Comparison of Cognitive-Behavioral Therapy and Relaxation Training for the Treatment of Depression in Adolescents." *Journal of Consulting and Clinical Psychology*, 1986, *54* (5), 653–660.

Ribner, N. G. "Effects of an Explicit Group Contract on Self-Disclosure and Group Cohesiveness." *Journal of Counseling Psychology*, 1974, *21*, 116–120.

Rice, C., and Rutan, J. S. "Boundary Maintenance in Inpatient Groups." *International Journal of Group Psychotherapy*, 1981, *31*, 297–309.

Rodin, J., and Langer, E. J. "Long-Term Effects of a Control-Relevant Intervention with the Institutionalized Aged." *Journal of Personality and Social Psychology*, 1977, *35*, 897–902.

Rose, S. D. "Group Training of Parents as Behavior Modifiers." *Social Work*, 1974, *19*, 156–162.

Rose, S. D. "The Effect of Contingency Contracting on the Completion Rate of Behavioral Assignments in Assertion Training Groups." *Journal of Social Service Research*, 1978, *1*, 299–306.

Rose, S. D. "How Group Attributes Relate to Outcome in Behavior Group Therapy." *Social Work Research and Abstracts*, 1981, *17*, 25–29.

Rose, S. D., and Edleson, J. *Children and Adolescents in Groups: A Multimethod Approach*. San Francisco: Jossey-Bass, 1987 .

Rose, S. D., Scobie, A. M., Saunders, D., and Hanusa, D. "The Development of a Role Play Test for Men Who Batter." Unpublished manuscript, School of Social Work, University of Wisconsin-Madison, 1989.

Rose, S. D., and Subramanian. K. *Leader's Guide to Pain Management*. School of Social Work, University of Wisconsin-Madison, 1987.

Rose, S. D., Sundel, M., Delange, J., Corwin, L., and Palumbo, A. "The Hartwig Project—A Behavioral Approach to the Treatment of Juvenile Offenders." In E. Ulrich, T. Stachnic, and J. Mabry (eds.), *The Control of Human Behavior*. Vol. 2. Glenview, Ill.: Scott, Foresman, 1971.

Rose, S. D., Tolman, R., and Tallant, S. "Group Process in Cognitive-Behavioral Therapy." *The Behavior Therapist,* 1985a, *8,* 71–75.

Rose, S. D., Tolman, R., and Tallant, S. *Leader's Guide to Stress Management Training.* Madison: School of Social Work, University of Wisconsin, 1985b.

Rose, S. D., Tolman, R. M., Tallant, S., and Subramanian, K. A. "Multimethod Group Approach: Program Development Research." *Social Work with Groups,* 1986, *9,* 71–88.

Rosenthal, L. *The Development and Evaluation of the Problem Inventory for Adolescent Girls.* Unpublished dissertation, University of Wisconsin-Madison, 1978.

Ross, A. L., and Bernstein, N. B. "A Framework for the Therapeutic Use of Group Activities." *Child Welfare,* 1976, *56,* 776–786.

Rotter, J. B. *Social Learning and Clinical Psychology.* Englewood Cliffs, N.J.: Prentice-Hall, 1954.

Rush, A. J., and Watkins, J. T. "Group Versus Individual Cognitive Therapy: A Pilot Study." *Cognitive Therapy & Research,* 1981, *5,* 95–104.

Sarason, I. G., and Ganzer, V. J. "Developing Appropriate Social Behaviors of Juvenile Delinquents." In J. D. Krumboltz and C. E. Thoresen (eds.), *Behavioral Counseling: Cases and Techniques.* New York: Holt, Rinehart & Winston, 1969.

Sarri, R. L., and Galinsky, M. J. "A Conceptual Framework for Group Development." In M. Sundel, P. Glasser, R. Sarri, and R. Vinter (eds.), *Individual Change Through Small Groups.* New York: Macmillan, 1985.

Saunders, D. G., and Hanusa, D. "Cognitive-Behavioral Treatment of Men Who Batter: The Short-Term Effects of Group Therapy." *Journal of Family Violence,* 1986, *1,* 357–372.

Schaefer, C., Coyne, J., and Lazarus, R. "The Health-Related Functions of Social Support." *Journal of Behavioral Medicine,* 1981, *4* (4), 381–406.

Schinke, S. P. *Behavioral Assertion Training in Groups: A Comparative Clinical Study.* Unpublished doctoral dissertation. University of Wisconsin-Madison, School of Social Work, 1975.

Schopler, J. H., and Galinsky, M. J. "The Open-Ended Group." In Sundel and others (eds.), *Individual Change Through Small Groups.* (2nd ed.) New York: Free Press, 1985.

Seaberg, J., and Gillespie, D. "Goal Attainment Scaling: A Critique." *Social Work Research and Abstracts,* 1977, *13,* 4-11.

Sermat, V., and Smyth, M. "Content Analysis of Verbal Communication in the Development of a Relationship: Conditions Influencing Self-Disclosure." *Journal of Personality and Social Psychology,* 1973, *26,* 332-346.

Shapiro, D. H. *Meditation: Self-Regulation Strategy and Altered State of Consciousness.* New York: Aldine, 1980.

Shapiro, D. H. "Overview: Clinical and Physiological Comparison of Meditation with Other Self-Control Strategies." *American Journal of Psychiatry,* 1982, *139,* 267-274.

Shaw, M. E. *Group Dynamics: The Psychology of Small Group Behavior.* (2nd ed.) New York: McGraw-Hill, 1976.

Shelton, J. L., and Ackerman, J. M. *Homework in Counseling and Psychotherapy.* Springfield, Ill.: Charles C Thomas, 1974.

Shelton, J. L., and Levy, R. L. *Behavioral Assignments and Treatment Compliance: A Handbook of Clinical Strategies.* Champaign, Ill.: Research Press, 1981.

Simonson, N., and Bahr, S. "Self-Disclosure by the Professional and Paraprofessional Therapist." *Journal of Consulting and Clinical Psychology,* 1974, *42,* 359-363.

Spence, J. T., and Helmreich, R. L. *Masculinity and Femininity: Their Psychological Dimensions, Correlates and Antecedents.* Austin, Tex.: University of Texas, 1978.

Spielberger, C. D., Gorsuch, R. L., and Lushene, R. E. *STAI Manual for the State-Trait Inventory.* Palo Alto, Calif.: Consulting Psychologists Press, 1970.

Spivack, G., and Shure, M. B. *Social Adjustment of Young Children: A Cognitive Approach to Activating Real Life Problems.* San Francisco: Jossey-Bass, 1974.

Stockton, R., and Morran, D. K. "Review and Perspective of Critical Dimensions in Therapeutic Small Group Research." In G. M. Gazda (ed.), *Basic Approaches to Group Psychotherapy and Group Counseling.* (3rd ed.) Springfield, Ill.: Charles C Thomas, 1982.

Stokes, J. P. "Components of Group Cohesion: Intermember Attraction, Instrumental Value, and Risk Taking." *Small Group Behavior,* 1983, *14,* 163-173.

Stokes, T. F., and Baer, D. M. "An Implicit Technology of Generalization." *Journal of Applied Behavior Analysis,* 1977, *10,* 349–367.

Stoyva, J. "Why Should Muscular Relaxation Be Useful?" In I. J. Beatty and H. Legewie (eds.), *Biofeedback and Behavior.* New York: Plenum, 1977.

Straus, M. A. "Measuring Intrafamily Conflict and Violence: The Conflict Tactics (CT) Scales." *Journal of Marriage and the Family,* 1979, *41* (1), 75–88.

Stuart, R. B. *Helping Couples Change: A Social Learning Approach to Marital Therapy.* New York: Guilford Press, 1980.

Subramanian, K., and Rose, S. D. "Group Training for the Management of Chronic Pain in Interpersonal Situations." *Health and Social Work,* 1988, *21* (3), 29–30.

Sundel, M., Glasser, P., Sarri, R., and Vinter, R. (eds.). *Individual Change Through Small Groups.* (2nd ed.) New York: Free Press, 1985.

Tallant, S., Rose, S. D., and Tolman, R. "New Evidence for the Effectiveness of Stress Management Training in Groups." *Behavior Modification,* 1989.

Taylor, C. B. "DSM-III and Behavioral Assessment." *Behavioral Assessment,* 1983, *5,* 5–14.

Teri, L., and Lewinsohn, P. M. "Group Intervention for Unipolar Depression." *The Behavior Therapist,* 1985, *8* (6), 109–111.

Tolman, R. M. "The Development of a Measure of Psychological Treatment of Women By Their Male Partners." *Violence and Victims,* in press.

Tolman, R. M., and Rose, S. D. "Stress Management Training in Groups: An Experimental Study." *Journal of Social Service Research,* 1989, *13* (2), 110–115.

Toseland, R. W., and Rivas, R. F. *An Introduction to Group Work Practice.* New York: Macmillan, 1984.

Toseland, R. W., Rossiter, C. M., Peak, T., and Hill, P. "Professionally-Led Support Groups for Caregivers." Unpublished manual, State University of New York-Albany, School of Social Welfare, 1988.

Toseland, R. W., and Siporin, M. "When to Recommend Group Treatment: A Review of the Clinical and the Research Literature." *International Journal of Group Psychotherapy,* April 1986.

Turner, J. "Comparison of Group Progressive-Relaxation Training and Cognitive-Behavioral Group Therapy for Chronic Low Back Pain." *Journal of Consulting and Clinical Psychology,* 1979, *50* (5), 757–765.

Vanderhoof, L. *The Effects of a Simple Relaxation Technique on Stress During Pelvic Examinations.* Unpublished master's thesis, University of Maryland School of Nursing, 1980.

Vinter, R. "The Essential Components of Social Group Work Practice." In P. Glasser, R. Sarri, and R. Vinter (eds.), *Individual Change Through Small Groups.* New York: Free Press, 1974.

Walls, R. T., Werner, T. J., Bacon, A., and Zane, T. "Behavior Checklists." In J. D. Cone and R. P. Hawkins (eds.), *Behavioral Assessments: New Direction in Clinical Psychology.* New York: Brunner/Mazel, 1977.

Watzlawick, P., Weakland, J., and Fisch, R. *Change: Principles of Problem Formation and Problem Resolution.* New York: Norton, 1974.

Whitaker, D., and Lieberman, M. *Psychotherapy Through the Group Process.* New York: Atherton Press, 1964.

White, W., and Boskind-White, M. "An Experiential-behavioral Approach to the Treatment of Bulimaria." *Psychotherapy: Theory, Research, and Practice,* 1981, *18,* 501–507.

Whitney, D., and Rose, S. D. "The Effect of Process and Structural Content on Outcome in Stress Management Groups." *Social Service Research,* 1988, *13* (2), 120–125.

Wolpe, J. *The Practice of Behavior Therapy.* (2nd ed.) Elmsford, N.Y.: Pergamon, 1973.

Yalom, I. D. *The Theory and Practice of Group Psychotherapy.* New York: Basic Books, 1985.

Yalom, I., Tinklenberg, J., and Giulula, M. "Curative Factors in Group Therapy." Unpublished study, 1968.

Zajonc, R. "Feeling and Thinking: Preferences Need No Inferences." *American Psychologist,* 1980, *35,* 151–175.

Name Index

A

Ackerman, J. M., 272
Alberti, R. E., 277
Alper, T., 93
American Psychiatric Association, 107
Anderson, K., 118
Anderson, M. P., 216
Antonuccio, D. O., 251
Ashby, W. A., 300
Ausubel, D. P., 68
Azrin, N. H., 176

B

Bacon, A., 111
Baer, D. M., 155, 271, 288, 291, 292
Bahr, S., 32
Bandura, A., 64, 164, 166–168, 172, 175, 178, 182, 188, 273
Barlow, D. H., 107, 134
Bates, P. E., 113
Beck, A. T., 6, 111, 134, 193, 204, 209, 211, 216, 222, 225
Bednar, R., 31, 109
Belfer, P. L., 29, 53, 68
Bellack, A. S., 114
Berger, R. M., 113
Bergner, M., 111
Berler, E. S., 176
Bernstein, D. A., 229, 233, 234
Bernstein, N. B., 19
Biddle, B. J., 33

Bion, W. P., 36, 37, 41, 42, 244
Birdwell, J., 147
Bloch, S., 31
Bloom M., 130, 132, 134
Bobbitt, R. A., 111
Booraem, C., 24
Borkovec, T. D., 15, 229, 233, 234
Boskind-White, M., 53
Brandt, L., 146
Brierton, D., 171
Brown, A., 24
Burish, T. G., 15, 228
Burlingame, G., 28

C

Campbell, D. T., 131
Carr, E. G., 179
Carrington, P., 238, 239
Carson, W., 114
Cartwright, D., 260
Cautela, J. R., 233
Chaney, E. F., 299
Chapman, D. G., 133
Clark, K. W., 113, 284
Coats, K. I., 24, 227
Cohen, C., 24, 227
Collins, F. L., 234
Cormier, L. S., 78, 156, 198, 201
Cormier, W. H., 78, 156, 198, 201
Costell, R., 24
Coyne, J., 95, 111, 222, 311
Cragan, M. K., 227, 228
Cytrynbaum, S., 147

D

D'Alelio, W. A., 53
D'Zurilla, T. J., 7, 113, 193
Davidson, W. S., 179
Decenteceo, E., 199
Deffenbacher, J. L., 227, 228
Delange, J., 113
Derogatis, L., 311
Deschner, J., 114
Dies, R., 24
Drescher, S., 28
Droppleman, L. F., 111, 134, 311

E

Edleson, J., xi, 3, 60, 133, 277
Eisler, R. M., 116
Ellis, A., 85, 193, 199, 200, 204, 299
Emmelkamp, P.M.G., 15, 52, 188, 189, 191, 192
Emmons, M. L., 277
Erbaugh, J., 111
Everly, G. S., 94, 229, 235, 238

F

Feldman, R., ix
Festinger, L., 63
Fiedler, F. E., 260
Fielding, J., 24
Fisch, R., 211
Fischer, J., 130, 132, 134
Flanagan, J., 171
Flores, T., 176
Flowers, J., 24, 31, 47, 53, 118
Fo, W.S.D., 18
Fuhriman, A., 28

G

Gaelick, L., 97, 284
Galinsky, M., 28, 35, 55
Gambrill, E. D., 111, 301
Ganzer, V. J., 171
Garvin, C. D., 52, 57
Garwick, G., 146
Gelder, M. G., 192, 298
Gillespie, D., 146

Ginath, Y., 147
Giulula, M., 31
Glasser, P., 20
Goldfried, M., 7, 113, 199
Goldstein, A. P., 15, 17, 52, 159, 166, 179, 250, 271, 295
Goodman, G., 118
Gordon, J., 299
Gorsuch, R. L., 111
Groden, J., 233
Grosscup, S. J., 93

H

Hafner, R. J., 15, 191
Hahnloser, R. M., 227
Hall, R. V., 133
Hand, I., 15, 54, 157, 192, 217
Hanusa, D., 62, 113, 114
Hartman, K., 24
Hartmann, D. P., 133
Hayes, S. C., 134
Heide, F. J., 15
Heller, K., 52, 159, 166, 250, 295
Helmreich, R. L., 111
Heppner, P. P., 7
Hersen, M., 114
Hewitt, J., 229
Hill, W. F., 126, 127
Hillenberg, J. B., 234
Hoehn-Saric, R., 68
Hudson, W. W., 111

I

Imber, S. D., 68

J

Jacobsen, E., 16, 234
Jannoun, L., 192
Jansson, L., 298
Jayaratne, S. L., 134
Jensen, S. H., 53
Jerremalm, A., 298
Johnston, D. W., 298

K

Kanfer, F. H., 97, 271, 284
Kanner, A. D., 111, 311
Kaplan, S. J., 176
Kaul, T., 31, 109
Kazdin, A., 300
Kelley, M. L., 187, 294
Kelly, G. A., 176
Kent, R. N., 111
Kiresuk, T. J., 146
Kirkham, M. A., 303
Kirshner, B., 24
Klein, A., 62
Koran, L., 24
Korzely, M. G., 15, 228
Kuipers, A.C.M., 15, 52, 189, 191

L

Lamontagne, Y., 15, 54, 157, 217
Langer, E. J., 160
Latham, G. P., 139
Lazarus, R. S., 95, 111, 175, 193, 311
Levendusky, P., 29, 53, 68
Levitt, J. L., 111
Levy, R. L., 134, 271, 279, 284
Lewin, K., xi
Lewinsohn, P. M., 6, 93, 118, 134, 251
Lieberman, M., 24, 27, 157, 159
Linehan, M. M., 6
Lloyd, M. E., 139
Locke, E. A., 139
Lorr, M., 111, 134, 311
Lott, A. J., 4, 27
Lott, B. E., 4, 27
Lushene, R. E., 111
Lydgate, T., 18
Lyles, J. N., 15, 228

M

MacPhillamy, D., 134
McFall, R. M., 182
McGihon, A. L., 127
McGovern, K. B., 53
McNair, D. M., 111, 134, 311
Magen, R. H., x, xvii, 309

Mahoney, M. J., 161, 193
Maletzky, B. M., 300
Marks, I. M., 15, 54, 157, 191, 217
Marlatt, G., 299
Marston, A. R., 182
Mash, E. J., 118, 127
Mathews, A. M., 192, 298
Maultsby, M., 271
Meichenbaum, D., 10, 14, 84, 193, 199–201, 203, 204, 221
Mendelson, M., 111
Middleman, R. R., 55
Miles, M., 24, 27, 157, 159
Miller, D. M., 133, 277
Minahan, A., 19
Mock, J., 111
Montvila, R. M., 127
Morran, D. K., 6
Murray, E. J., 53
Myers, C. R., 15, 17

N

Nelson, R. O., 107, 134, 193
Nezu, A., 193
Nixon, H. L., 6
Novaco, R. W., 111

O

O'Donnell, C. R., 18
O'Leary, M. R., 299
Oldham, R. K., 15, 228
Osborne, J. G., 146
Ost, L. G., 298

P

Patterson, G., 277
Paul, G. L., 234
Peak, T., 126
Pincus, A., 19
Piper, W. E., 127
Pollard, W. E., 111
Pow, G., 284
Prinz, R. J., 111

Q

Quinsey, V. L., 239

R

Rathus, S. A., 111
Redl, F., 37
Reid, W. J., 111, 271
Reynolds, W. M., 227, 271
Ribner, N., 24
Rice, C., 68
Richey, C. A., 111
Rivas, R. F., 17, 303
Rodin, J., 160
Rose, S. D., xiii, 3, 5, 12, 24, 37, 60,
    66, 67, 95, 109, 113, 114, 124, 127,
    133, 159, 171, 198, 263, 273, 277,
    309, 318
Rosenfeld, R., 94, 229, 235, 238
Rosenthal, L., 113
Ross, S. M., 19
Rossiter, C. M., 126
Rotter, J. B., 159
Rush, A. J., 6
Rutan, J. S., 68

S

Saari, L. M., 139
Sarason, I. G., 171
Sarri, R. L., 20, 38, 62
Saunders, D. G., 62, 113, 114
Schaefer, C., 95, 111, 311
Schilling II, R. F., 303
Schinke, S. P., 113
Schopler, J. H., 28, 55
Schwartz, B., 31, 47, 53
Scobie, A. M., 113, 114
Seaberg, J., 146
Sechrest, L. B., 52, 156, 159, 250, 295
Sermat, V., 32
Shapiro, D. H., 229, 238, 239
Shaw, M. E., 6, 139
Shelton, J. L., 271, 279, 284
Shure, M. B., 7
Simonson, N., 32
Siporin, M., 6, 109
Smyth, M., 32

Spence, J. T., 111
Spielberger, C. D., 111
Spivack, G., 7
Stanley, J. C., 100
Steinmetz, J., 251
Stockton, R., 6
Stokes, T. F., 27, 155, 271, 288, 291,
    292, 294
Stone, G. W., 133, 277
Straus, M. A., 111, 118
Stuart, R. B., 299
Subramanian, K., xiii, 198, 277
Sullivan, M. J., 93
Sundel, M., 20

T

Tallant, S., xiii, xvii, 5, 12, 67, 95,
    198, 277
Taylor, C. B., 108
Terdal, L. G., 118, 127
Teri, L., 6
Thomas, E. J., 33
Tinklenberg, J., 31
Tolman, R. M., ix, xiii, xv, xvii, 5,
    17, 67, 95, 109, 111, 198, 277
Toseland, R. W., 6, 17, 109, 126, 303
Turner, S., 114, 227

U

Upper, D., 232

V

Van der Hout, A., 191
Vanderhoof, L., 236
Varney, G. W., 239
Vinter, R., 19, 20, 70

W

Walls, R. T., 111
Watkins, J. T., 6
Watzlawick, P., 211
Weakland, J., 211
Wehr, P., 179
Weinberg, L., 199

Weinstein, M., 93
Werner, T. J., 111
Whitaker, D., 24
White, W., 53
Whitney, D., xvii, 24, 37, 159
Wildman, B. G., 176
Wilson, G. T., 300
Witkin, S. L., 60
Wolpe, J., 157, 217

Y

Yalom, I., xi, 24, 27, 31, 41, 52, 67, 157, 159, 251, 269, 293
Yamashita, D., 284

Z

Zajonc, R., 195
Zander, A., 260
Zane, T., 111

Subject Index

A

Absolutizing, 204–206, 210, 317
Accountability, 57
Advocacy, 301, 303, 304
Affective responses, 85–86
Agenda, 16, 23, 40, 97, 122, 154, 155, 163, 239, 244, 255, 268, 315
Agoraphobics, 276
Agoraphobic group, 2, 15, 47, 53, 156, 157, 188, 190, 192, 240, 276, 298
Alcohol and drug abuse group, 35, 56, 62, 154, 166, 303, 331
Altruism, 269, 293
Anger control, 46, 62, 70, 116, 271, 291, 331, 339
Anger control group, 116, 271, 291
Anorexics, 47
Antecedent conditions, 13, 78, 338
Antitherapeutic norms, 30, 31, 304
Anxiety, 10–12, 15, 29, 39, 46, 47, 53, 59, 61, 68, 74, 76, 80–83, 111, 113, 139, 141, 159, 189–196, 199, 203–205, 211, 217, 222–229, 234–239, 257, 276, 278, 282, 296, 298, 311, 313, 332, 333, 335, 340
Anxiety management group, 83, 293
Assertion inventories, 111
Assertive training, 46, 47, 64, 124, 127, 263, 294, 326
Assertive training group, 64, 143, 263, 293, 294, 326
Assertiveness, 64, 113, 143, 164, 326
Assessment, 61, 72, 73, 75, 76, 84, 94,
96, 98, 105, 108, 109, 149, 173, 284, 311, 312, 313, 327, 328
Assessment group, 46, 48
Assignments, 5, 13, 36, 55, 69, 97, 108, 117, 127, 128, 148, 156, 171, 175, 179, 225, 226, 264–266, 271, 274, 285, 297, 311, 316. *See also* Homework; Extragroup tasks
Attendance, 27, 28, 31, 58, 96, 119, 128, 129, 155, 246, 247, 268, 312
Attitudes toward Women Scale, 111
Attraction to group, 269. *See also* Cohesion; Group cohesion

B

Back-to-back talking, 262
Behavior Approach Test (BAT), 298
Beck Depression Inventory (BDI), 111, 134
Behavioral interactive tasks, 274–276, 280
Behavioral response, 77, 81
Behavioral specificity, 175, 185. *See also* Specificity
Board game, 239, 295
Booster session, 293, 300, 301, 305, 326
Bowling, 100, 161, 240, 302, 304
Brainstorming, 5, 146, 150, 173, 175, 211, 246, 247, 248, 254, 257, 264, 267, 269, 270, 281, 318, 322
Breathing control, 227, 229. *See also* Respiratory control

Buddy system, 15, 17, 18, 246, 280,
   283, 294, 301, 304
Bulemia, 47, 53, 228

C

Cancer, 3, 158, 195, 196, 228
Caregivers of the elderly, groups for,
   2, 127, 302, 330
Case study, 102, 104, 130, 136, 145,
   259, 279
Catastrophization, 204
Centering, 204, 205, 211
Chained situations, 80
Checklists, 98, 106, 110–112, 134, 135,
   313
Clinically standardized meditation,
   238
Coaching, 12, 13, 164, 171, 173, 181,
   192, 222
Cognitions, 82–86, 93, 104, 140, 149,
   279, 296, 325
Cognitive modeling, 216, 222, 287,
   308
Cognitive rehearsal, 199, 212–218,
   222, 223, 280, 284, 285, 325
Cognitive responses, 74, 77, 105, 274,
   276, 292
Cognitive restructuring, 14, 17, 78,
   157, 158, 195–200, 202, 217, 220,
   222–224, 226, 228, 240, 248, 255,
   273, 274, 276, 310, 327
Cognitive task, 275, 276
Cohesion, 6, 25, 27, 31, 36, 39, 40, 59,
   62, 63, 120, 246–248, 250, 252,
   256, 270, 332, 334, 337, 338, 340.
   See also Group cohesion
Coleaders, 55, 56, 65, 159, 166, 255,
   261
Common treatment goals, 3, 138
Communication structure, 6, 35, 36,
   252–256
Composition, 63–66. *See also*
   Group composition
Computer, 173, 282
Confidentiality, 69, 207, 252, 307
Conflict, 16, 37, 38, 39, 40, 42, 59, 65,
   67, 94, 95, 111, 118, 270, 278, 298,
   344

Conflict Tactics Scale, 111, 118
Confrontation, 89, 107, 157, 159, 255
Consequences, 75, 77, 88, 89, 99,
   108, 295, 303
Construct validity, 146
Contract, 37, 63, 68–71, 118, 152–
   154, 232, 266, 281, 284, 294, 295,
   312. *See also* Treatment contracts
Coping skill training, 227, 228
Corrective information, 195, 196
Couples groups, 47, 282
Critical moment, 86–88, 100, 108,
   180, 234, 320, 321
Criticism, 2, 11, 18, 29, 41, 42, 68,
   114, 125, 133, 151, 154, 159, 164,
   184–186, 211, 250, 252, 257–259,
   267, 276, 299, 310, 327
Cue card, 166, 181
Cueing, 166, 195, 234, 246, 282, 291,
   292, 299
Cues, 291, 292, 294, 295, 297
Curative factors, 30, 31, 37, 251, 269,
   293

D

Dating, 11, 47, 53, 164, 276
Dating group, 53, 276
Decentering, 211
Delegation of leadership, 250, 260,
   263, 293. *See also* Involvement of
   members
Delegation of responsibility, 160.
   See also Involvement of members
Dependency, 28, 40, 41, 44, 133, 246,
   257, 265, 266, 270, 272, 307
Depression, 1, 2, 6, 11, 12, 53, 61, 64,
   70, 85, 191, 227, 228, 257
Depression groups, 6, 12, 53, 64, 70,
   93, 102
Diagnosis, 107, 108
Diary, 97, 98, 101, 104, 225, 276, 278,
   306, 315, 326
Disputation, 199, 200, 202, 209, 212,
   285
Distribution of participation, 246,
   264, 270
Divorce adjustment groups, 2, 95,
   97, 157, 228, 292, 293, 299, 300

Dominance, 31, 35, 253, 264
Drop-out, 15, 24, 28, 37, 300, 324
Drug abuse, 35, 56, 299
Drug abuse group, 299. *See also*
Alcohol and drug abuse group
DSM-III-R, 107, 329
Duration of sessions, 54

E

Effective listening, 16
Elderly, groups for, 76, 113, 160,
278, 296
Emotional arousal, 206, 217
Emotional group processes, 40-42
Empowerment, 36, 37, 269
Encounter groups, 252
Escape, 11, 245
Evaluation, 10, 13, 36, 49, 73, 77, 85,
87, 102, 105, 106, 109-112, 114,
117, 118, 129, 130, 134-136, 142,
150, 155, 193, 194, 204, 212, 237,
264, 269, 290, 316, 319, 324, 327
Exaggeration, 10, 204, 205, 209, 258
Excessive self-demand, 204, 205
Extragroup tasks, 13, 133, 189, 225-
226, 266, 271-273, 278, 279, 285,
288, 293, 294, 312, 314-316, 318,
319, 323-326
Extragroup intervention, 19, 20

F

Fading, 52, 202, 215, 216, 219, 222,
224, 265, 283, 297, 298
Family service agency, 57, 59, 60
Family violence group, 35
Feedback, 4, 5, 12, 13, 24, 30, 33, 34,
39, 41, 51, 84, 91, 113, 114, 117,
154, 155, 157, 159, 161, 164, 171,
178, 181, 182, 184-186, 192, 197,
199, 202, 214-216, 219, 222, 226,
243, 247, 258, 259, 262, 263, 267,
279, 293, 294, 315, 318, 319, 322,
323, 327
Fees, 58, 69, 201
Field trips, 161, 296, 302
Fight or flight process, 42, 44, 265,
267

Fixed membership groups, 46, 49
Fixed role therapy, 187, 192
Flexible membership groups, 49, 50
Flooding, 188, 335
Folk dancing, 161
Follow up, 130, 135, 298, 301, 302,
305, 337
Frequency of group meetings, 52
Friendship, 5, 247, 252, 302

G

Gender issues, 23, 64-66, 71, 83, 170,
174, 176, 177, 290
Generalization, 40, 224-226, 287,
288, 305, 307, 323, 325, 328
Goal attainment scaling, 110, 118,
134, 135, 146-149
Goal formulation, 137, 140, 143-145
Goal setting, 7, 94, 108, 136, 137,
139, 141, 142, 146, 149, 162, 163,
173, 294, 321
Goals, 3, 7-10, 24-27, 37, 42, 43, 53,
77, 83, 94, 108, 110, 118, 120, 133-
153, 157, 162, 163, 167, 173, 203,
225, 238, 240, 243, 244, 247, 252,
255, 261, 264, 266, 268, 276, 282,
290, 294, 321, 322
Group activities, 22, 153, 256, 307
Group climate, 259
Group cohesion, 27, 227, 247, 313,
325, 327. *See also* Cohesion
Group composition, 63, 152. *See also*
Composition.
Group contagion, 6
Group contingency, 227, 228
Group counselor, 21
Group data, 119, 128, 129
Group development, 26, 38, 39, 40,
41-43
Group exposure, 15, 47, 54, 157-159,
161, 163, 188, 190-192, 217, 276,
282, 297, 304. *See also* Agora-
phobic group
Group feedback, 202, 219
Group goal attainment scaling, 148
Group goals, 3, 8, 18, 24, 26, 136-
138, 147-149, 235, 242-244, 247,
252, 256, 257, 260

Group intervention, 19, 20, 109, 110, 114, 129–132, 150, 152, 153, 228, 300
Group observations, 106
Group norm, 228, 257, 259, 267, 270. *See also* Norms
Group plan, 152–154, 255
Group pressure, 284
Group problems, 39, 42, 43, 243, 244, 245, 253, 259, 263, 264, 267, 268, 269, 316, 319, 324, 325, 327
Group process, 24–26, 30, 31, 38, 42, 43, 52, 129, 135, 148, 182, 243, 256, 267, 270, 274
Group satisfaction, 246, 247, 249. *See also* Satisfaction
Group setting, 17, 131, 158, 164, 297
Group size, 18, 24, 48–52, 71
Group structure, 23–26, 36, 43, 44, 68, 119, 148, 243, 270
Group tasks, 13, 133, 189, 266, 271–273, 278, 279, 285, 288, 293, 294, 296, 312, 314–316, 319. *See also* Homework
Group therapist, 21, 36, 41, 67, 85
Group *v* individual treatment, 191
Group worker, 21
Guests as models, 177, 251

H

Hallucination, 62
Handouts, 100, 196, 249, 277, 317
Hassles, 102, 258, 287, 293
Hassles inventory, 111, 311
Heterogeneous groups, 47, 53, 63, 172, 296
Hill interaction matrix, 127
Homework, 31, 39, 49, 55, 96, 99, 121, 145, 146, 148, 155, 179, 184, 225, 226, 228, 234, 266, 271, 276, 282, 285, 286, 291, 293, 297, 315, 316. *See also* Extragroup task
Hyperventilation, 235

I

Imagery, 84, 216, 217, 224
Imagery training, 216, 217

Imitation, 165–169
Impediments to treatment, 97, 98
Incentives, 58, 166. *See also* Reinforcement
Incest victims, 56, 147
Independence, 272, 286, 293
Independent behavior, 289, 293, 305
Individual goals, 4, 110, 138, 147, 260
Informed consent, 158
In-group behavior, 250
In-group observation, 119
Insight, 25, 41, 54, 120, 158, 340
Institutions, 48, 55
Intake interviews, 48
Interaction (Conflict) Behavior Questionnaire, 111
Intervention plan, 151–153, 163
Inventories, 105, 107, 110, 111, 135, 136
Involvement of members, 11, 18, 20, 22, 25, 28, 75, 94, 139, 150, 154, 157, 160, 177, 184, 247, 250, 252, 260–264, 269, 279, 284, 293, 294
Irrational ideas, 199, 200
Isolation, 296

J

Jargon, 249
Job preparation groups, 47, 167

L

Larger pattern, 91, 292
Leader competency, 159
Leader self-disclosure, 32
Leadership, 36, 37, 255, 260, 265, 293, 294, 304
Leadership functions, 22, 25, 37, 39, 41, 49, 260, 262, 263, 265, 293, 321, 323, 327
Leadership structure, 36, 37, 43, 260
Limit setting, 53, 154, 159
Long term consequences, 75
Long term goals, 137, 138, 143, 144

M

Maintenance, 36, 49, 51, 52, 54, 57, 64, 70, 150, 155, 252, 260, 287,

289, 294, 299–302, 305, 307, 325–327, 329, 336, 339, 341
Maintenance groups, 54, 70, 301, 302
Maintenance of change, 289, 305, 326, 327
Marathon groups, 55
Measurement, 26, 109, 110, 114, 117, 129–132, 135, 136, 149, 336
Mediated generalization, 291
Medication, 49, 75, 94, 230
Meditation, 227, 229, 237, 331
Men who batter, 46–48, 53, 56, 60, 62, 64, 111, 113, 114, 118, 132, 333, 341, 342
Men who batter, groups for, 46, 56, 111, 114, 118
Mind reading, 205, 209
Modeling, 4, 5, 12–15, 17, 18, 31, 33, 48, 51, 63, 78, 79, 107, 147, 152, 154, 157, 158, 161, 163–173, 175–182, 185, 186, 188, 189, 191, 192, 199, 200, 202, 208, 209, 212, 213, 216, 218, 222–224, 226, 237, 240, 263, 274, 275, 278, 279, 288, 290, 291, 295, 299, 312, 319, 322, 323, 327, 340
Modeling sequence, 12–15, 18, 152, 157, 158, 163, 164, 173, 186, 192, 223, 312, 322, 323, 327
Modeling theory, 164, 192
Monitoring, 5, 10, 20, 56, 82, 102, 110, 116, 117, 136, 151–153, 189, 197, 230, 235, 236, 238–241, 252, 255, 263–265, 269, 273, 276–278, 283, 285, 286, 314, 319, 326, 353
Motivation, 96, 97
Multiple monitoring sources, 283
Mutual aid, 101, 157, 171
Mutual member tasks, 274, 276

N

Negative self-talk, 255, 275
Networking, 4
Non-interactive tasks, 276, 278
Non-verbal behavior, 165

Norms, 263, 314. *See also* Group norms
Novaco Anger Scale, 111
Number of group leaders, 55

O

Observation, 12, 26, 32, 35, 82, 106, 112, 117–119, 124, 125, 127, 148, 158, 164–166, 170, 171, 262, 278, 288
Observation system, 106, 148
Observational tasks, 274–278
Observers, 254, 255, 262
Off-task behavior, 126, 154, 246, 252, 257, 270, 304
Open ended group, 48, 50
Organization, 50, 57, 83, 290, 300, 302, 327
Organizational attributes, 51, 56
Orientation, 3, 4, 7–9, 21, 30, 38, 39, 45, 46, 48, 50, 51, 54, 61, 66–68, 70, 71, 83, 154, 161, 196, 197, 203, 230, 252, 313, 328
Orientation group, 48, 54, 67

P

Pain management, 47, 56, 66, 75, 111, 162, 277, 341
Pain management groups, 47, 50, 66, 75, 111, 162, 277
Pairing off, 16, 31, 36, 41, 42, 44, 244, 265, 270
Parent training groups, 61, 126, 141, 153, 172, 264, 285, 295, 299, 303, 304
Participation, 9, 17–19, 23, 24, 27, 34–36, 39, 62, 69, 92, 124, 125, 160, 170, 187, 190, 207, 229, 247, 253–255, 261, 264, 267, 268, 270, 313, 315, 321, 323, 327, 334, 337, 345–347
Phase of treatment, 45–48, 50–52, 76, 78, 98, 136, 188, 211, 240, 261, 278, 283, 293
Phobic disorders, 2, 107
Physical attributes, 93, 94
Planning, 3, 7, 20, 45, 46, 50, 66, 70,

71, 73, 98, 107, 108, 136, 139, 149–
151, 154, 156, 160, 162, 163, 178,
192, 245, 252, 256, 269, 279, 282,
283, 286, 288, 298, 306–308, 318,
325, 326, 354
Point-counterpoint, 216
Positive self talk, 289–291, 305
Post session questionnaires, 23, 26,
28, 45, 119, 120, 148, 149, 198,
248, 249, 294, 314, 316, 318, 323
Pranyayma, 235. See also Respira-
tory control
Pregroup interviews, 228
Preliminary treatment contract, 70,
71
Preparation, 127, 135, 162, 179, 188,
212, 217, 218, 239, 240, 274, 275,
277, 280, 281, 297, 298, 304, 336
Pre-post design, 130, 131
Presenting problem, 46, 51, 53, 63,
66
Pre-test, 298
Prevention, 268
Private commitment, 284
Private practice, 56–58, 66
Problem cards, 118, 136
Problem situation, 8, 13, 90, 106,
140, 145, 146, 170, 171, 175, 178,
192, 291, 296
Problem-solving, 3, 7, 8, 10, 12, 14,
21, 22, 36, 38, 42, 43, 49, 65, 70,
72, 95, 139, 162, 163, 206, 221,
228, 243, 245, 249, 250, 253, 257,
259, 263, 264–270, 273, 274, 286,
289, 293, 295, 316, 318, 319, 323,
326, 328, 332, 335, 340
Productivity, 27, 127, 128, 263, 264,
270, 273, 274, 286, 294, 327
Profile of Mood States (POMS), 111,
134, 311, 338
Progressive relaxation, 229, 330, 336
Promptness, 96, 119, 128, 129, 246,
312, 314
Prophesizing, 204
Psychodynamic theory, 25
Psychodynamically oriented group,
268
Psychological Maltreatment of
Women Inventory, 111

Public commitment, 226, 283, 284,
326
Punishment, 158, 159, 167, 256
Put-down, 126, 247, 257, 258, 259

R

Racial composition, 65
Racial issues, 65, 66, 71, 77, 168–170,
177, 237
Rapid-assessment instruments, 111,
337
Rating scales, 118, 123, 146
Rational emotive therapy, 199
Recapitulation, 255, 256
Recovering alcoholics, groups for,
154–155, 298
Recreational activities, 227, 229, 239.
See also Socio-recreational activi-
ties
Reframing, 211
Reinforcement, 2, 4, 5, 10, 13, 14, 16,
17, 19, 20, 23, 29, 32, 40, 52, 53,
68, 88, 92, 93, 101, 117, 125, 126,
133, 153, 159, 161, 167, 169, 178,
191, 196, 197, 226, 250–252, 276,
281–285, 290–292, 294, 295, 298,
314, 327, 352, 353
Reinforcement schedule, 298
Reinforcement survey schedule, 92
Relapse prevention, 298–300, 305
Relational skills, 228
Relationship, 4, 12, 15–17, 25, 27,
29, 32, 44, 54, 62, 64, 68, 71, 84,
88, 103, 137, 142, 143, 149, 151,
153, 168, 177, 200, 215, 247, 250,
268, 273, 277, 288, 297, 303, 319,
335, 337
Relaxation, 1, 11, 15, 17, 20, 56, 94,
161, 191, 217, 226–239, 241, 242,
257, 264, 273, 274, 282, 292, 310,
312, 316, 318, 323, 325–327, 330–
332, 335, 336, 338, 340, 343, 344
Relaxation training, 227, 228, 229,
274
Reliability, 111, 112, 116, 117, 146
Rerehearsal, 185, 214
Research, 3, 6, 7, 12, 15, 20, 21, 24,
52, 54, 63, 69, 107, 109, 127, 136,

159, 160, 168, 192, 196, 227, 235, 238, 241, 284, 289, 300, 304, 330, 331

Research design, 130–135, 331

Resources, 7, 49, 61, 69, 72–74, 88, 91–95, 98, 107, 108, 134, 141, 170, 194, 234, 235

Respiratory control, 229, 235, 236, 241

Risk, 27, 96, 142, 169, 183, 196, 290, 298, 321, 343

Risk taking, 27, 343

Role instruction, 186, 187, 260

Role play test, 84, 105, 108, 112–114, 127, 136, 341

Role structure, 33–35

Roleplaying, 1, 13, 104–106, 110, 112–114, 127, 136, 167, 170, 171, 173, 175, 177–182, 184, 185, 186, 215, 222, 223, 271, 275, 280, 282, 287, 295–297, 319, 322–324, 341

Roles, 13, 18, 23, 25, 33–35, 37–39, 42, 56, 157, 158, 166, 172, 187, 222, 244, 260, 263, 297

Round-robin exercises, 18, 216

Rules, 19, 25, 28–30, 39, 67, 176, 335

S

Satisfaction, 16, 23, 35, 42, 51, 52, 68, 74, 78, 89, 90, 95, 113, 120, 122, 123, 129, 205, 246–250, 253, 257, 262, 264, 268, 293

Selection, 59, 60, 71, 111, 137, 148, 156, 160, 162, 163, 192, 212, 238, 259, 279, 288, 289, 293, 335

Selective perception, 204, 205

Self-control groups, 162, 163

Self-defeating statements or thoughts, 200–203, 206–213, 277, 317

Self-disclosure, 23, 26, 27, 30–32, 36, 41, 79, 96, 120, 123, 163, 170, 207, 246, 251, 317, 318, 319, 327

Self-efficacy, 273, 286, 329

Self-enhancing statements or thoughts, 200–203, 206–208, 212–214, 216, 316

Self-esteem, 197, 210, 293

Self-help groups, 127, 302, 306, 339

Self-instructional training, 14, 195, 200, 217, 220, 222, 224–226, 228, 240

Self-management, 10, 336

Self-modeling, 170

Self-monitoring, 10, 56, 102, 116, 117, 197, 278, 314

Self-monitoring card, 117

Self-rating, 110, 111

Self-reinforcement training, 196, 197, 226, 281–282, 292

Self-report, 111, 117, 332

Sensitivity to change, 111

Setback, 288, 298, 305

Setback list, 306

Setting limits, 154

Sexual disorders, 2, 11, 53, 62, 196, 273, 274, 282

Shaping, 161, 322

Short term goals, 137, 138, 140, 143, 151, 153

Sickness Impact Profile (SIP), 111, 330

Side effects, 49, 94, 157, 158, 160, 185, 192, 230, 236, 238, 239, 241, 286, 316

Significant others, 175, 177, 178, 180, 181, 275

Simulated tasks, 274, 275

Single parents groups, 250

Situational analysis, 72, 73, 76, 78, 79, 89, 98, 106–108, 295

Sleeping disorders, 274

Smoke-enders groups, 47, 56

Social network, 95, 290, 303, 306, 353

Social skill training, 48, 50, 176, 228, 239, 310

Social skill training group, 10, 55, 102, 116, 176, 228, 262, 277, 331

Social skills, 10, 11, 13, 19, 48, 50, 63, 101, 111, 113, 164, 176, 262, 330–333, 340

Social support, 94, 95, 97, 290, 303, 306

Socio-recreational activities, 16, 19, 227, 229, 239–241

Socio-recreational group, 302

Sources of models, 168, 169

Specificity, 16, 81, 185, 271, 279, 280, 286

State-Trait Anxiety Inventory (STAI), 111

Stress, 1, 2, 6, 10–15, 37, 47, 50, 56, 61, 64, 68–70, 75, 79, 80, 82, 84, 88, 91, 95, 102, 107, 111, 113, 116, 126, 127, 155, 159, 161, 163, 170, 191–205, 208, 212, 215, 216, 217, 226–229, 233–241, 257, 261, 264, 275–278, 287, 301, 306, 309–327, 332–337

Stress management group, 163, 257, 264–265, 283

Stressful situations, 1, 10, 11, 91, 116, 155, 193, 199–201, 208, 212, 228, 234, 264, 278, 301, 313, 318, 319, 324, 325

Subgrouping, 17, 18, 246, 256, 257, 327

Subgroups, 36, 97, 190, 240, 246, 256, 257, 265, 266

Supervision, 15, 237, 239, 272, 273, 304

Support, 3, 10, 15, 19, 24, 27, 32, 34, 35, 37, 46, 47, 49, 54, 55, 60, 65, 68, 94, 95, 97, 115, 127, 156, 157, 159, 160, 188, 189, 191, 195, 198, 227, 228, 236, 241, 243, 244, 251, 253, 276, 277, 284, 290, 299, 301, 303, 306, 342, 344

Support groups, 94, 160

Symptom Check-List-Revised (SCL-90-R), 311

Systematic desensitization, 157, 217, 332

T

Taping, 171, 256

Task completion, 119, 127, 129, 263–265, 273, 283, 286

Task completion rate, 129, 264, 265, 274

Task groups, 34

Tasks, 8, 13, 50, 84, 127, 128, 133, 170, 186, 188, 189, 191, 193, 220, 226, 261, 263, 266, 271–286, 288, 293, 294, 296, 297, 309, 312, 314–316, 319, 324–326, 349

Termination, 22, 28, 38, 40, 53, 55, 95, 132, 135, 239, 251, 281, 287, 291, 301, 302, 304, 306, 307

Termination of groups, 300, 301, 304, 306, 307

Tests and measures, 84, 105–108, 111–114, 127, 134, 136, 149, 298, 311, 312, 327

Themes, 35, 46, 64, 85, 106, 111, 217, 240, 253

Time-out, 154

Transfer of change, 5, 18, 155, 225, 272, 275, 286, 304, 305, 307, 313, 326, 335

Transition, 48, 49, 310

Transition group, 48, 49

Transitional statements, 212–215

Treatment contracts, 67–71

Treatment goals, 3, 8, 9, 53, 57, 73, 93, 94, 97, 98, 108, 119, 126, 138, 142–146, 148, 170, 243, 251, 253, 260, 276, 277, 293

Treatment planning, 3, 7, 73, 282, 298

Triads, 18, 42, 244, 246, 256

V

Validity, 111, 112, 117, 131, 132, 146

Values, 14, 18, 27, 71, 81

Videotape, 67, 166, 170, 171, 216

Violence, 35, 64, 70, 118, 128, 133, 147, 151, 152, 277, 303

Victims of men who batter, groups for, 47, 56, 142

W

Waitlist, 59, 60

Weight loss groups, 47, 56, 265, 300, 302, 329

What-if exercise, 299

Y

Yoga, 235, 326

Z

Zen, 235